American Stonewares

The Art & Craft of Utilitarian Potters

Georgeanna H. Greer

Revised 3rd Edition

4880 Lower Valley Road, Atglen, PA 19310 USA

This beautiful punch bowl is 8-1/2" high and 15-1/2" in diameter. It was made as a presentation piece for a marriage and is inscribed "C CRANE - ELIZABETH CRANE/MAY 22nd, 1811." It is salt-glazed inside and out and decorated with cobalt in a vivid blue. The exterior is decorated with a scallop design coggled just beneath the rim. Under this an incised undulating vine encircles the bowl. Flowers, leaves, and fruits extend from this stem and are incised and filled with cobalt. A large fish is incised and colored with cobalt in the center of the bowl interior. Attributed to John Crolius, New York City. *Courtesy of Barry Cohen, Photographer: Henry Cox.*

AMERICAN STONEWARES

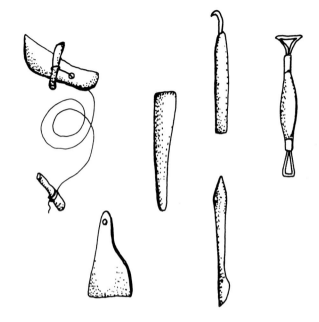

738.3

Revised price guide: 1999
Copyright © 1981, 1996, 1999 by Georgeanna H.
Greer
Library of Congress Catalog Card Number:99-60784

ISBN: 0-7643-0856-4
Printed in China
1 2 3 4

Published by Schiffer Publishing Ltd.
4880 Lower Valley Road
Atglen, PA 19310
Phone: (610) 593-1777; Fax: (610) 593-2002
E-mail: Schifferbk@aol.com
Please visit our web site catalog at
www.schifferbooks.com

This book may be purchased from the publisher.
Include $3.95 for shipping. Please try your bookstore
first.
We are interested in hearing from authors
with book ideas on related subjects.
You may write for a free printed catalog.

In Europe, Schiffer books are distributed by
Bushwood Books
6 Marksbury Avenue
Kew Gardens
Surrey TW9 4JF England
Phone: 44 (0)181 392-8585; Fax: 44 (0)181 392-9876
E-mail: Bushwd@aol.com

TO SAM

WHOSE LOVING ENCOURAGEMENT
AND GENEROUS SUPPORT HAVE
MADE ALL THIS POSSIBLE.

The prices in this book were compiled by Lynn D. Trusdell of Crown & Eagle Antiques, New Hope, PA. Lynn has been in business since 1968. She is a certified appraiser and has been a collector of stoneware for over 37 years. Prices are **approximate**, based not only on condition, uniqueness, provenance, craftsmanship, and quality of design, but on location and date of purchase. Neither the author nor the publisher are responsible for any outcomes resulting from consulting this guide.

ART WORK: TINA GRIESENBECK

PHOTOGRAPHY: CHRIS WILLIAMS

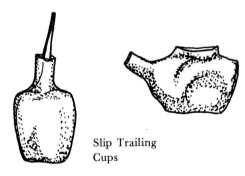

Slip Trailing
Cups

Preface

Ceramic objects have had a fascination for me for almost as long as I can remember. The beautiful doll dishes at my grandmother's first entranced me as a child. Then, during a year that my family lived in Arizona, I collected miniature American Indian pots. As we traveled in Mexico during subsequent summers, I collected miniature Mexican pots. Little did I dream that this interest would result in a rich and rewarding preoccupation in my later life.

With the passing of childhood, my life soon became more involved, and there was no time to devote to a hobby during the years of college, medical school, marriage, and early motherhood. Only after my older children were in school was I able to take advantage of classes at the San Antonio Art Institute. There I studied the throwing of pottery upon a wheel, as well as the decorating, glazing, and firing of high temperature ceramics. Since that time the study of one phase or another of stoneware pottery production has been a part of my life almost daily.

Ten years of working at throwing pots upon a wheel brought me to the realization that this was a much more difficult craft than it had first appeared. I then understood that those who toy at this craft late in life are rank amateurs when compared with the craftsmen who make it their means of livlihood.

My ceramic instructor at that time had investigated the early manufacture of utilitarian stoneware in Ohio, and, at his suggestion, I read John Ramsey's *American Potters and Potteries* and Lura Watkins' *Early New England Potters and Their Wares*. These books started an entirely new interest for me. When I also learned that there had been a number of early potteries in our local area, I was on the search for information which has continued for more than fifteen years.

This book represents an accumulation of knowledge begun in my early days of making pots and extending through years of investigation into historical utilitarian stoneware manufacture. I have collected bits of information here and there along the way, many of which I cannot refer back to a particular author or a single interview.

I have visited abandoned pottery sites, operating potteries, old potters and the descendants of potters, collectors, museums, and conferences. My European travels have greatly enriched my background and have given me a much clearer view of the pottery traditions that were brought to America.

The very kind and friendly acceptance, cooperation, and encouragement which I have received from my many friends along the way has made this work a pleasure.

I should like to thank my former ceramics instructor, George Palovich, for putting the original "bee in my bonnett" about historic American stoneware.

Harding Black has been a friend, teacher, mentor, and kiln-hunting companion for all these many years. It is from him that my major knowledge of ceramic bodies, glazes, and firing techniques has come. Without his patient explanations and answers to my multitude of questions, I might long ago have given up this quest. I am most grateful for having been able to learn from such a knowledgable teacher.

Dorothy and Walther Auman have long been very special friends. Their own involvement in the potter's craft as their means of livlihood, as well as their rich background and understanding of the craft, have made my visits with them most important. The opportunity to live within the American pottery tradition has been mine during visits with them. I am deeply grateful to both of them for many things, but especially for having given me an insight into the world of the traditional potter which I could hardly have gained otherwise.

Acceptance and encouragement by Curtis Tunnell, Stanley South, Charles Fairbanks, Jim Neely, and Kathleen Gilmore, professional archeologists all, has given me the courage to feel that I have something worthwhile to say. This has been enhanced by my friends in the museum world. Malcom Watkins' advice and encouragement have been a great help. Cecelia Steinfeld and Jack McGregor of the San Antonio Museum Association as well as Joe Nicholson of Trinity University Press gave me great confidence as they steered me through the production of my first book and museum exhibit.

The traditional potters who have taken the time to talk or correspond with me have given my understanding a depth that can come only from first-hand information. I am grateful to the late James E. Richter, Frank Meyer, E.J. Brown, and Arthur Cole for information and cooperation that will long be remembered. Bill Gordy, Lanier Meaders, Wesley and John Ellis, E.J. Humphreys, Herman Cole, Norman Smith, Bascome Craven, "Duck" Craven, Melvin Owen, Charlie Owen, and Vernon Owen have all been extremely kind and helpful.

Although I am indebted to many friends for their kindness along the research road, I should especially like to thank those friends, both old and new, who have allowed me to use photographs of pots from their collections or institutions or have assisted me in many ways with the research on this book. These friends are Jerry Banta, Norman Barka, John Burrison, Lelyn Branin, Daisy Bridges, Barry Cohen, Ellen Denker, Kurt and Marsha Dewhurst, Mel Davies, Charles Dietz, Jonathan Fairbanks, Steven and Terry Ferrell, Eulalie Genius, W.E. Grove, George Hamell, Eric McGuire, Bob and Beka Mebane, Ron Michael, Susan Myers, David Newlands, Edwa Osborn, Elizabeth Reeb, Peter Schreiber, Stu Schwartz, Bob Sherman, Sam Smith, the Ralph Strongs, Nancy and Bob Treichler, Jack Troy, Dean Zimmerman, and Terry Zug.

William Barnhill's permission to use his beautiful photographic soliloquy on the Reems Creek Pottery has enabled me to set a mood for the background of traditional potteries that would otherwise have been difficult to achieve.

I also thank Dot Auman, Harding Black, and Marsha Jackson for taking time to read the manuscript to be sure that I made no major errors.

Helen Simons has kindly edited my sentence structure and, she insists, merely lent her knowledge of prose to my knowledge of pots. She has also been ever-ready to answer my questions and help me with all of the little details of publication. For all of this I am sincerely grateful.

Chris Williams, my photographer, has labored long hours to produce photographs which pleased me. His bouyant good spirits have persisted even when I cast out many of the photographs from a session of work. Chris has done my photography for many years and I appreciate his good work.

Tina Griesenbeck, my artist, has worked hard sketching and making plates which please me. I am grateful for her help, and considerable talent.

My father and mother are to be thanked for providing me with an excellent education as well as a rich intellectual and research oriented background. This has served me well in my ceramic research.

My own family is to be thanked most of all. They have allowed me the freedom of travel and time necessary to do this research. My husband has fostored my work from the early beginning and most of all, has supported it. My oldest daughter, Cassie, has valiently read my cramped notes and mistyped text to produce the final typewritten manuscript, a long and arduous task. My son, Mac, has moved pots by the hundreds, and driven me to sites that could not be reached except in a four wheel drive vehicle. My youngest daughter, Gretchen, has been my companion on many field trips, putting up with sun, rain, ticks, and redbugs without complaint. Without all of this family cooperation, my research and writing could never have come to a productive conclusion.

Georgeanna H. Greer

March 23, 1981

TABLE OF CONTENTS

Chapter 1
Antecedants, Immigrants, and Pioneers

The celebration of two hundred years of existence of the United States as a free nation has made Americans more aware than before that our past is worthy of consideration and reflection. In addition to the potitical and military history that we have long been taught, we are now developing an interest in our cultural and social history. Public interest first turned to the study of the original inhabitants of North America, primarily through the disciplines of ethnohistory and archeology. In the last two decades a widespread effort to preserve and study later ethnic and regional differences has come into being, and the folklore, history, and architecture of the many different peoples who immigrated to the United states is becoming a part of our national heritage.

A large part of this renewed interest must inevitably be directed toward our European heritage, simply because the majority of early colonists as well as later immigrants came from the European nations.Out social and cultural history is unalterably linked to Europe through those immigrants. During the three hundred years or so since the earliest immigrants came to America, arts and crafts in North America have generally derived from those of Europe. This is not to say that the traditions remained distinctively British or French or German, for over the years various traditions have melded together to form new types that are distinctly American. In addition, especially in the southwestern states, native arts and crafts of the remaining original Americans are a continual source of influence and inspiration in both folk and artistic expressions.

Nevertheless, American utilitarian stoneware, which is our principal concern, is primarily northern European in origin. Genealogical links to known European families of potters can be traced in the American tradition, and the influence of historic European pottery centers is readily apparent. The Rhenish stoneware center of Raeran is one of these areas. The names Corselius, de Wilde and Lent are all old family names of potters from area. These same names appear among potters working in the New York - New Jersey area in the late eighteenth century. Pottery has historically been a "family" craft, a trade passed on from father to son, and this tradition persisted throughout the long period in which utilitarian stonewares were produced in North America.

SOURCES OF THE POTTERY TRADITION

In nearly every portion of the world, pottery traditions manifest themselves as soon as native cultures pass the simple stone implement state. Clay is a more or less ubiquitous material, available practically the world over. Historically, strong cultures have imposed many of their social and cultural traditions on the peoples they conquered, and historians and archeologists have thus been able to trace the roots of certain traditions back in time for many centuries. Since ceramic material remains are extremely durable, the pottery tradition of a culture is one that lends itself to later investigation. Evident in both surviving vessels and archeological remains of early North American potteries are strong influences from the British, German, and French traditions.

These northern European cultures had centuries earlier been heavily influenced by the Roman during periods of Roman occupation, while the Roman culture had been heavily influenced by the earlier strong Greek culture, and so on into antiquity. Each new culture received something from its background cultures but also added something of its own, producing characteristic variations within any given art or craft. The use of the potter's wheel and of well-constructed kilns was one of the important advances in ceramic technology that spread over most of Europe during the periods of Roman occupation. The inhabitants of the occupied areas learned to produce wheel made ceramics as well as brick and tile and to fire their wares in well-constructed kilns. Over several centuries, new nations, each one having its own special cultural and craft traditions, developed within the areas of Roman occupation.

Northern European potters, in turn, immigrated to and settled in the upper North American continent, imposing their earthenware and stoneware traditions on the areas in which they worked. Because the United States and Canada share, in general, the same pattern of settlement and because of the passage of potters across the border between the two countries, Canadian pottery traditions essentially follow those of the United States. In contrast, South and Central America and Mexico, occupied during the colonial period primarily by Spanish and Portuguese, developed a pottery tradition influenced heavily by that of southern Europe. The forms as well as the glazes used by Spanish and Portuguese colonials were, and still remain, primarily Iberian in type. Southern Europe traditionally produced only earthenware ceramic vessels. In that area, after the fourteenth century, potters developed the tin enamel type of glaze brought to Spain by the Moorish invaders and called majolica. This is a much more sophisticated form of earthenware than plain lead-glazed wares. Mexico is the only North American nation in which the tin enamel earthenware glazes have been employed widely in the production of majolica wares. No traditional stonewares have been produced in Mexico or in any of the South American countries.

CLASSIFICATION OF CERAMICS

Before we consider the establishment and development of the American stoneware tradition, let us consider first exactly what utilitarian stonewares are and how they differ from earthenwares.

Since utilitarian vessel types represent two different branches of ceramic classification, some points of the differentiation must be explained. The old traditional earthenwares, as well as the newer stonewares for use in ordinary households, were produced by potters trained in these crafts. This was true in northern Europe as well as North America. There are only two relative firing ranges for ceramic objects, and these are spoken of as high and low temperature ranges. There are, however, three distinct types of ceramic ware produced: earthenware, stoneware, and porcelain. Stoneware and porcelain belong in the high temperature range, while the low temperature range includes all forms of earthenware, be they coil formed earthenware vessels made by primative cultures or later, fine bodied, ornate and molded tablewares. The point of differentiation in ceramic classification is determined by the clay and the temperature at which it must be fired to produce a durable ware.

Common clays such as those suitable for making ordinary brick are used to make earthenwares. Although common utilitarian earthenwares are sometimes called red-wares, the body of an earthenware pot may be of any natural clay color, just as the body of a stoneware pot may be of any natural clay color. This color varies mainly according to the amount of iron present in the clay. Before firing, clays may be blackish or bluish in color from organic material, but this burns out in the firing. Colors after firing may be anywhere from a pure white, in the absence of iron, to a deep red-brown or gray. The development of artificially prepared and colored clay bodies will not be considered in this discussion of traditional utilitarian wares.

Stonewares must be made from clays that can be fired in an intense heat without loss of form. These clays in their natural state are often called fire clays or potter's clays. Porcelain is made from the purest of clays, kaolin. Kaolin, or china clay, is iron free and combines with feldspar at very high temperatures to produce the pure white, completely vitrified ware which we call porcelain and respect as the highest achievement of the potter's art. Fired stoneware clays may vary as earthenware clays in color, from near white to deep red browns and grays. When available, the lighter clays are usually preferred for stoneware vessels.

In firing earthenwares the temperature must be sufficient to fuse the clay into a firm, durable body, but not vitrify it. Earthenware clays are less resistant to heat than those used for stonewares and slump rapidly in the kiln when overheated. Since the clays themselves do not completely fuse in such firing, earthenware remains permeable to water and other common liquids and must be lined on the interior to prevent leaking. The usual practical glaze that will melt at earthenware temperatures is a glaze containing some form of lead. Common European and American earthenware was traditionally lined with a glaze containing raw lead oxides. Now many improvements have been made, and our tablewares are lined with glazes containing lead in an insoluble form or other more suitable fluxes. Because of the incomplete fusion of the body, all earthenwares, glazed or unglazed, give off a characteristic low or hollow tone when tapped with a metal tool, such as a knife.

Stoneware derives its very name from its dense and hard nature. The clays suitable for the production of stoneware are coarser than those used for porcelain but are capable of fusing by slowly melting together or vitrifying at high temperatures without losing their original form. Even as late as the nineteenth century, small pottery shops had little in the way of aids to control kiln temperatures and to determine the exact vitrification points of natural clays. These early potters fired by trial and error and for that reason — even though all wares fired at reasonable stoneware temperature ranges should theoretically be vitrified, but it is not uncommon to find poorly vitrified old stoneware pots. Well vitrified pots will give a high, clear ring or tone almost identical to that of a good grade of glass when tapped with a metal tool. Poorly vitrified as well as cracked pots will give off lower tones, all the way down to the hollow, dull tones of earthenware.

A rough approximation of temperature ranges for the firing of these two forms of ceramic ware may give the reader an idea of the very high temperatures needed for the successful production of stonewares and porcelains. These temperatures cannot be reached without properly constructed kilns to contain the heat. Earthenware bodies in the low temperature range must be heated between 1000 degrees and 1100 degrees C, while those in the upper earthenware range must be heated to approximately 1100 degrees to 1200 degrees C to mature. (Orton ceramic cones 06. through 01. and cones 1 through 5.) Rarely, clays will vitrify naturally at temperatures of 1175 degrees to 1190 degrees C and vessels made of this clay may be classed as stoneware because of the vitrification. There is no simple procedure for determining the temperature at which a vessel was fired.

Stoneware bodies are generally supposed to mature or vitrify in the temperature range between 1200 degrees and 1300 degrees C (cones 6 - 11), although some refractory stoneware bodies may need temperatures as high as cone 14 (1390 degrees C) to mature.

Porcelain is distinguished from stoneware by its finer white body paste. It is necessary to fire porcelain bodies to a temperature between 1250 degrees and 1400 degrees C for proper vitrification of the porcelain. A consideration of the advanced industrialized techniques involving the addition of artifical fluxes to clay body mixtures, making them vitrify at lower temperatures, is not necessary in the case of the utilitarian ware made in small shops.

The higher firing temperature was the

essential reason that stoneware and porcelain were later developments than earthenware. In Asia as well as in Europe, technology allowing such temperatures to be achieved within the fairly large, closed space of a kiln had to develop before stoneware and porcelain manufacture was possible. The basic differences in the fusion of the clay particles is one of the major points of separation between the techniques of manufacture as well as the manner of use suitable for high and low temperature ceramic vessels. In considering this, only utilitarian earthenware and stoneware will be compared here.

Prior to the development of stonewares, earthenwares were relegated to all sorts of household use, mainly the storage, preparation, and cooking of foods and beverages. The permeability of what one might call the "open body" of earthenware led to the use of impermeable linings. Generally glazes were used in the late historic period which we are discussing. Lead oxide combines with clay at a relatively low temperature to produce a smooth, glassy sheet or glaze over the areas to which it is applied. Other oxides that will produce a glass or glaze when combined with silica at low temperatures are highly alkaline. They also have different expansion and contraction ratios than the clays and tend to crack or crackle upon cooling. This form of glaze does not seal the body well because of this defect, and therefore does not correct the problem of liquids seeping through the earthenware body. Highly alkaline glazes were not used in early European pottery traditions.

Lead is soluble in weak acids when used in simple low temperature glazes, and the fact that poisonous compounds result when acid mixtures are stored in such lead glazed vessels became a serious drawback to their use for food storage. Earthenware, with its open body and high sand content may, on the other hand, be used very successfully in cooking because the body is able to absorb the expansion and contraction that occur when vessels are exposed to heat. Lead glazed vessels are perfectly safe when used as cooking, serving, or tablewares for relatively short periods of time.

It is long exposure to acidic mixtures that causes decomposition of the glaze and subsequently lead poisoning when the contents of the vessel are consumed. The manufacture of traditional utilitarian earthenware persisted in the United States throughout the nineteenth century because the ware was entirely suitable for the preparation, cooking and storing of many foods and for use as common tableware as well.

Stoneware theoretically does not need a glaze to prevent leaking. Many vessels have no interior glaze. Poorly vitrified stoneware does leak, and the interior is usually slightly rough. Glazes enhance the appearance of stoneware and also render it impermeable, smooth, and easy to clean. It therefore became the custom here to glaze stoneware both inside and out by the mid-nineteenth century. Stoneware was durable, leakproof, and acid resistant and so became the preferred ceramic medium for household storage of many foods. All manner of acid foods such as vinegar, wine, cider, sauerkraut, and various forms of pickles could safely be stored in these vessels. Since they were impermeable, stoneware vessels were also better for use as chamberpots and milk containers because they could be readily cleaned and remained free of odors. Stoneware largely replaced earthenware for the storage of foods and other utilitirian needs, but its tight, vitrified body made it unsuitable for cooking use.

DEVELOPMENT OF THE AMERICAN STONEWARE TRADITION

THE EUROPEAN BACKGROUND

Although strong earthenware traditions were present in northern Europe prior to the medieval period, a new form of ware evolved from the medieval Pingsdorf and Schinveldt sintered, or hard-burned, earthenwares. From this improved technology the development of the manufacture of stonewares occurred in areas along the Rhein River and in parts of northern France during the twelfth and thirteenth centuries. By the early fourteenth century, true vitrified stoneware was being produced in centers from Beauvais, France, to Seigburg, West Germany. During that century unglazed, flame-licked stonewares became well developed.. Brown loam or slip coatings, which were thinly applied and did not form a true glaze coating, were also sometimes used. This firm, durable, vitrified ware was immensely popular, and large producing centers developed. Heavy fly ash glazes also occur upon some of this ware manufactured in Siegburg. This was presumably accidental, but may have been purposeful. Rather suddenly — probably accidentally at first, then purposefully — the development of an unprecedented form of glaze on the exterior of the Rhenish wares was seen, the salt glaze.

Glazing with salt began early in the fifteenth century in the major centers along the Rhein River — Seigburg, Cologne, and Raeren. During that century these Rhenish potters became masters of salt glazing and firing techniques as well as of the wheel throwing of many new ornate ceramic forms and the decoration of the exterior vessel surfaces by all manner of sprigged and incised decoration. The sixteenth century was the period of the flowering of this art. At that period cobalt as an agent to produce a decorative blue when applied prior to the glaze was added to the color palette, which prior to this period had included only ferruginous browns. Manganese, producing purplish brown, was added by the mid-seventeenth century.

The British had long been importers of Rhenish stonewares, and during the seventeenth century British entrepreneurs began to try to imitate the Rhenish potters and produce salt-glazed stonewares. John Dwight is probably the best known of these early salt-glaze stoneware potters. He obtained a patent to produce salt-glazed stoneware at his shop at Fulham in 1671. The Ehlers brothers are also known to have brought knowledge of the methods of manufacture of both red-bodied unglazed stoneware and typical Rhenish salt-glazed stoneware to England. By the mid-eighteenth century large amounts of salt-glazed stoneware were being manufactured in England. The technique was applied to some utilitarian wares, but still was used mainly for expensive, highly decorative wares, especially fancy tablewares. During the eighteenth century, Josiah Wedgewood developed cream-colored earthenware, with its perfect background for hand-painted or transfer printed decoration. The manufacture of the "perfect" high temperature ceramic, true porcelain, also began in Europe during this period. Salt-glazed stoneware consequently dropped to the lower position of sturdy utilitarian ware in both Great Britain and Germany. It is in this form that the salt-glaze stoneware tradition persisted throughout the nineteenth century in both northern Europe and North America. It became a form of utilitarian folk pottery often decorated by the potters themselves or untrained painters in a folk or simple tradition rather than a elegant one.

AMERICAN TRADITIONS BEGIN

Colonial settlers and later immigrants arrived in North America having all of the rich background of European cultural development in the arts and crafts. European potters brought with them the tools necessary for the clearing of land and the manufacture of both utilitarian earthenware and stoneware. They were able to begin the manufacture of ceramic wares in this country at nearly the same point of development that they had reached in Europe. However, a certain time lag was necessary for the clearing of land and the setting up of a business. For this reason a time lag is also visible in the work of the pioneering potters moving westward across North America. American decorative art forms remained ten to twenty years behind those of European cultures in style.

Such works produced in pioneering western areas of the United States, particulary in architecture, furniture, and ceramic wares, remained stylistically some ten to twenty years behind the fashionable pace of the eastern seaboard states during the nineteenth century. Tremendously improved communication during the twentieth century has eliminated this lag in fashion.

Potters, primarily from Germany and England, arrived in America, each bringing with them cultural preferences in form and decoration for their wares. A few French potters immigrated to the provinces of Canada and to Louisiana, producing a French type of common earthenware in these areas, but no potteries producing characteristic French stoneware have been reported in North America.

German stoneware potters brought their bulbous jar, long-necked jug, heavily banded cylindrical mug, and cask forms with them. They brought as well a taste for rather ornate decoration accomplished by incising into the clay and brushing on a cobalt solution for color under the salt glaze. Their preferred glaze was the salt glaze, but they were also knowledgeable about natural clay or slip glazes. British potters of the eighteenth and early nineteenth centuries were also accomplished users of the salt glaze as well as slip glazes. They brought with them a more restrained style of stoneware: simple cylindrical jar forms; full, shorter-necked jug forms; and considerably lighter, straight cylindrical mug forms. Their preferred decorative techniques involved dipping the upper and sometimes lower portions of vessels into a ferruginous mixture before firing, producing banding areas of brown on the tops or tops and bottoms of their vessels. Occasionally simple incised bands were also used as decoration, and small, rather simple plaques or figures were sprigged on the pots.

Manifestations of the purer British and Germanic styles may be seen in eighteenth century American pots. Few of these survive, but the mugs excavated from the site of William Rogers' factory at Yorktown show manifestations of British styling. An ornate inkstand which was signed and dated by William Crolius of Manhattan could well be mistaken for a piece of German Westerwald stoneware without the inscription, showing the strong influence of this potter's Germanic background.

Mugs excavated at the Yorktown factory of William Rogers. They have typical British cylindrical form and ferruginous dips of the tops under a salt glaze. *Courtesy of The National Park Service.*

An inkstand consisting of hand-thrown ink and sand containers in a heart-shaped stand formed using slab techniques. There are five quill holes between and in front of the containers. Elaborate stamping was done all around the top and bottom exterior edges which makes these edges appear scalloped. Hand incised floral and leaf patterns cover the top and side walls and are filled with cobalt blue. Hand-inscribed on the bottom "New York / July 12th, 1773 / William Crolius / Tyler." Height: 2-1/4". Maximum diameter: 5-3/4". *Photographer: Henry Cox. Courtesy of Barry Cohen.* $8500-10,000, unique.

During the last decade of the eighteenth century and the early nineteenth century many pieces of American stoneware illustrate a blending of these two traditions and the subsequent development of singularly American forms and manner of decoration in stoneware. The pots produced at the Boston factory of Johnathan Fenton and Frederick Carpenter between 1793 and 1797 demonstrate mixed traditions. Both men were born in America to parents of British background. They are both also known to have worked with potters in the New Haven, Connecticut, area before coming to Boston. Fenton's work frequently shows manifestations of Germanic traditions in long-necked, full-bellied jugs and ovoid jars decorated with cobalt painted within incised designs. Carpenter's work, on the other hand, remains more or less true to his British background, as is evident in the brown ferrugenous dips on the upper and lower portions of his pots and in his production of some absolutely cylindrical jars. The use of the stamp, possibly for the factory, which produced BOSTON in impressed letters on the vessels of both men, was an American innovation. A jug, produced in East Dorset by Fenton's son, Richard L., about thirty years later, is illustrative of a typical American stoneware jug of the early nineteenth century. The company name and location have been impressed with a stamp on the throat of the jug; the neck is typical, the rather short American style of the period; and a free cobalt floral design was brushed on the front of the jug. Fenton's son, Christopher W. became involved with the Bennington, Vermont, factories and the production of stoneware pots as well as the ornate earthenwares for which Bennington is well known.

As the general population began to multiply and expand westward across North America, craftsmen of every sort were a part of the wave of expansion.

Potters were somewhat limited in the selection of a homestead in the wilderness, since the proximity to good clay, water, and wood was essential for the practice of their craft. Since clays occur most often in areas suitable for agriculture rather than in mountainous areas, pioneer potters frequently farmed on a small scale and practiced their craft on a part-time basis in small, one or two man shops. As the population increased, the need for storage vessels increased, and potters established larger shops, eventually moving toward industrialization of the craft.

Clusters of small shops frequently developed in areas where good clays were abundant. As small communities developed into towns, pottery shops often lay at the outer edge of the community. The fact that the presence of pottery kilns created a serious fire hazard was perhaps the major

A one-gallon jug with "BOSTON" impressed just under the long neck. Decorated with cobalt at the end of the handle and within the "J. F." cartouche. This shows much Germanic influence but was made by Jonathan Fenton between 1793 and 1797. The one-gallon cylindrical preserve jar bears the same mark, but has been dipped in a ferruginous solution to color the top and bottom of the jar. This British manner of decoration was commonly used by Fredrick Carpenter, a partner in the Boston pottery. 1793-1797. Both salt glazed.

A four-gallon jug of an ovoid form made by R. L. Fenton, a son of Jonathan Fenton, about 1835. It is salt glazed with a crude cobalt floral design on the front and "R. L. FENTON & CO. / EAST DORSET" impressed. $395

A semi-ovoid form of wide-mouthed jar. It is salt glazed on the exterior and unglazed on the interior. "L. MASSILOT" impressed and "3" and "1836" in cobalt. Atttributed to Ohio. *Courtesy of The Western Reserve Historical Society.* $550

A tall, ovoid, four-gallon capacity jug. The exterior is a buff to pale gray salt glaze and the interior is unglazed. Impressed: "A.A. AUSTIN & CO./ COMMERCE, MO." c. 1850. *Courtesy of Robert Sherman.* $750

reason for their location at a distance from the community center. Since transportation of raw clay was arduous, shops were frequently located near the source of clay. One other reason for the distance of potteries from homes and stores applied to salt glazing potters only. The somewhat dangerous and very unpleasant emission of chlorine and hydrochloric acid fumes during the salting period dictated a location away from well-populated areas.

The manufacture of utilitarian stonewares increased tremendously during the nineteenth century in North America. Small stoneware potters in most parts of the United States and Canada provided impermeable, easily cleaned, safe vessels for the storage of all types of foods, even highly acid vinegars and pickles. This major role of stoneware for food storage was extremely important in the productive, agrarian culture of North America during this period. Farming methods had improved, and greater production of foods during the warm seasons made storage of this food for the unproductive seasons most important. Stoneware vessels were considerably more durable and cleaner than the previously used earthenware or staved wooden containers and much less expensive than metal vessels. Glass storage vessels during this period were still expensive and relatively small in size. Stoneware vessels were by far the most suitable containers for the storage of the large amounts of foods conserved by the relatively large farm households.

As the manufacture of stoneware became more common, other vessel forms suitable for the daily chore of milk conservation and the separation of cream, as well as the making of butter, were produced. Still other forms for use in the barnyard and household—such as poultry feeders and waterers, flowerpots, and chamberpots—became common in stoneware because of their durability and impermeability. Very, very few tablewares were made in stoneware, and cookingwares were not commonly produced in this medium until technology became advanced at the end of the nineteenth century and special bodies capable of withstanding the thermal shock imposed on cooking vessels could be developed.

The history of the development and early technology of the American utilitarian stoneware industry has gained in importance with the passing of the industry's flowering. Only a few potters remain who can tell us some of the story firsthand, answer our questions, or correct our **false** interpretations.

A very ovoid one-gallon preserve jar in a light gray salt glaze. The interior has a deep brown slip glaze, probably local. Impressed: "D.L. ATCHESON / ANNAPOLIS, IA." Annapolis, Indiana 1841-1850. *Courtesy of Indianapolis Museum of Art. Photographer: Robert Wallace.* $550

A very ovoid four-gallon preserve or storage jar in a pale gray salt glaze. The interior is unglazed. Impressed: "DAN'L CRIBBS / TUSCALOOSA" c. 1860. The Cribbs family is known to have come to Alabama from Ohio before 1860. $1650

A tall, slightly ovoid churn with a wooden lid. This churn is a pale gray to beige alkaline glaze inside and out. Two incised lines as for ii indicate the gallon capacity. Rusk County, Texas, c. 1850. $300

A one-quart pitcher with a tan to brown mottled alkaline glaze inside and out. The initials "T. L." for Thaddeus Leopard are impressed near the handle. Winston County, Mississippi. c. 1880. *Courtesy of the Mississippi State Historical Museum.* $500

A three-gallon churn with lid and dasher. This churn is glazed in a caramel brown slip local glaze inside and out. Impressed: "D. BRANNAN / SAN ANTONIO" Daniel Brannan, San Antonio, California c. 1860. *Courtesy of The National Museum of History and Technology, Smithsonian Institution.* $1000

Bennington, Vt. _Dec_ _27_ 1847.

No.

Cambridgeport Mass.

E. F. Cuttings

Bought of **JULIUS NORTON,**

Manufacturer of every description of Stone Ware.

			per dozen.	$	CENTS.				per dozen	$	CENTS
JUGS.	Dozen 4 gall.		$8.00					Amount bro't forward.		9	87½
Ditto,	" 3 "		6.50			**BUTTER POTS**	Dozen 6 gall.		$14.00		
Ditto,	" 2 "		4.50			Ditto,	" 5 "		12.00		
Ditto,	" 1 "		3.00	3	17	Ditto,	" 4 "		10.00		
Ditto,	" 1-2 "		1.75	6	88	Ditto,	" 3 "		8.00		
Ditto,	" 1-4 "		1.00	0	51	Ditto,	" 2 "		6.00		
Ditto,	" 1-8 "		0.75			Ditto,	" 1 "		4.00		
POTS.	" 6 "		12.00			Ditto,	" 1-2 "		3.00		
Ditto,	" 5 "		10.00			**PITCHERS.**	" 2 "		4.50		
Ditto,	" 4 "		8.00			Ditto,	" 1 "		3.00		
Ditto,	" 3 "		6.50			Ditto,	" 1-2 "		1.75		
Ditto,	" 2 "		4.50			Ditto,	" 1-4 "		1.00		
Ditto,	" 1 "		3.00			**FLOWER POTS.**	" 2 "		4.50		
Ditto,	" 1-2 "		1.75			Ditto.	" 1 "		3.00		
CHURNS.	" 6 "		12.00			Ditto.	" 1-2 "		1.75		
Ditto.	" 5 "		10.00	2	50	Ditto.	" 1-4 "		1.25		
Ditto,	" 4 "		8.00			Ditto.	" 1-8 "		1.00		
Ditto,	" 3 "		6.50			**FANCY** do.	" 2 "		7.50		
Ditto,	" 2 "		4.50			Ditto.	" 1 "		5.00		
JARS. Cov'd.	" 4 "		8.50			Ditto.	" 1-2 "		3.50		
Ditto,	" 3 "		7.00			**STOVE TUBES**	1st size		6.50		
Ditto,	" 2 "		5.00			Ditto.	2d "		4.50		
Ditto,	" 1 "		3.50			Ditto.	3d "		3.00		
Ditto,	" 1-2 "		2.00			**CHAMBERS.**	1st "		2.00		
Ditto,	" 1-4 "		1.50			Ditto.	2d "		1.50		
PUDDING POTS.	Dozen 1 gall.		3.00			**INK STANDS.** Founts	doz.		2.00		
Ditto,	" 1-2 "		1.75			Ditto, common	1st size		1.00		
BEER BOTTLES.	" 1-4 "		1.00			Ditto.	2d "		0.50		
SPITTOONS.	1st size		6.00			**MUGS.**	Dozen quart		1.00		
Ditto.	2d size		1.00			Ditto.	" pint		0.75		
						WATER FOUNTAINS.	Per gal. 25 cents.				
	Carried forward.					Ditto, Urn Shape (ornamented)		50 cents.			

Chapter 2
From Clay to Pot

THE CLAY SOURCE

Naturally occurring stoneware clays are abundant in many parts of the United States. Early potters found good sources on Manhattan Island, on Long Island, and in New Jersey, Pennsylvania, Virginia, and the Carolinas. Westward expansion brought about the discovery of clay in a great many areas of the nation. "Prospecting" for clay was the first stage in the establishment of a pottery shop, and most of the early shops were founded within easy reach of a good source. Near-at-hand supplies of water, wood for firing, and a good clay were essential for the establishment of an early shop. It was not common in the interior of the country for clays to be shipped any distance or for advantageous shop locations for the distribution of the wares to be considered of importance. New England and New York State potters had, however, been transporting the excellent stoneware clays of Long Island and New Jersey to their locations even before the beginning of the nineteenth century. Their local clays, more suitable for earthenware, were usually mixed with the stoneware clay.

When the pioneer potter began looking for a new clay source, he examined ravines and hillsides where exposures of clay might have weathered out and where there was little overburden of soil and vegetation. Areas with clay free of large amounts of roots, soil, sand, or rock were sought. The selected clay was felt between the fingers for grit, tasted (a "sour" clay is generally not a good stoneware clay), moistened (often with saliva), and rolled between the palms to make a coil. This little coil was then looped around a finger to test for

plasticity—bending without cracking.

Availability, absence of extraneous material, plasticity, wet strength (the ability to hold up when turned on a wheel), dry strength, and little shrinkage are the most important factors in determining a good clay. Good clays are frequently found in boggy areas. Bog clays are usually rather dark in color, containing a moderate amount of iron and much organic material, and are very plastic. The clays suitable for stoneware have no typical natural color and in the raw state may be a creamy white, bluish gray, buff, yellow, ochre, or even brownish.

Iron content is the major factor in producing permanent color. The more iron present, the darker the fired color. Organic matter in raw clay may produce a blue to gray color, but it burns out in firing. Thus the stoneware clay made into a pot may be almost white, buff, gray to black, or salmon to red brown in color after firing. It is for this reason that the term "red-ware" is a poor name for common earthenware, since stonewares also can be red-bodied.

If the clay found by the pioneer potter was fresh, clean, and plastic, samples were taken home to be tested for drying, shrinking, and firing abilities. Desirable qualities for stoneware potter's clay are plasiticy, good wet and dry tensile strength, a moderate or very small amount of iron, minimal shrinkage, suitable vitrification point, and adequate silica content if it is to be salt glazed. Stoneware may be made from a single clay or a combination of clays. The combination is necessary when no single clay that is available to the potter possesses good working and firing properties. At times only fine sand need be

A general view of the Reems Creek Pottery in Western North Carolina about 1915. The groundhog kiln is in the center of the picture, its mouth opening under the shed on the left. The pillar of brick on the right is the chimney. Behind this the sweep of the clay mill is visible against the log shop. This is the first of a series of photographs of this pottery taken by William A. Barnhill. *Courtesy of The Library of Congress and W. A. Barnhill.*

added to a single clay to "open" it up, that is, to improve its drying qualities and lessen a tendency to crack. Sand also supplied added silica for a clay low in silica and therefore not suitable in its original state for the production of salt-glazed vessels.

Surface availability and depth of the deposit were important factors in the pioneer potter's selection of a clay. Until the later days of mechanical mining, clay was dug by hand with picks and shovels and either thrown up to the surface or pulled up in a basket. One large wagon or ox-cart load was usually removed in the one digging and taken to the shop for processing. Four or five wagon loads might serve a potter for an entire year. At times a year's supply of clay was dug during the winter months, allowed to weather out of doors, and processed as it was needed.

If the new-found clay proved suitable for stoneware after the initial testing, the potter could begin to establish a shop. Early potters who migrated from one part of the country to another carried within their heads all of the necessary information on how to make brick, build a kiln, build a wheel, turn pots, glaze, and fire.

A close view of the log shop at the Reem's Creek Pottery. Various unsold pots may be seen in the foreground. The one window allowed light over the wheel. *Courtesy of the Library of Congress and W. A. Barnhill.*

The potter is mixing clay with water in his bin. The mule is attached to the sweep of the clay mill and will begin to walk his circular path as soon as the mill is filled with damp clay. *Courtesy of the Library of Congress and W. A. Barnhill.*

BUILDING THE KILN

The clays used for brick for the construction of a kiln did not need to be as clean or as high burning as those for stoneware, although the kiln itself was the most important structure at the shop site. Bricks were made by patting a heavy paste of sandy clay into a small wooden form divided into four or six comprartments of wet brick size. The formed bricks were then turned out to dry. No formal kiln was necessary to fire the brick. A new kiln might even be built entirely of raw brick and then fired very slowly at a rather low temperature to cure them. More often pillars of raw brick were stacked and wood laid in channels between the pillars. The remaining raw brick were then laid up into a long rectangular form with corbelled arches over the channels. Slow burning for two or three days fired the brick within this informal "clamp" or "skove" kiln. The clamp was dismantled when cool, and the bricks that were most exterior and not well burned were placed within the pile with more raw brick over them for a second firing. The fired bricks were ready for use in construction of a kiln and other shop features as needed.

With no more than the simplest of tools—shovel, trowel, hammer, saw, and plumb line—a kiln of a simple round or rectangualr form could be constructed. Kiln floors were usually simple sand, brick, or earth covered with bits of crushed quartz rock. Rock was not necessary to the early potter but was a helpful accessory and cheap building material when avail-

A close view of the clay or "pug" mill. In this instance it is in a pit in the ground and the clay is removed from the top. A shed for drying pots can be seen at the far left. *Courtesy of the Library of Congress and W. A. Barnhill.*

Several balls ready for throwing are on the end of the bench. This rough, dirt floored interior is typical of the log shops of 19th and early 20th century potters in remote areas. *Courtesy of the Library of Congress and W. A. Barnhill.*

able. Rock was sometimes used as a building material under the floor, against the exterior walls, or as an exterior wall. Although occasionally an entire kiln may have been built of rock, the interior was usually lined with brick. Perpendicular brick kiln walls were built up in the desired fashion with a mortar of sand and clay. When the walls had reached the desired height, arch boards were used to lay the vault bricks, and their position could be changed as the vault became dry and relatively stable. The purpose of these boards was to maintain a uniform arch of the proper curve for the kiln. The boards cut in the proper curve supported a lath work over which brick was laid. The completed kiln was allowed to dry and then tested with a low firing cycle. Kilns could either be left exposed to the elements or lightly covered with an open shed. Some in cold climates were even within buildings. The kiln chimney always rose above any adjacent roof to avoid burning the protecting cover.

THE POTTER'S SHOP

The potter's shop, constructed like the kiln from the materials at hand, varied from a rather stable structure, sometimes of brick or stone in the cold climates, to a simple, dirt-floored log building in warm southern regions. Within the shop were one or two, perhaps more, wheels for throwing. Although all are rotary, the exact forms of potter's wheels may vary considerably. The most common wheel employed by American potters, certainly between 1850 and 1930, was the wood-framed wheel at which the potter worked in a standing position using a treadle bar kicked with the left foot to keep the wheel in motion. This form of wheel has a small disc or head at the top, a shaft with a special crook for the attachment of the wooden treadle bar, and a heavy bottom fly wheel. As the laterally projecting treadle is pushed back by the potter's foot it turns the shaft and the attached wheel head and fly wheel. After 1930 most wheels were equipped with an electric motor and pulley system. In the shop, wheels were usually positioned in front of the windows for light.

There were also racks to hold the boards upon which the pots were put to dry. A low benchlike table stood nearby, usually against a wall, with a taut wire strung from the table's outer edge to the wall. This table was used to work up or "wedge" the clay that had been prepared and to make balls of clay of the proper weight for different vessels. The wire served to cut the clay as it was worked or wedged to an even consistency. Above the table a set of very simple balance scales usually hung. The scales were to weigh the balls, which were made in specific sizes. Vessel size was primarily determined by a specific weight of clay. Often an apprentice did this work for the man throwing on the wheel.

A small area within the shop or under an adjacent lean-to was reserved for glazing. Large tubs or vats and the raw materials needed to prepare the glaze solutions were stored nearby. If the potter needed to grind his own glaze materials, a glaze quern or mill stood here also. As a rule, this was nothing more than a large stone basinlike form with a drip spout. A smaller stone fit within the basin and could be turned by hand with a stick fitted into a hole on its top. The mill was placed on a sturdy bench or small table. Glaze ingredients mixed with water were put into the basin and the movable upper stone was used to grind glaze ingredients much as a mortar and pestle are used.

In the vicinity of the shop, areas were set aside for the storage and weathering of the unprepared clay. Weathering or exposure to the elements for a few months has a definite advantage in that it increases the plasticity of the clay.

PREPARING THE CLAY

Certain areas near the shop were set aside for preparation of the clay. Some potters were faced with the problem of too much grit or undesirable particles such as lime within the clay. These potters had to first wash and screen the clay, a process which consisted of making the clay into a creamy

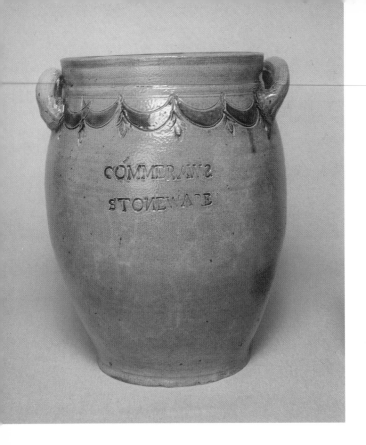

An ovoid, three-gallon wide mouthed jar with a pale gray salt glazed exterior and a toasty brown unglazed interior. A band of decoration filled with cobalt in the form of swags and tassels extends around the base of the neck. Bilateral open loop horizontal handles have been bent upward to nearly adjoin the body. Impressed with cobalt on stamp: "COMMERAW'S/STONEWARE" on this side "N' YORK/CORLEARS HOOK" on the reverse. Thomas H. Commeraw, c. 1800-1810. $3900

A 1-1/2 gallon jug of ovoid form. It has a pale gray salt-glazed exterior and brown slip glazed interior. A large eagle with spread wings and a sheaf of arrows in his claw sits upon a rope swing. All is incised with considerable detail and colored with cobalt blue. Impressed "BARNABUS EDMONDS & CO'/CHARLESTOWN" Charlestown, Mass. between 1812 and 1850. $18,500

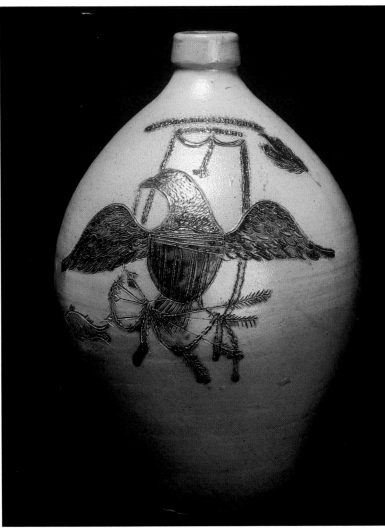

A bird ornately trailed and decorated in cobalt colored slip adorns the light gray to beige salt-glazed exterior of this 1-1/2 gallon jug. Albany slip glazed interior. Impressed: J. & E. NORTON/ BENNINGTON, VT." 1850-1859. $4750

Three salt-glazed vessels showing varying color in a salt glaze. The low jar on the left has no lining and a pale gray salt glazed exterior, the center churn has a light beige salt glazed exterior and an Albany type slip glazed interior. Decorated with a floral spray in blue and green produced by cobalt and copper coloring oxides. The deep jar on the right has a mottled dark gray and terra cotta colored salt glaze produced by varying amounts of oxidation and reduction in firing and a moderately large amount of iron in the body clay. No interior glaze. All second half of the nineteenth century. L-R: $600; $500; $275

George Donkel finishing the lip of a pitcher which he has just thrown on his wheel. The wheel is next to the window for light. *Courtesy of the Library of Congress and W. A. Barnhill.*

solution with water (called a "slip") and then passing it through a series of mesh screens into a vat of some sort where evaporation could take place. The clay was poured or funneled into the vat until the layer was at least eight or ten inches in depth. After sufficient water had evaporated in the vat, the clay was cut into blocks and stored in a dry state for "pugging," or mixing for throwing. At one pottery the vat might be no more than a brick-lined trough, while at others large open vats with low walls and floors of earth, wood, or brick were constructed out of doors. The large open-air vats are called "sun-pans." Present-day washed clays are prepared industrially in a mechanical device called a filter press. The slip is strained before entering the press, which is essentially a vacuum dehydrator that removes excess water from the clay.

The early potter's dry clay, if washing was not necessary, was coarsely crushed with a sledge hammer or in some sort of simple mill, then mixed with water to make it the proper consistency for throwing on the wheel. This is a slightly soft state about the consistency of bread dough. For centuries this mixing was accomplished by working a large mass of clay with the hands or treading upon it with both feet. With mechanization came clay "pugging" mills consisting of a cylindrical vat in the center of which a shaft was fitted with wooden or metal rods placed in a spiral pattern and extending from the shaft out almost to the vat wall. This form of mill, called a pug mill, was usually turned by a horse or mule walking in a circle around the mill, and was used in most parts of the United States during the major period of stoneware production.

The clay may be taken out of the pug mill from a hole at the base or from the top. It is then made into a long log-shaped form, a "bolt," weighing at least twenty pounds. In mechanized pug mills, clay is extruded in a cylindrical form and broken or cut into bolts for storage. Larger plants and even many artist potters today still use a mill of the pug type, but one that has been modernized and fitted with an electric motor. Other simple forms of mixers, working like giant potato ricers, were sometimes used to mix the clay and eliminate any harder lumps.

Visiting in the deep South a few years ago, I thought that I had come upon a potter who still used the traditional horse power, since the pug mill and the sweep which attached to the horse were in front of the pottery. His answer to my questions about using a horse was "No, I use my wife." Two years later the mystery was solved. As I drove up the road I saw his wife driving a small tractor attached to the sweep and thereby turning the mill.

THE POTTER'S SKILL

Potters in traditional shops still use the old guild method of designation of training periods. The first stage is Apprenticeship. During this period the learner is taught to throw upon the wheel but also has to do many menial tasks around the pottery such as making balls for the main throwers, making handles, preparing clay, loading, and helping fire the kiln. After two years of experience, the apprentice should be able to throw most utilitarian vessel forms with accuracy and a fair amount of speed. The second period is the Journeyman period. After two years of work under a Master potter, mainly improving his throwing skill, the potter can be considered a Master. The Master potters usually operate the shop, oversee and finish the firing of the kiln, prepare the glazes, and throw the larger pieces, such as five and ten gallon vessels, and fancy wares. They also have to arrange for the marketing of the wares.

Industrialized shops have broken this old traditional and rather personal method of pottery manufacture down into an assembly line process where specific jobs are done by separate persons. There are separate groups who do only single functions, such as preparation of the clay, throwing, molding, or jiggering. Other workers only glaze, and still others are kiln loading and firing specialists. The turners or throwers even in industrialized shops still follow the three traditional periods of Apprentice,

A group of four vessels glazed with an Albany type of slip glaze. The black pitcher at the far left was fired in an oxidizing kiln. The small green pitcher at its foot has a "frog-skin" glaze produced by very light salting over an Albany type glaze. The tall churn in the center shows a ruddy phase of the slip glaze while the one gallon jug on the right shows the usual shiny chocolate-brown of Albany type glazes with yellowish bleaching on the shoulder caused by the deposition of fly ash during wood firing. All last quarter of the nineteenth century or early twentieth century. L-R: $350; $275; $600; $200

Three pieces of salt glazed ware from the Seagrove area of North Carolina. They show the greenish tint and runs of salt glaze often seen in that area as the result of heavy overhead salt glazing in groundhog kilns over dark clay bodies. All second half of the nineteenth century. L-R: $750; $950; $380

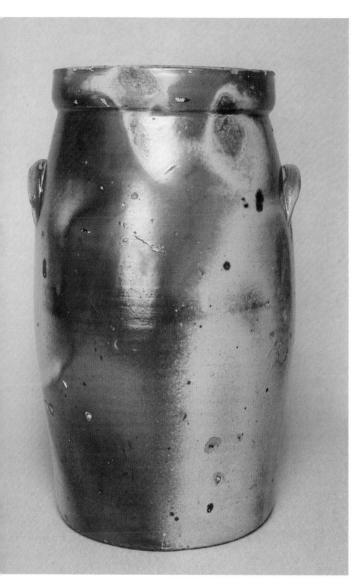

A three-gallon churn glazed with an Albany type slip glaze. Striking yellow areas appear on all sides of this pot and were caused by contact with fly ash, salt vapor, and possibly direct flames within the kiln during its firing. Attributed to William Saenger, St. Hedwig, Texas c. 1880. $600

Three pieces of stoneware glazed with the Leon slip glaze and made at the Meyer Pottery, Bexar County, Texas probably between 1900 and 1940. They show a deep brown phase with creamy speckles, a green to yellow green phase, and a mustard yellow to brown variation. Varying amounts of iron in different batches of clay as well as atmospheric and temperature variation within the firing kilns caused these color variations. L-R: $200; $375; $200

George Donkel handing pots into the kiln. An assistant within (on hands and knees is placing them on the floor of the firing chamber. This kiln has an opening in the rear chimney wall for loading. It is closed with brick during firing. *Courtesy of the Library of Congress and W. A. Barnhill.*

Wood is being placed within the firebox at the front of the kiln. Very modern metal door covers in this kiln are unusual. A slow fire will be lit and increased after about 4 or 6 hours. Notice that this part of the kiln is under a shed roof. *Courtesy of the Library of Congress and W. A. Barnhill.*

Journeyman, and Master, but they take no part in the other processes. There were some shops in the past, particularly in the rural South, where an entrepreneuer might build his own shop and kiln and perform all of the relatively unskilled work, with the exception of the throwing, himself. Accomplished "turners" or throwers who were really master potters moved from shop to shop. They helped the owner with the throwing or did all of the throwing to "fill the shop," moving on then to another shop to do the same thing. There were many stages between simple one-man shops and totally industrialized shops.

Although women are the potters in many primitive societies, few women have worked as professional utilitarian potters. This was a male occupation. The very few instances in which a woman's name has been associated with any American stoneware potteries present no evidence that the woman was associated with work in the pottery, but was the owner of the pottery. Women were and still are frequently employed as decorators in many branches of the industry. With the advent of studio potteries many women have also learned to throw upon a wheel.

"Throwing" upon a potter's wheel, is a craft that usually can be learned in three or four years of study, but varying degrees of skill may be developed. Some potters will throw very rapidly and can produce over one hundred five-gallon jars a day. Others may be slower but their work thinner and more even. In the past the manner of payment was by the number of

Three vessels with alkaline forms of glaze to show the wide range of color and textural variations. The pitcher on the left has a pale, straw-colored alkaline glaze inside and out. The tall jug shows a very common olive green color glaze with only slight texture while the jar on the right shows heavy agglutinated streaks and runs in a deep caramel brown with a few iron spots that have turned a deep iron red. L-R: $795; $1400; $395

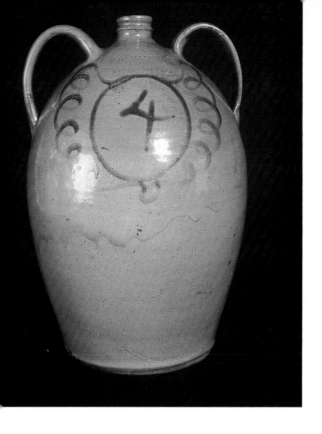

A four-gallon capacity ovoid jug with two strap handles. The smooth, transparent alkaline glaze is yellowish green, but becomes bluish green where an added coat of glaze pooled as it ran down the pot. Decorated with a "4" within a circle surrounded by loops trailed in a brown ferruginous slip. Impressed: "CHANDLER/ MAKER" Thomas Chandler, Edgefield are, S. C. c. 1850. $2500

A large jar of about 10-12 gallon capacity. It has four handles of the wheel thrown, flaring type attached around the shoulder area. Decoration consisting of tulips and leaves painted in a dark brown slip and outlined in white slip appears on the surface between three handles, a sunflower in brown slip outlined with appears in the fourth space. The streaks made by the thickness of additional alkaline glaze are olive in color, while the thinly glazed background is brownish. Attributed to Collin Rhodes, Edgefield, S. C. c. 1850. $9500 rare.

An almost globular five-gallon jug with two strap handles affixed to the upper shoulder. This jug is covered with a smooth, transparent straw yellow alkaline glaze. A bold floral form is brushed on each side in a dark brown slip and outlined in a trailed white slip. This side shows the capacity numeral "5" worked into the design in place of a flower. The reverse shows the same essential design with a flower in the proper place. Attributed to Collin Rhodes, Edgefield, S. C. c. 1850. $6000

43

Stoking the kiln at night. Since most firings lasted 12 to 18 hours in these small kilns, night stoking took place regularly. *Courtesy of the Library of Congress and W. A. Barnhill.*

The Meyer Pottery at Atascoca, Texas about 1910. The large open air vats into which the strained clay was placed to dry are visible at the left front. These may be called "sun pans." The sweep of the clay mill is seen in front of the shop at the center of the photograph. *Courtesy of Frank O. Meyer.*

Treadle Kick Wheel

Some potter's tools. Top: a set of lifters for one- or two-gallon vessels. Center: a pair of lifters for small jars or vases. Bottom: far left: plaster of paris capacity numbers. Left to right: three wooden ribs, one plain and two with notches for rim contours.

A two-quart pitcher glazed inside and out with a pale yellowish, lightly textured alkaline glaze. Decoration was achieved by the pouring of a much darker batch of glaze in four areas around the pitcher. Dark stripes resulted with variegated iron reds and blacks streaking down the lower portion of the pot. *Attributed to John Leopard, Rusk County, Texas c. 1875.* $7500

A three-gallon jar of ovoid form with bilateral pulled lug handles on the upper shoulder. The alkaline glaze is of the form typical of the Catawba River Valley area of North Carolina and shows a speckled white and pale blue color developing on top of a dark brown background. These white and sky blue flecks are produced by iron in the presence of titanium and calcium which seem to be indigenous to that one particular are. Maker unknown. Last quarter of the nineteenth or early twentieth century. $775

A spaniel doorstop made in a press mold at the McDade Pottery, McDade, Texas about 1920-1930. He stand 8-1/2" high and is covered with a white Bristol glaze decorated with a few spots and features brushed on in cobalt. $1500

Three pieces of stoneware glazed in a form of Bristol glaze. The pieces vary from a blue white to creamy white to cream mottled with light beige (over an iron-speckled body). The jar on the left is a florist's vase decorated with sprayed bands of cobalt, the churn shows two cobalt painted bands and a stamped cobalt mark and capacity number. The jug on the right is representative of the Albany and Bristol glaze combinations with a stamped advertisement for a merchant. All first half of the twentieth century. L-R: $220; $350; $650

Marcus Allie Broach with his wife and daughter at the Evans Pottery, Dexter, Mo. about 1900. The elegant jardinieres with their combed bases would make any potter proud. Notice also the flowerpot and saucer with fluted edges. *Courtesy: daughter of M. A. Broach.*

gallons turned in one day, which promoted rapidity. Nineteenth-century masters in this country took great pride in their craft and were very demanding of their workers. Pots from that period usually have thinner, more even walls and more pleasing forms than those of the twentieth century.

In pots produced under conditions of industrialization and mechanization we find a loss of individual characteristics and little evidence of artistic pride on the part of the individual potter. Modern pots usually are heavy, have poorly defined features such as rims and handles, and are monotonous in form and glaze. This applies both to pots thrown by hand and those made in jigger machines.

The process of throwing clay upon a flat revolving disc called a wheel head appears easy and effortless when it is done by a proficient potter. This is far from true, and only an amateur who has tried his luck at throwing can know how very much experience it does take. The process is relatively rapid, for it is important that the clay not become too wet or "overworked."

The accomplished thrower usually has an assistant who prepares the balls of clay in the proper size by weight for the vessel to be made. Sometimes called the ball-boy, **this assistant often is a young apprentice.** After preparing the balls ready for the thrower, the assistant then takes away the full boards of ware for placement upon the drying rack. Often the assistant applies handles to the vessels as well.

After placing the clay ball upon the middle of the wheel head with a forceful movement so that it will stick, the thrower then moistens his hands and applies pressure to the clay as the wheel revolves, making it into an even, slightly flattened, solid cylinder. This is called "centering." After centering, if a very large clay ball is being used, such as twenty pounds or so to make a large churn or jar, the thrower may use a leverlike instrument attached to the side of the wheel frame. This is called a ball-opener. When lowered onto the centered clay cylinder, it opens a hole in the middle of the ball, being set so that it leaves an even thickness of about ½ inch for the interior bottom. If the clay mass is

Mr. J. E. Ricter of Berg's Mill, Texas using a ball opener to start a one-gallon jar. The height gauge may be seen between the lever of the ball opener and the waterpan. Taken about 1968 when Mr. Richter was 86 years old. *Photographer: Harvey Belgin.*

smaller, the ball is usually opened with the thumb or forefinger, and the centered clay then forms a simple cylinder with thick walls and an opening in the center. The walls are then pulled upwards once or twice to the desired height by using the fingers of one hand inside and those of the other hand outside, pulling in a gently upward motion as the wheel spins. Some potters use a wooden tool called a rib to smooth out the exterior throwing lines as they pull upwards.

The finishing touches and smoothing, such as pulling in the mouth and rolling the rim and smoothing the clay surface with a wooden rib, are then accomplished. After a final flourish, often accomplished with a pointed tool to make an incised line marking the level of the handles, or even several lines for decoration, the thrower cleans up the base by making a swift cut around it with the pointed tool. The pot is cut from the wheel by drawing a plain or twisted cord or wire under it as close to the wheel head as possible. With both hands for small vessels or a set of lifters for larger ones, the potter lifts the vessel and places it on the drying board. Vessels that have become out of round during the lifting process may be jiggled to return them to round. Potters also usually blow a puff of air into small-mouthed vessels such as jugs to give them a fuller form. Handles are applied as soon as the drying process stiffens the pot enough that it is not distorted by the handling process. If the clay becomes too dry, the handles will not secure well.

Traditional utilitarian potters formed a large number of vessels of one size and type in a single session of throwing. There was an attempt at uniformity in these vessels in the use of uniform weights of clay for specific vessels. Four pounds was the usual

A water cooler made at the Meyer Pottery about 1925 for Tinsley School. This cooler consists of three eight-gallon jar size cylinders placed one on top of the other. Green Leon slip glaze inside and out. Height: 33-1/4". Capacity: about 24 gallons. $2200

ball size for a one-gallon jug. After the first vessel of the day was formed, the height gauge attached to the wheel frame was fixed at the level of the top of the vessel. All subsequent identical vessels were made to conform with this height. All sorts of individual characteristics such as the basic form of the pot, the type of rim preferred for various vessels, the manner of attachment as well as the shape of various handles, and even different ways of cutting the pot off of the wheel and finishing the bottom appeared during the throwing and handling processes. These are often all that we have to separate different potters in a local area, especially in the absence of potters' marks. Although these individual characteristics fade out as industrialization takes over, the pots from later potteries are much more often marked.

There are a number of different modifications in wheel throwing used by different potters and traditions. Orientals sometimes use very large lumps of clay and center only the small top section, making a number of small bowls or cups from one large lump. This method was not commonly used by American traditional potters. The manner of making large vessels may also vary. A potter might make a large vessel (over three gallons in size) by forming the base and then a separate top section, joining the two while they were still damp. This is termed "topping" by most potters. Some form of caliper is necessary to do this accurately. In wheel turning very large vessels, such as those of 15 or 20 gallon capacity, a sturdy lower section must be made and allowed to stiffen somewhat by drying. A second method of forming a large pot may then be employed. One or more rolls of damp clay may be added to the top of this base and worked by turning and pulling up to finish the vessel. After the application of each section, a period of drying is necessary so that the base will be firm enough to support the added section. Evidence of splicing of either type can usually be seen on the interior of the pot.

MODERN POTTER'S METHODS

Although other methods were used, wheel formation of the vessel was the most common manner of producing utilitarian stoneware vessels in the United States during the nineteenth century. The other methods have now almost supplanted basic wheel throwing. The "jigger and jolly" machine began to be commonly used after 1850 in industrialized potteries where production of a large amount of ware to be sold at a very cheap price was important. This machine is commonly called a "jigger wheel" in the United States.

The jigger has a large base that revolves when powered by energy (now usually electric) and plaster molds of various forms can be placed in this base. A relatively unskilled workman can place a ball of clay within the mold and with his fingers or a simple inside template (the jolly) pull it up around the walls as the wheel revolves, forming a rather heavy but adequate pot. The plaster absorbs some of the water out of the clay, and the formed pot can be removed from the mold in an hour or so for further drying. One of the advantages of the machine is that is is inexpensive to operate, since the operators do not have to be skilled potters. Decorative patterns can be formed on the exterior of the pot if desired and can be incorporated in the mold. The disadvantages are that the pots are heavy and must be open in form. The mouth of the vessel has to be at least as large as the base, and no undercutting may be present in the form. Most of the graceful variations that can be expressed in hand turning are obliterated in the forms that are produced by this machine. The pots are always rather heavy and very "plain Jane" in appearance. Flower pots are often made in this machine for this reason. Jugs of the shouldered form can also be produced with the jigger by using two molds—one for the cylindrical base and another to make the top of the jug upside down. The two sections of the jug are then put together while still damp with the use of a thick clay suspension in water, commonly called "slip." Although jigger machines are still in use, mechanical

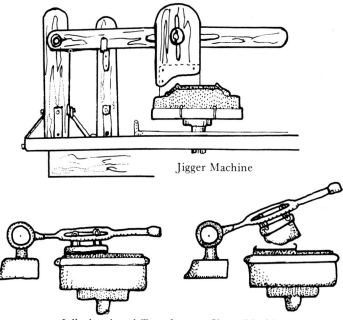

Jigger Machine

Jolly head and Template on Jigger Machine

A whimsical cartoon painted in cobalt under a Bristol white glaze. The bail handled, jiggered jar dates c. 1900 or later. A scrawny horse is out of sight around the right side. The cartoons issuing from the mouths of the men say "Guy, the mare is thin, but she hasn't had any grain." and "John, I will take her at $85.00 and have her fat, too." Said to have been made in the Zanesville-Lancaster area of Ohio. *Courtesy of the Ohio Historical Society, Ohio Ceramic Center at Roseville.* $7500

A one-gallon bowl made in a jigger mold and having an ornate ribbed pattern on the exterior. Albany type slip glaze inside and out except the broad heavy rim. This bowl was stacked with a group of others like it in the kiln and only the rim was exposed and salt-glazed during firing. Middlewestern U.S.A. late 19th century. $750

presses presently employed have taken over the production of common objects such as flower pots.

Another method used for forming stoneware vessels, mainly employed in an industrial situation, is the use of bisqued clay or plaster of paris molds, mainly of one, two or three parts. In one-part molds rather firm clay can be pressed by hand into the interior or over the mold and allowed to dry and shrink. Simple "drape" molds in which the clay was draped over the mold were once commonly used for pie baking dishes. In the more elaborate molds, commonly used for pitchers, spittoons, and decorative items, a thick solution of the clay (slip) is prepared and poured into the mold. The entire mold is filled, but after the plaster absorbs enough water and a wall of the proper thickness can be seen separating from the plaster, the excess slip may be poured back into the slip tub to be mixed and used again. This is called slip casting and is the manner in which most ornate wares are formed. Mold lines formed by the joints between the two or more parts of the mold can usually be seen on the exterior of coarse wares formed in this manner, but fine wares are carefully trimmed by hand to remove this excess clay. Handles for such vessels are frequently made in another mold and attached as soon as the forms are dry enough to remove from the plaster. The vessels are always more thin-walled, therefore lighter in weight than those formed by any other ordinary method.

Some limited varieties of pots as well as hand-formed or press-molded whimseys were made by workers in sewer pipe factories in many parts of the country. Occasional planters and a few other jar forms were made using pieces of extruded pipe. Extra clay was often applied to the exterior and the surface combed coarsely to resemble tree bark. Some of these planters have only a single opening, while others have pieces of pipe of smaller diameter affixed to the sides to resemble branches of a hollow tree. Since men employed to make sewer pipe were not really potters in the true sense of the word, their artistic efforts were usually limited to the use of the extruded forms or to clay pressed into molds, a technique used by some of the more enterprising and artistic workers. Considerable hand modelling of figures such as turtles and alligators also was done. The pieces were then placed into one of the kilns when dry and salt glazed along with a load of vitrified sewer pipe. This work is certainly a part of the history of our stoneware heritage and is more representative of folk art expression than many of the plain turned pieces. The sewer pipe pieces often can be recognized by their very coarsely textured clay body.

The continued decrease in the number of potters trained for production wheel throwing has made the use of other methods of production of pots even more important in our present ceramic industry. I know of only one pottery in the United States today employing a group of men throwing utilitarian stoneware forms on the potter's wheel in a production manner. This is the Marshall Pottery in Marshall, Texas. All of the clay preparation, drying, glazing, and firing of the stoneware is industrialized in assembly lines at this pottery. The stoneware production is a small part of the output of the factory, which presses red clay flower pots and saucers by the thousands in other departments.

The art of throwing clay upon the potter's wheel is the province of "artist potters" in the United States today. Traditional utilitarian potters have become relatively unneeded, and therefore their numbers have declined nearly to extinction.

A happy lion doorstop made at the Grand Ledge, Michigan Sewer Pipe Factory. It is 9" long and 5-1/2" tall. Artist unknown. Grand Ledge Sewer Pipe Company, Grand Ledge, Michigan. First quarter of 19th century. *Courtesy of the Folk Arts Division, The Museum, Michigan State University.* $3500-4000

This planter was formed by adding branches of smaller diameter to a central piece of sewer pipe of about 10" diameter. It has been coarsely combed all over to make it resemble a tree stump. The name "Nellie Flynn" is hand inscribed in a plain medallion on the upper front. Salt glazed, dark ruddy brown color. Height: 22". Made at the Summit Sewer Pipe Company, Akron, Ohio about 1925-1930. *Courtesy of Nancy and Bob Treichler. Photographer: Doug Moore.* $600

Chapter 3
Form Follows Function

THE VARIETIES OF FORM

There is an old adage among designers and craftsmen that the primary form of an object follows its function. This is very true of utilitarian American stonewares. They were manufactured as necessary household items to perform certain specific functions. Vessels with small mouths such as jugs and bottles are designed to hold relatively thin liquids such as water, wine, cider, vinegar, syrups and distilled liquors. These small mouthed vessels can be securely corked to keep the contents from spilling, evaporating, or being contaminated by insects, animals, or dirt. Bowls are relatively wide and not deep so that foods can be mixed within them easily, and those designed for the separation of milk are often especially wide so that the cream may be easily skimmed from the surface.

Each vessel, therefore, has a basic form associated with its function, but many, many variations are seen within each specific grouping. These may follow a general traditional pattern, a temporal pattern, a regionally preferred pattern, or even the personal preference pattern of the individual potter or owner. The influences upon variation are so numerous that it is impossible to present more than generalties in a study of this scope. There will always be exceptions that can neither be anticipated nor explained.

Temporal change in form during the nineteenth century was very evident in both the United States and Great Britain. Rhenish jugs also lost their earlier full middles and became tall slender cylinders. Essentially the change was from the centuries old ovoid, globular, or full-bellied form for jars, jugs, and even churns to vessels in which the major portion of the sides of the body were straight, making the vessels cylindrical rather than ovoid. Shoulders were higher, sharper, and better defined. Undoubtedly developments toward industrialization of the craft as well as in kiln forms and size influenced this change. Cylindrical vessels may be very neatly and closely stacked inside of a large kiln.

An economic arrangement of ovoid vessels with a kiln is practically impossible. Fuel was becoming more expensive and larger amounts were needed as larger kilns became common. It was therefore more economical to pack the vessels tightly. Potters, having the adaptability of soft clay to work with could change their forms easily. With the increasing industrialization of the craft, it was necessary that the produce of the small individual shop be modified so that it could be sold as inexpensively as possible to compete in the market with the products of industrialized potteries.

Consumers in remote, economically depressed rural areas were not so influenced by this trend and were usually quite satisfied with the wares produced by their local potters. It was in these areas that regionally preferred patterns remained strong. For example, we see ovoid forms persisting in vessels produced in the Piedmont area of North Carolina and central and northern Georgia until the beginning of the twentieth century. The temporal change to cylindrical forms there was at least thirty or forty years later than it was in the industrialized areas of Pennsylvania, New York, or Ohio.

Regionally preferred patterns are evident in a number of stoneware forms. The

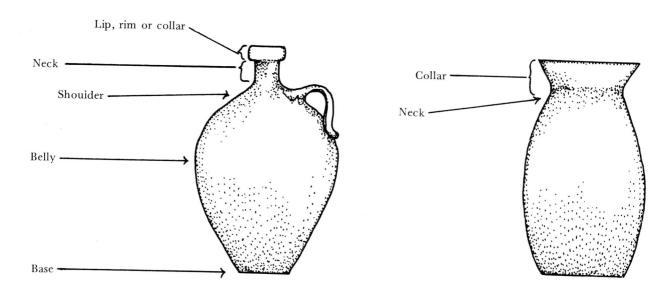

wheel-thrown handles on most ovoid jars glazed in an alkaline glaze are certainly a regional preference in the deep South. Milk bowls are commonly a deep pan form in the upper South and mid-Atlantic areas and a wide and shallow pan form in the deep South.

The persistence of a pattern personally preferred by the potter may be demonstrated by the unglazed water coolers produced during the twentieth century at the Meyer Pottery of Bexar County, Texas. At the very same time that Meyer was producing cylindrical jars and jugs, the Meyer's water coolers retained a slightly ovoid jar shape with bilateral strap handles affixed so that they extended outward. This was essentially the form of the utilitarian wide-mouthed jar of nineteenth century German potters. The water coolers therefore show retention of a traditional form from the land of the potter's birth and period of his youth being used at the same time that the potter had "Americanized" or "modernized" most of his other products. The pots of Germanic form and decoration produced by Jakob Wingender and his sons during the earlier period of their New Jersey pottery also demonstrate the survival of a pattern preferred by the potter.

Personal modification of a form to perform a function, other than that for which it was designed, may be even more variable. An elderly lady who likes to make her own butter, but has need for a very little, may have a wooden lid and dasher made to convert a one-gallon preserving jar into a churn that is large enough for her needs. She may also feed her chickens from a large ceramic milk bowl. We cannot anticipate this sort of modification or function, only attempt to explain it when we find it.

Some common variations of each basic form produced in utilitarian stoneware will be discussed and illustrated in this chapter.

The illustrations show temporal as well as regional variations. Most of the forms were made on a potter's wheel and for those that were not, the method of manufacture will be specified.

To enable accurate description of form for utilitarian pots, terms to describe elements of the primary form of the vessel (such as the lips, necks, handles, and feet) must be established. Therefore, discussion of the primary forms and lists of descriptive terms precede the discussion of specific examples of form.

There are definite chronological changes in the form of the common stoneware vessels. These follow a pattern, but the dates of these changes are relative and not exact, just as the dates of changes in manner of decoration or types of glaze preferred are relative. Exact dating is not possible except in those few instances in which a date appears on the vessel. Relatively accurate dating can be accomplished when the potter's or the pottery's name is marked on the vessel and their dates of operation are known. Unmarked vessels may then be compared with marked vessels of known relative dates produced in the same general area and a rough date covering a quarter of a century may be assumed. A consideration of the glaze type and manner of marking and decoration (if any is present) of the vessel under study also gives keys that assist in rough dating. However, there is some temporal variation in preferred form and glaze types regionally within North America. Therefore, any applicable regional studies of area potteries which may exist should be consulted in any attempt to determine more accurate identification and dating of unidentified American stoneware vessels.

There are in existence a fair number of price lists from mid- to late-nineteenth century potteries operating mainly in the northeastern United States. Several of these lists have been reprinted in previous studies of American stoneware. They give us a vast amount of information as to just what vessels were made at the time, what they were properly named by their manufacturers, and in what size capacities they were manufactured. Some of these lists have small outline drawings of the vessels in each category as well, giving us a fairly accurate idea of the form preferred at the particular date of the list. Unfortunately, there are no lists for the earliest periods of manufacture and essentially none for potteries operating in the deep South.

All of the drawings and descriptions of vessels and vessel parts in this chapter are based on actual American stoneware vessels. An attempt has been made to use marked vessels for as many of these examples as possible so that the provenience and a relative date are known. Because there are always variations in the

work of one potter from the next-even in known father and son relationships-only the rather loose categories covering locally prevalent vessel forms and glazes may be applied to the determination of the age and the provenience of unknown pots. Some studies of stoneware manufacture in different regions of North America have already been produced, and perhaps in the future we may have a more or less complete set of regional studies. These will enable interested persons to determine a great deal more about their unknown pots than I can possibly provide in one book.

My general descriptions of form used for stoneware vessels, as well as the examples of each different major form which follow are mainly those of forms made on a potter's wheel or made with a jigger or jolly machine. Both of these methods of manufacture, since they operate upon the principle of centrifugal force, restrict the horizontal form to a circular shape. The diameter may be varied, producing a number of different three-dimensional forms. The usual vessel form, while still soft, might be modified at times for specific effects. For example, flattening of the sides of small jug and bottle forms to make them resemble glass or metal flasks was not uncommon. Press molding and slip casting do not limit form in this manner and these methods were used occasionally in utilitarian potteries to produce ornate or unusual forms. The occasional hand modeled whimseys produced were not limited by method and could be made in any shape desired.

TYPES OF VESSEL FORMS

The various stoneware vessel forms manufactured may be divided into the most common (or major), which were produced at almost every utilitarian pottery; the fairly common, which were produced in smaller numbers at most potteries; and the unusual. The later types may be whimseys, toys, or special forms produced to supply a particular neighborhood demand. Jugs, jars with both wide and narrow mouths, churns, and bowls were the common forms produced by most nineteenth and early twentieth century utilitarian stoneware shops. Bowls were less commonly made in some areas in which earthenware bowls were being produced, either by small traditional potteries or industrialized potteries. Pitchers (always termed so when this form is manufactured in the United States but usually called "jugs" in Great Britain) and chamber pots were also frequently produced in small numbers. Plain flower pots, usually unglazed and partially vitrified, having been fired in the cooler sections of the kiln, were also a common product of potteries in well populated areas. There was less demand for such wares in pioneering areas.

With the exception of mugs, tablewares were seldom produced by utilitarian potteries. It seems that this form of production was favored only when potteries were in remote, unpopulated areas or areas shut off from their usual importation routes by war. This was particularly true in some areas of the South during the Civil War. Industrially produced tablewares were generally favored during the nineteenth century and most of those used in this country during that period were imported from Great Britain.

All of the other forms considered in this discussion are unusual. Their production varied from pottery to pottery and area to area. Production of unusual forms increased mainly in areas where competition was keener and during the twentieth century when the need for the basic forms was declining.

An unglazed but hard-fired water container of about 5 gallon capacity made by William Meyer at his pottery. This form of a slightly ovoid pot with bilateral pulled strap handles just under the upper rim is in exactly the same form as German wide-mouthed jars of the same period. Bexar County, Texas 1887-1920. $550

A medieval castle in gray salt glaze with cobalt applied decoratively in many areas. Stamps like those used on other Kirkpatrick pieces appear in some area. It is 7" high and 12" in maximum diameter. This piece was purchased from Kirkpatrick descendants and is known to have been made at the Ann Pottery. Probably a sculpture to be used in a fishbowl and made in the late 1860s. *Courtesy of Barry Cohen. Photographer: Henry Cox.* $9500

Bennington, Vt., Jan. _____ 1862.

M _____ _____ _____

Bot of **E. & L. P. NORTON,**

ORDERS BY MAIL PROMPTLY ATTENDED TO.

EDWARD NORTON.　　　　　　　　LUMAN P. NORTON.

JUGS.

	Per Dozen	Dols. Cts.
Doz. 4 Gallon,	-	$9.00
" 3 "		7.00
" 2 "		4.50
" 1 1-2 "		3.75
" 1 "		3.00
" 1-2 "		2.00
" 1-4 "		1.00
" 1-8 "		0.75

OPEN CREAM POTS.

Doz. 6 Gallon,		12.50
" 5 "		10.00
" 4 "		9.00
" 3 "		7.00
" 2 "		4.50
" 1 1-2 "		3.75
" 1 "		3.00
" 1-2 "		2.00

COVERED CREAM POTS.

Doz. 4 Gallon,		10.00
" 3 "		8.00
" 2 "		6.00
" 1 1-2 "		5.00
" 1 "		4.00

CHURNS.

Doz. 6 Gallon,		12.00
" 5 "		10.00
" 4 "		9.00
" 3 "		7.00
" 2 "		5.00

COVERED PRESERVE JARS.

Doz. 4 Gallon,		9.00
" 3 "		7.50
" 2 "		6.00
" 1 1-2 "		4.75
" 1 "		4.00
" 1-2 "		2.25
" 1-4 "		1.50
Bean Pots. Doz. 1 Gallon,		3.00
" 1-2		2.00
Pudding Pots. Doz. 1 Gallon,		3.00
" 1-2		2.00
Beer Bottles, per doz.		1.00
Quart Mugs, " "		1.25
Pint Mugs, " "		0.75
Soap Dishes, " "		2.00
Water Kegs, per gallon.		33 1-3

BUTTER POTS, COVERED.

	Per Dozen	Dols. Cts.
Doz. 6 Gallon,	-	$15.00
" 5 "		12.00
" 4 "		10.00
" 3 "		8.00
" 2 "		6.00
" 1 1-2 "		5.00
" 1 "		4.00
" 1-2 "		3.00

COVERED CAKE POTS.

Doz. 4 Gallon,		10.00
" 3 "		8.00
" 2 "		6.00
" 1 "		4.00

PITCHERS.

COVERED BATTER PITCHERS,

Doz. 2 Gallon,		6.00
" 1 1-2 "		4.75
" 1 "		4.00
" 1-2 "		2.50

COMMON PITCHERS,

Doz. 2 Gallon,		5.00
" 1 1-2 "		4.00
" 1 "		3.00
" 1-2 "		2.00
" 1-4 "		1.25

FLOWER POTS.

Doz. 4 Gallon,		9.00
" 3 "		7.00
" 2 "		5.00
" 1 "		3.50
" 1-2 "		2.00
" 1-4 "		1.50
" 1-8 "		1.00
Stove Tubes, Doz. 1st size,		6.00
" 2d "		4.50
" 3d "		3.00

SPITTOONS.

Doz. 1st size,		6.00
" 2d "		4.00
Chambers, Doz. 1st size,		2.50
" 2d "		2.00

MILK POTS.

Doz. 2 Gallon,		4.50
" 1 1-2 "		3.75
" 1 "		3.00

TOMATO JARS.

Doz. 1-2 Gallon, (with corks,)		2.37
" 1-4 "		1.25

A price list from the Bennington pottery of E. and L. P. Norton, 1862.

GENERAL FORMS

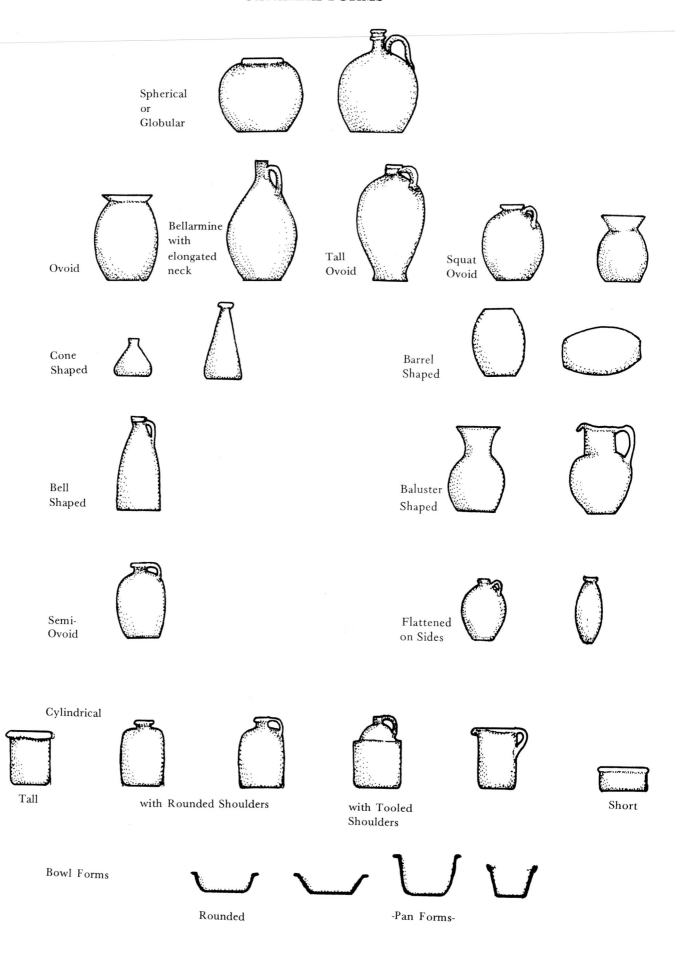

Spherical
or
Globular

Ovoid

Bellarmine
with
elongated
neck

Tall
Ovoid

Squat
Ovoid

Cone
Shaped

Barrel
Shaped

Bell
Shaped

Baluster
Shaped

Semi-
Ovoid

Flattened
on Sides

Cylindrical

Tall

with Rounded Shoulders

with Tooled
Shoulders

Short

Bowl Forms

Rounded

-Pan Forms-

60

GENERAL FORM

Terms for Describing General Form of Most Stoneware Vessels.

BALUSTER SHAPED: This term may be used to describe vessels which show a combination of cylindrical and ovoid or globular forms used in the turning of the vessel. The same word applies to wooden turned pieces in which both cylindrical and different ovoid, and globular forms are combined on one piece to form fancy support columns. The word actually derives from the Greek term for the pomegranate fruit, which exhibits a globular base with a cylindrical top.
This is the commonest form used for pitchers in stoneware and exhibits a globular or ovoid lower section and a cylindrical upper section taking up about one third of the body. This form may also be employed for decorative vases.

BARREL SHAPED: This form is very much like the semi-ovoid form with its gently rounded midsection and fairly wide base. The top section, however, is sharply cut in from the sides and flat. It is a direct imitation of the staved keg or barrel form and was most popular for small keg-like vessels for hard liquor and water collers. It appears throughout the period of stoneware manufacture in America in nearly the same form. Very early barrels may have slightly smaller bases and tops, but there is little other difference. This form may be finished to rest either in an upright or horizontal position.

BELL SHAPED: This form is characterized by a long slope from the neck to the midsection or belly of the pot, which eliminates the usual shoulder curve as the form tapers in toward the mouth. It seems to have been more common in the deep South than in any other region. The form is occasionally seen in jugs two gallons and under in size during the same period that the larger jugs of the same potter were ovoid in form.

BOTTLE SHAPED: This is a rather self explanatory term which may be applied to wheel-made stoneware vessels turned in direct imitation of glass bottles. This may be more closely defined by saying that it is an imitation of ordinary glass bottles which exhibit a cylindrical lower section, a well defined shoulder, and straight, narrow neck.

BOWL FORMS: Since bowls are open forms they do not fit into the general descriptive patterns for form. A few more specific terms must be listed to aid in their general description. The shallowness or depth and the character of the rim and base may be separately described.
Pan Form: This implies that the bowl has a perfectly flat base and that the sides rise to the rim at an angle with little or no curve.
Rounded Form: This form is more generally seen in bowls which were made in a Jigger machine. They may have a small base or foot ring so that the bottom is not flat. The sides rise to the rim in a definite curve. Although this form may easily be turned, for some reason most utilitarian potters preferred the pan form for turned utilitarian bowls.

CONE SHAPED: In this form there is no visible shoulder or belly, only a long taper from a wide base up to a smaller mouth. It was generally used for containers for liquids and is an imitation of glass ink, catsup, hot sauce, beer, and wine bottles. Churns made in imitation of staved wooden churns may have a slightly conical tapered form.

CANTEEN SHAPED: This form consists of a short and wide cylinder which is turned on its side in imitation of a wooden canteen. Two low bowl forms may also be joined on the edges to make this form.

CYLINDRICAL: In this form the major portion of the pot consists of walls rising directly vertically from a broad base, forming a perfect cylinder. These may be short, fat, tall, or slender. Although some early jars of this form are seen, by the twentieth century almost all of the major vessel forms manufactured in stoneware in America assumed this form. It may be seen in jugs, pitchers, and jars of the wide mouth or narrow mouth types. If the vessels have a mouth smaller than the diameter of the base in cylindrical forms, a sharp and well defined shoulder turns in toward the mouth. Late churns are usually more or less in this form. "Shouldered" or stacking jugs have a very sharp angle at the point of the inward shoulder turn, and this is tooled into a flat ledge to permit the stacking of a jar of the same dimensions upside down on this ledge. After a ledge of about three quarters of an inch has been tooled flat, the shoulder rounds or angles upward to the mouth.

FLASK SHAPED: This term is reserved for wheel made bottle forms which have been flattened on two sides after they were turned so that they have the appearance of blown glass flask.

GLOBULAR: See Spherical.

OVOID: This term, meaning egg-shaped, is used to describe vessels that have a central or belly portion which is fuller than the base or the top. There are tall ovoid forms and short ovoid forms, but all tend to have a gentle inward and upward slope to the neck or mouth and a similar slope inward and downward from belly to the base. Jugs and large and small preserve jars with small mouths as well as early wide mouthed storage jars often show this form.

Its uneconomical occupation of space in a kiln as well as its rather top-heavy nature led to the phasing out of this form after the mid-nineteenth century. It was very seldom used during the twentieth century except for essentially decorative vessels, but it was perhaps the most common form used for early American stoneware.

PAN FORM: See Bowl Forms.

RING SHAPED: A form which involves throwing two short walls parallel to each other in a circle then closing these walls together to form a ring-shaped vessel. A separate, thrown spout is usually added.

SEMI-OVOID: This term is used to describe vessels that have, usually, a wide base, gentle rounding of the midsection, and a little better defined shoulder. Jugs, large and small mouthed preserve jars, and churns may take this form, especially during the second half of the nineteenth

century. Usually, vessels of this form are transitional between the period in which the main vessel forms tended to be ovoid and the late straight cylindrical vessel forms.

SPHERICAL OR GLOBULAR: Either of these terms may be used to describe a more or less completely rounded form in which the shoulder area curves rather rapidly towards the mouth. There is usually little or no obvious neck. This form is generally reserved for storage jars or vase and tableware forms. It is a relatively early storage jar form. Although seldom used for jugs in American stoneware, fifteenth and sixteenth century Rhenish stoneware jugs and seventeenth century English Delft jugs are often of this form.

A pair of bottles of about one quart capacity each. These lipless bottles were formed in a three-part mold - the mold lines may be seen on the exterior. They are glazed inside and out with a shiny brown to black Albany type slip glaze. Bleached areas on the shoulder tops are golden yellow and the result of fly-ash deposits during wood firing. Limestone County, Texas c. 1900. $250 ea.

Jug and Bottle Necks and Mouth Rims

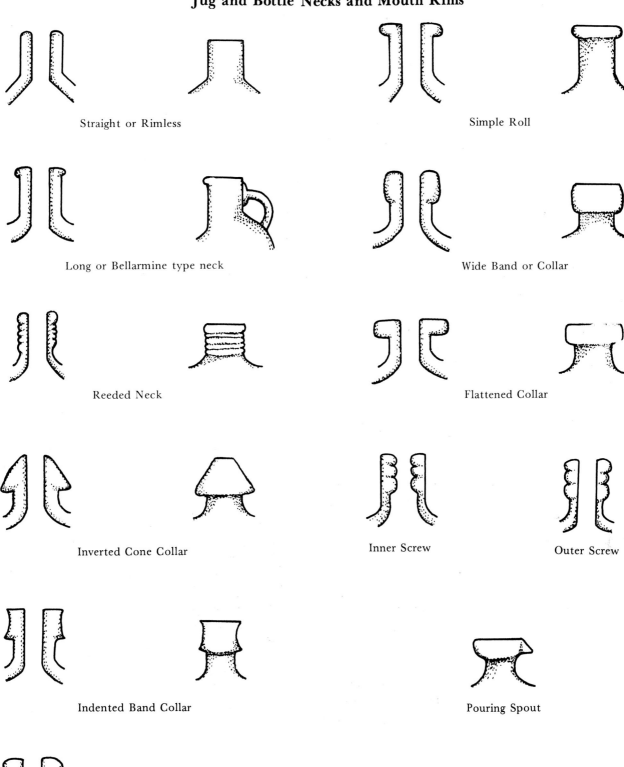

Straight or Rimless

Simple Roll

Long or Bellarmine type neck

Wide Band or Collar

Reeded Neck

Flattened Collar

Inverted Cone Collar

Inner Screw

Outer Screw

Indented Band Collar

Pouring Spout

Ringed or Fancy Collar

Neckless with Single Roll

JUG AND BOTTLE NECKS

Terms for Describing Jug and Bottle Necks

AVERAGE, SHORT, OR LONG NECKS: Jug necks as well as bottle necks may be long or short. Average necks on jugs may range from one half of a centimeter up to two and a half centimeters in length. Although there is usually a fairly well defined cylindrical section just below the mouth rim, at times there is no visible space between the rounding in of the shoulder and the terminating ring or band around the mouth of the jug (these vessels are neckless). The length of the neck, its definition, and the form of the rim around the mouth are all individual characteristics of the potter. An unusually long neck is usually associated with earlier vessels, since the form of European seventeenth- and eighteenth- century stoneware jugs incorporated a long neck. Any jug neck three centimeters or more in length may be considered unusually long; decoration was often used on unusually long necks.

RHENISH NECK FORM: The unusually long neck seen on Rhenish seventeenth- and eighteenth- century jugs appears only on very early American stoneware forms. The one positive example that I can think of is that of the jugs made by Johnathan Fenton in Boston between 1793 and 1797. It is associated with a pear-shaped, tall, ovoid body. The term BELLARMINE is often erroneously applied to this form, as it is to such jugs in Great Britain. I prefer to call this a Rhenish neck form.

TOOLED NECKS: These are usually somewhat longer necks which exhibit decorative tooled rings incised into the neck area. Sometimes these rings were deliberately rounded to look as if a reed was wrapped around the neck. These may be called reeded necks, but fit into the tooled neck group.

JUG AND BOTTLE MOUTH RIMS, COLLARS, OR LIPS

Terms for Describing Jug and Bottle Mouth Finishes

Cone: A terminal ring in the form of a heavy cone is formwd at the mouth of the vessel so that there is a sharp inward angle toward the exterior shoulder from the base of the cone. This was a common form of rim used for beer and ale bottles so that the cork could be secured in with wire.

Fancy Collars: Many potters fashioned rather ornate neck rings around their jug mouths. These may consist only of a single wide band which has a middle indentation, while some have even double or triple rings fashioned within the defined collar. The reverse curves occurring between these rings may make the term "ogee curved" applicable.

Flattened Lip: A flattened extension of a mouth ring is everted so that it projects at right angles to the mouth, producing a broad flat lip.

Pouring Spout: The mouth rim may be fashioned into a small bowl or saucer shape with a pouring spout pulled opposite the handle position. These were usually formed on jugs made to contain molasses and syrups and bottles for ink.

Rimless: These vessels usually have a rather distinct neck, but no finishing collar or ring around the mouth opening.

Screw Mouths, Inner and Outer: The grooves for a screw cap are molded into the jug mouth with a special tool. Only industrialized potteries used this mouth form, and it is very rare in America. The stoppers may be cast in stoneware to fit the screw, or metal and wooden stoppers made to fit.

Simple Roll: The mouth is finished off with a very simple single roll. This was the most common mouth finish prior to 1850.

Wide Band or Collar: One of the most common finishes is a heavy flat band of one centimeter or more in width and height around the mouth. This is common on relatively neckless jugs especially after 1850.

Rims: Jar, Bowl, and Churn Mouth and Rim Types

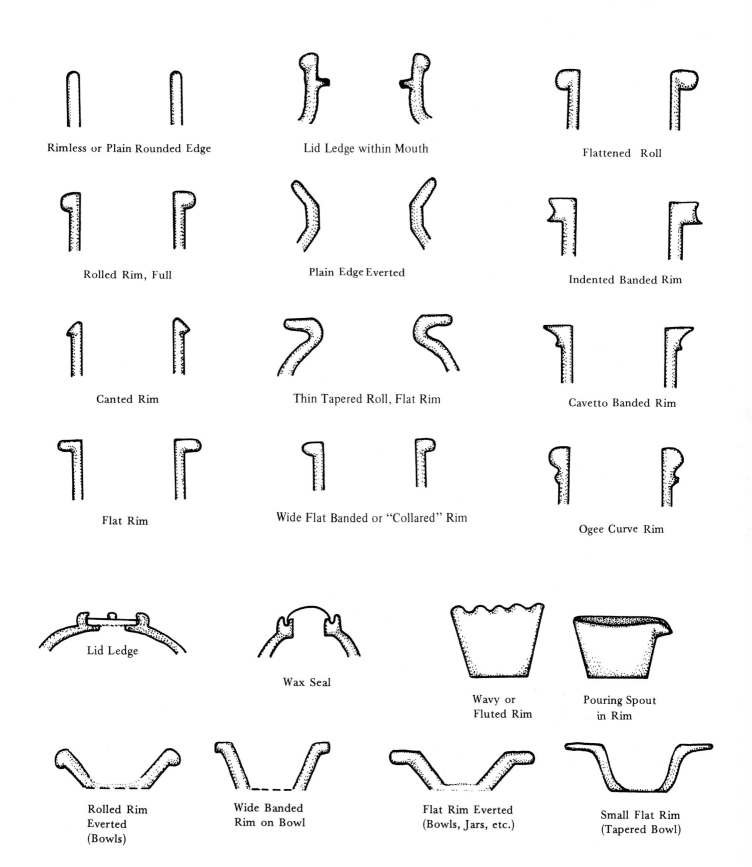

Rimless or Plain Rounded Edge

Lid Ledge within Mouth

Flattened Roll

Rolled Rim, Full

Plain Edge Everted

Indented Banded Rim

Canted Rim

Thin Tapered Roll, Flat Rim

Cavetto Banded Rim

Flat Rim

Wide Flat Banded or "Collared" Rim

Ogee Curve Rim

Lid Ledge

Wax Seal

Wavy or Fluted Rim

Pouring Spout in Rim

Rolled Rim Everted (Bowls)

Wide Banded Rim on Bowl

Flat Rim Everted (Bowls, Jars, etc.)

Small Flat Rim (Tapered Bowl)

65

Other Rims and Lips

These descriptive terms apply generally to rims occuring on jar, churn, and bowl forms. These rims are generally parallel to the walls of the pot and are, therefore, usually somewhat everted when used on wide flaring vessels such as bowls. The very top of the rim is, however, usually parallel to the base of the vessel. If indwelling lids were to be used on the vessels, small projections or ledges were present within the mouth ring, a centimeter or two beneath the top of the rim. Churn and small-mouthed preserve jar lids were usually indwelling. Small-mouthed preserve jars of both large and small sizes exhibiting a strong projecting rim or lip of some sort and no lid ledge within the mouth were common before the mid-nineteenth century and are spoken of as having "tie-down" rims. This means that the strong projecting rim made it possible to tie down a cloth cover tightly over the mouth opening of the vessel.

A specially tooled groove was made in the upper rim of certain late-nineteenth-century stoneware preserve jars. This mouth opening had to be made in a more or less exact diameter so that domed metal lids, which were also manufactured for early glass preserving jars, could be used on the jars and secured with sealing wax or tree resin. This grooved rim is seen in smaller sized stoneware jars of pint, quart, and half-gallon capacities. I shall call this a "wax-seal" rim.

Late forms of preserve jars sometimes have ledges around the outside of the mouth or a very flat top to the rim to receive the rubber rings necessary with a patented closure. Most of these jars were produced in industrialized potteries and formed in molds.

Terms for Describing Other Rims and Lips

Canted Rim: A little of the clay remaining at the top of the vessel wall is pressed downward in a cant away from the mouth of the vessel. This is not a common rim.

Cavetto Banded Rim: This is a form of an indented banded rim, but the lower section of the band is less wide than the upper, producing a cavetto form.

Fancy Ogee Curved Rim: This is a very fancy rim in which a second and sometimes even third curve has been made to produce ringlike projections beneath the heavy top ring. It was employed particularly in the production of fancy flower pots.

Flat Rim: This rim may be formed by simply flattening the top of a rolled rim. It is also sometimes done by turning back the top centimeter or so of a plain finished mouth to form a slightly projecting, firm rim. It is a common tie-down rim.

Flat Tapered Rim: This rim or lip is formed by turning back the upper centimeter or so of the mouth in which the walls have been tapered thinner towards the edge. It also is a common form of tie-down rim.

Indented Band Rim: The heaviness of a solid wide banded rim is broken by an indentation made between the upper and lower edges, usually with one finger.

Indwelling Lid Ledge: This is a feature of any vessel which properly has a lid fitted within the mouth. The exterior finish of the rim may be accomplished in any manner desired by the potter, but is usually a simple band or roll.

Rimless or Plain Edge: This term is really self-explanatory. The tops of the vessel walls are rounded or squared off and no defining lip or rim is to be seen.

Rolled Rim: An obvious roll of clay terminates the vessel form. It may be small or large and heavy.

Spouted Rim: This is a rim in which a pouring spout has been intentionally formed after the turning. This is a standard feature of pitchers and ink bottles, but is also sometimes used on bowls which are to be used for liquids such as milk.

Wavy or Hand Fluted Rim: This second very fancy rim is produced by hand fluting a finished plain rim after the turning of the pot has been completed. It appears almost exclusively on fancy flower pots or vases.

Wax Seal Rim: A tooled groove is present within the top of the mouth rim into which a form of metal domed lid may be fitted.

66

Bottoms and Feet

Flat or
without
Foot

Wire cuts sometimes
seen on flat bases

Plain
base

Tooled
foot
flange

Flat
Base

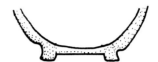

Hand Tooled
or Cut

Foot Ring
Sometimes
double

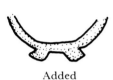

Added
Foot Ring

Base

Added Separate
Hollow Feet
-wheel made-
(as in pipkin
handle, has
tiny hole)

BASES AND FEET: Terms for Bases and Feet of Wheel-Made Vessels.

Wheel-Made Vessels

Most wheel-made vessel bases or bottoms are very simple flat bottoms cut from the potter's wheel. At times, however, the finished forms of certain vessels may be raised upon feet of one type or another.

FLAT OR UNFOOTED bottoms are the most common form seen in wheel made utilitarian stoneware of North America. Three different types of cuts may be seen on these bases:

a. Crossed twisted wire cut - this cut shows a pattern of oval grooves made as the twisted wire was pulled under the vessel in a loop. This may result from pulling one of the wires through the clay while holding the other taunt.

The mark left when a twisted wire is pulled in a loop to cut the pot from the wheel.

67

b. Plain cut - a single wire was passed through the clay rather than a twisted one, and no pattern of grooves was made. This is the most common cut, although it appears about the same as one of the other forms which has been smoothed with a damp sponge after cutting.

The smooth cut made by a single wire pulled across under the base of a pot to cut it from the wheel.

c. Straight plain twisted wire cut - shows transverse grooves resulting from the passage of a twisted wire through the soft clay to cut it from the wheel.

A stoneware jar base showing the typical mark left by a twisted wire which is pulled through the pot straight from the side to side.

ADDED SEPARATE THROWN FEET: Occasionally small thrown feet, either in the form of solid or hollow knobs, may be added to a form. These are rare, but are used to convert jug forms to pig-like forms at times. If these happen to be hollow, a pinhole must be left open for the relief of air expansion during firing or these feet will blow off.

ADDED THROWN FOOT RING: If a rather fancy foot is desired to give the vessel a more elegant form, a hollow cylinder of clay may be thrown on the wheel and attached as a base when it is firm, or one may even be thrown directly on the base of the vessel which has been fixed upside down on the wheel. This sort of foot is uncommon, but was used for fancy water coolers or jardiniere forms at times.

HAND TOOLED FOOT RING: A thick bottom is left as the pot is cut from the wheel and then the vessel is turned upside down on a potter's wheel when slightly dry and the center is cut down for one-half centimeter or so to leave a small foot ring at the outerbase. This is a tooled foot ring, common on most oriental stoneware and porcelain thrown vessels, but uncommon on American ones.

JOLLY MOLDED BASES

Terms for Describing Bases Formed in a Jolly Mold

MARKS AND NUMBERS ON BASES: These are seen most often in raised profile on juggered vessels. It was possible to cut these into the plaster mold and have them appear on the pot bottoms as raised designs. They are not uncommon on such vessels.

The base of a bowl with a central ribbed design within the foot ring and a ribbed pattern on the walls of the vessel. Made in a jigger mold.

SHALLOW ROUNDED FOOT RINGS: Very low, rounded rings which may be continous or interrupted are usually present upon the bases of Jolly molded forms, especially bowls. These rings characteristically have a very low and rounded profile necessary in this form of mold. The sharp profile of a tooled cut foot is absent.

A low foot ring of the rounded type frequently seen on a bowl formed in a jigger mold.

SQUEEZED CLAY LINES: These distortions look like fine radiating lines which may be formed by squeezing the clay into a mold. They frequently show up around the outer edge of the bases of vessels made in these molds. They are formed as the clay is pressed with the template into the mold.

The "squeezed" lines in the clay around the edges of a wide-mounted jar made in a jigger mold.

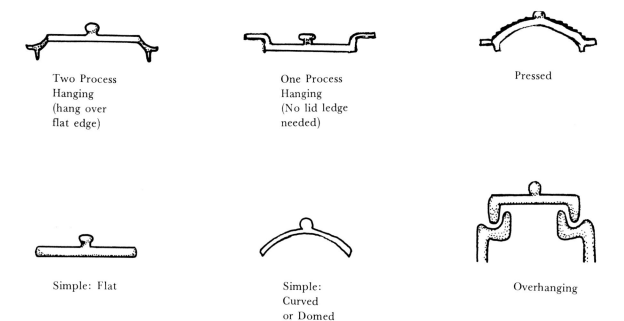

Two Process
Hanging
(hang over
flat edge)

One Process
Hanging
(No lid ledge
needed)

Pressed

Simple: Flat

Simple:
Curved
or Domed

Overhanging

CHARACTERISTIC OF LIDS

Not all potters seem to have bothered to make lids for their vessels and many vessels were made purposefully without lids during the earlier part of the nineteenth century. During that period cloth or paper were often substituted as a covering when one was desired. Early potteries did, however, manufacture lids for most vessels having a lid ledge visible within the mouth. These are all termed "indwelling lids," since they sit within the vessel mouth. Occasionally lids were made with a side taper to enable them to sit within a vessel mouth in the absence of a lid ledge. This form is most common in churn lids. Wide-mouthed vessels were usually fitted with "hanging" lids, a type of lid having a flange that hangs on the upper rim of the vessel. The "overhanging" lid is less common in utilitarian stonewares, more common in decorative wares. It fits over the mouth and upper lip of the vessel and may bear weight upon the top of the vessel or upon a ledge cut a centimeter or so below the top rim on the outside of the

vessel. Ceramic lids are rarely completely glazed. The hanging forms generally have the well-like area on the top side glazed, but not the lip flange. Most of the small flat lids for preserve jars have no glaze at all on them. Unfortunately, the original lids usually are not found on old stoneware vessels.

Terms Used to Describe Indwelling Lids

CHURN LIDS: Churn lids are generally made just as flat lids, but the central inch or so of the disc is left open about two to three centimeters so that a dasher handle may pass through it. Various forms of cups from very low rings two or three centimeters out from central opening to deep cup forms which center around this opening are seen on these lids. The latter is usually the older form.

A second basic form of churn lid may have the outer edge of the disc thrown into a free flange which is turned up to make about a 45 degree angle with the wheel. This makes it possible for the lid to slide down into the outward angled type of churn mouth for a short distance. It may or may not rest on a lid ledge.

DOMED LID: A slightly domed simple lid is seen rarely. It is made to rest upon a lid ledge within the mouth of a vessel. The lid is thrown upside down as a small bowl, but lacks the extra flange of the hanging two-process lid. It must be turned over when it is dry enough and a small knob added on the top center. Its most frequent use was on sugar bowls.

PLAIN FLAT LID: The is the simplest form of lid and sits upon the ledge provided for it just inside of the mouth. It is usually also provided with a small solid knob thrown at the same time.

Terms to Describe Hanging Lids

HANGING ONE-PROCESS LID: This lid is formed in one piece flat upon the wheel, but with a free flange around the edge which rises upwards about one to two centimeters above the central well formed by the lower section of the lid. It also has a small solid knob thrown at the original period of throwing in the middle of the lid. The flange rests upon the top of the upper rim of the vessel. It is the most common lid for wide mouthed storage jars.

HANGING TWO-PROCESS LID: This lid is made from a thrown shallow pan or bowl form which has a flat projecting exterior edge or lip as well as a one or two centimeter tall vertical projection up from the inner part of the ledge. The form is then turned upside down so that it rests on the upper rim of the jar when in use. The vertical edge fits down inside the vessel. A knob is added to this form by turning it upside down and throwing a small solid knob in the center of what is the top of the lid — hence the two processes. The top may be flat or slightly domed.

OVERHANGING LIDS: This form of lid is made to hand over the upper rim of the pot. It also must be made in two processes. The small pot form is made in the position that will be the reverse of its intended position and is then turned over when firm and a knob added unless the lid is very small. This is a decorative lid as a rule and uncommon in utilitarian wares. Overhanging lids are often seen on oriental jars.

CHURN LIDS

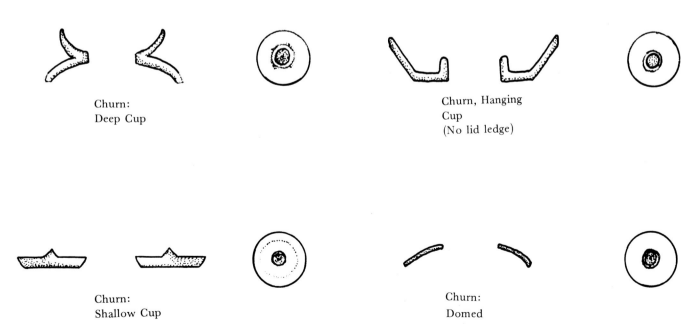

Churn:
Deep Cup

Churn, Hanging
Cup
(No lid ledge)

Churn:
Shallow Cup

Churn:
Domed

HANDLES

Strap: usually attached vertically

Occasionally
attached over
the top

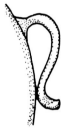

Pulled Attachments

Laid on

Loose
end

pulled on,
attached end

Lug:

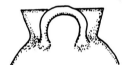

attached at ends only
Open Loop

attached along length

round, attached along length

cupped or straight
wheel made

Pipkin Type

Hollow thrown
(usually has a
small hole)

attached along full lengths:

Flat

Crescent

Projecting
straight

Projecting
cupped

-wheel made-

Knobs: Solid thrown

Flat

Round

Cupped

Cupped

72

CHARACTERISTICS OF HANDLES

Handles are probably the most varied of all of the appendages seen on pottery and they are not always "ears." The form of a handle is also very characteristic of individual potters. The handles with their manner of attachment in conjection with the consideration of body clays, form, glaze, and specific rim finish may help to identify an unmarked pot as coming from a particular pottery from which known vessels exist or from which comparative sherds have been collected. This is especially true in the case of unmarked pots appearing within the vicinity of the area in which the particular pottery existed.

The majority of the handles used for utilitarian stonewares were made by the "hand pulled method" in which a piece of clay was pulled out into a long strip by one hand, which had been well-lubricated with water. After the proper length had been pulled out, the handle was cut off with two fingers acting like a pair of scissors. Some handles, after being attached to the pot, were extended by further pulling.

A few handles, especially those used as lateral handles or lug handles on some alkaline-glazed stonewares, were formed by turning a low, hollow cylinder on the wheel and then cutting this form into four or six pieces to be placed on the pots as handles. Knob handles and the hollow thrown handles used on pipkins were also thrown on the wheel.

A third method of forming handles was by the use of a device something like a cookie press in which the clay could be extruded through a template of the desired form and pieces cut off and used as handles. These are "extruded handles." A few small, simple handles were modeled in press molds. Very fancy handles, such as those in the form of a lion's head, were also made in press molds. The little knobs and protuberances attached to the sides of pots to receive the metal ends of bail handles were often hand modeled or made in a very simple press mold.

The majority of handles may be defined as either strap or lug handles. This implies that long straps are formed and affixed to the pot with open loops remaining through which the fingers may be placed for the handling of the vessel. Strap handles are most commonly attached to the pot vertically. Lug handles, on the other hand, have a rim or flange extending out from the pot in which the tips of the fingers may be placed to lift or move the pot. They are most generally affixed in a horizontal direction and attached to the pot along their entire inner margins. "Ears" are properly only the very small, molded projections added to a pot as a simple handle or those made to receive a wire for a bail handle. The latter resembles an ear in that it has a central opening to receive the wire of the metal bail handle. Pipkin or hollow thrown handles or knobs are also identified as separate types. Solid knobs are a specific category.

Terms Used to Describe Handles

STRAP HANDLES: Strap handles are formed by pulling a piece of clay to form a handle and then cutting and attaching it to the vessel. There is, therefore, an area of origin and an area of insertion for these handles. Handles applied to jug and pitcher forms are nearly always strap handles, but they may be used on churns and jars as well as across the top of poultry waterers and a few other forms. They begin or arise near the upper portion of the vessel as a rule, but in the case of jugs they may arise from the rim around the mouth, from the neck just below the mouth rim, or from the upper portion of the shoulder. Two methods of application are used.

In the "laid on" method the upper section of the handle is gently rolled over and pressed down on the body of the pot. This produces the most attractive origin, but not the most common.

In the "pulled on" method, the rather thick, upper, cut end of the handle is pushed firmly into the area of desired origin. After this has been firmly fixed to the pot, the handle is pulled lengthwise gently again to smooth and lengthen it, then looped, cut, and inserted at a selected point. The "pulled-on handle" is the most common form of strap handle. These handles may be formed wide and flat with decorative grooves made by the fingers along their length, or they may be any shape between this flat type and a fully rounded form. The manner of attachment of the insertion or lower end also varies. Some ends are simply cut off at right angles and pushed down firmly at the point of insertion. This point may then be worked and flared out or smoothed into the body of the pot, or it may be tacked down firmly with a single impression made by a finger. Tapered tips may also be fashioned by cutting the handle end into a point. These may or may not be affixed with a single firm impression. Occasionally on fancy mugs, pitchers, or vases the point of insertion occurs a centimeter or so before the end of the handle, and the remaining bit of handle is allowed to have an upward curl at its tip as a final flourish.

Extruded handles may be applied in the very same ways, but are relatively uncommon in American utilitarian stonewares. The European form of strap handle produced by rolling a flat strip of clay into a hollow tube is not seen in America. It is characterized by the presence of a small hole pierced through the wall to allow the expanding air to escape during firing.

LUG-TYPE HANDLES: These handles are affixed horizontally, usually in pairs, on opposite sides of jars and churns to assist in the lifting of the vessels. Many of the earliest storage vessels show a form of open-loop lug handle affixed in a horizontal position on the shoulder of the pot. These are almost transitional between strap and lug handles, but I prefer to place them in the lug category since they are placed horizontally on both sides of the pot. These open loop handles were frequently bent upward after application so that they could be used by the fingertips of both hands to lift the pot. By the second quarter of the nineteenth century lug handles were being fixed along their entire length to the walls of the pot and this type became the common form of lug handle. During the mid-twentieth century they became practically rudimentary in some cases. The open loop is still used in Germany on storage jars.

Lug handles are most often pulled initially from a piece of clay just as strap handles are. An attempt is made not to narrow the pulled end, and narrowed ends are cut off and discarded. The portion which is used for the handle is of even width and, if tapering takes place, both ends are tapered to produce a crescent—shaped handle. These handles may be either flat or rounded. One side of a lug handle is fixed to the wall of the vessel, while the other side of the handle extends outward; the ends, as a rule, are firmly fixed by smoothing into the vessel wall. Sometimes single, deep, finger impressions may characterize the ends. Some lug handles appear to have been made from coils of clay rather than pulled. The infinite variations cannot all be described, but were often an identifying characteristic of the work of a particular potter.

Alkaline glazed stoneware, in particular, commonly had a different form of lug handle. This type was formed by throwing a bottomless cylinder wall in a ring upon the wheel and cutting this wall into four or six sections for application as handles. These are fixed to the pot along the cut made at the base of the ring. The ends may be cut to fit, left projecting, or cupped downward and worked into the vessel wall. The rounded, smooth edge made during the turning forms the exterior edge of the handle and is usually the key to the identification of this form of handle. This type is deeper than most pulled handles and shows a characteristic outward flaring appearance. At times four rather than two of these handles are used on large jars.

Another type of lug handle may occur, but is not common. A small, flat piece of clay is formed in a press mold and pairs of these are fixed to the pot horizontally as lug handles.

EARS: This type of handle occurs as small pieces of clay affixed in pairs to the sides of late vessels, usually churns and jars. Ears may have a small central opening to admit the wire for a bail handle. They may have been hand-formed of small balls or half-circular flat slabs of clay or may have been pressed into molds.

HOLLOW THROWN HANDLES:
These as well as the small knobs formed in the same manner on the wheel are more common on earthenware vessels than stoneware. They may be almost balls of two to three centimeters in diameter when used for feet, or elongated tubes ten or more centimeters in length when used as unilateral handles on small porriger-like vessels. These are often called a "pipkin" type handle because of their use on this type of earthenware vessel. Occasionally such handles are knob-shaped but remain in this category when hollow.

SOLID KNOBS: This form of handle has been briefly discussed with lids, for most lids are topped with knobs. They are made upon the potter's wheel and may either be formed at the time of the initial turning or added later. They are small, solid bits of clay and may be fully round in form, flattened, or turned up into a cuplike form. The flattened knob is the most common. I have seen knobs affixed bilaterally to the upper sides of a very few jars and presume that these knobs were applied so that the jar could be suspended by a rope or a wooden frame for ease in tipping to pour. Knobs are not often seen on any form other than lids.

THE COMMON FORMS

JUGS

Jugs are probably the most common form of stoneware manufactured. The jug form is designed as a storage vessel for liquids and has a relatively small mouth, which is usually designed for closure with a stopper of some sort, commonly of cork or wood. Jugs were used in large sizes for water, mineral water, hard liquors, wines, vinegar, oils, syrups, and such liquids. Smaller sizes were used for product samples, hard liquors, inks, turpentine, beer and ale, and stains or shoe blacking. Occasionally small sizes were used as containers for medication and antiseptics "for man or beast." These smaller forms were often handleless and called bottles, from their resemblance to glass bottles.

This three-gallon jug was decorated completely around its exterior surface with a remarkable whaling scene in cobalt slip. In this view a large whale surfacing, a small whale spouting, and a tiny sailing ship may be seen. Salt-glazed, Albany type slip glazed interior. Impressed on the shoulder: "F. T. WRIGHT & SON / TAUTON, MASS." c. 1860. *Courtesy of Eric McGuire.* $7500-8000

J. Fenton
Boston
1793-1797

Paul Cushman
Albany, NY
Dated-1809

N. Clark
Athens, NY
1815-1830

Julius Norton
Bennington, VT
1838-1844

Thos. Chandler
Edgefield, SC
c. 1850

John M. Wilson
Guadalupe Co.,
TX c. 1860

C.W. Braun
Buffalo, NY
1865-1877

J.D. Craven
Randolph Co.,
c. 1875

E.A. Jaegglin
Booneville, MO
1880-1896

Shouldered

Minnesota
Stoneware Co.
Redwing, MN
c. 1900
(jigger molds)

Shouldered

Star Pottery
Bexar Co., TX
c. 1905

Meyer Pottery
Bexar Co., TX
1900-1940

Large jugs may be considered those of from one- to five- gallon capacities. Rarely six-, eight-, or ten-gallon jugs may be seen. Most jugs above four gallons in capacity have double strap handles so that they may be carried or lifted by two persons. This is necessary because of the considerable weight of such a jug when filled with liquid. All true jugs have one or more handles. Occasionally the mouth is varied by the addition of a flared, bowl-like form in which a pouring spout is pulled. This is termed a syrup jug. The point of origin of the handle on a jug, whether from mouth rim, neck, or shoulder, was usually the result of the preference or habit of each individual potter.

There is a definite temporal change in the form of jugs during the nineteenth century. Early ones usually exhibit the longer necks and more pear shaped forms reflective of seventeenth- and eighteenth-century European forms. During the first half of the nineteenth century the full—bellied or ovoid form was general. After mid-century the sides began to move inward, and more definite shoulders were formed. Transition to the straight cylindrical form was complete in most areas of North America before the end of the first decade of the twentieth century. This late transition period was in most areas also the period of transition from small, family—owned shops to large industrialized shops. Many individual characteristics were lost during this period, since the economics of production were becoming more important and larger numbers of vessels were being produced by itinerant potters in large, partially industrialized shops.

A five-gallon, double-handled jug of tall, ovoid form. This jug is salt glazed on the exterior and has a thin brown local slip glaze lining. Impressed: "H. WILSON & CO.," and "5." Guadalupe County, Texas c. 1875. $650

A short, almost globular one-gallon jug. The beautiful handle was pulled and cut at the inserting end, then simply smoothed on to the neck of the jug. This is typical of the form of handle made in the Seagrove area of North Carolina. Heavy salt glazed exterior, brown slip lining glaze of the Albany type. Impressed: "WRENN BROS." c. 1894. $550

A one-half-gallon jug made in two pieces in a jigger mold. It has a bail handle and is covered with a thick, white Bristol form of glaze inside and out. The bottom bears the raised mark: "MANUFACTURED BY F. W. WEEKS, AKRON O. / STYLE XXX / pat. pending." Akron, Ohio c. 1890. $150

FANCY JUG FORMS AND BOTTLES

A large number of fancy or unusual forms were made modifying the original jug form. A good many of these were really whimseys. Small and miniature jug forms were almost always in demand as gifts or containers for small amounts, even samples, of various products. Some miniature jugs may be too small to contain anything. Many are the usual sample size of two-ounce capacity. Most of the other fancy forms vary from half pint to half gallon in capacity. They are mainly rather ornately turned modifications of ordinary jug forms.

One of the most common modifications of the ovoid jug form to produce a rather fancy effect is the flattening of two sides to make the jug resemble the glass flask form. These "fancy" stoneware flasks were very often also inscribed and decorated. A handle may or may not be present. **Stoneware flasks are uncommon after the mid-nineteenth century.**

The field or harvest jug is made with two openings on the shoulder area. One is in the form of an added spout from which to drink, the other, either central in position **or opposite the drinking spout, is a ringed** mouth opening through which to fill the jug. These jugs are usually handled with a ceramic strap or metal bail handle across the top. During the late nineteenth century in the industrialized potteries of Ohio, this form was often highly decorated and inscribed. The main body of these particular Ohio fancy jugs was frequently formed in jigger molds.

Grotesque and puzzle jugs were made as special pieces. Early anthropomorphic grotesque jugs may have been made as witchcraft pieces, but later examples were (and still are) manufactured as a sort of curiosity or souvenir piece popular for tourist sale. Most grotesque jugs made in America have facial characteristics representing a male Negro. Eyeballs and teeth may be a white clay. Teeth were also represented by broken bits of white ironstone china. They were produced mainly in the deep southern states and in Ohio.

Puzzle jugs, like mugs of the same type, are so constructed that inner secret tubes or openings make them dribble or spill when used in an ordinary fashion. They are highly variable in form.

Batter jugs are almost more pitcher than jug forms, since they have an added spout and a large mouth opening. At times they were fitted with overhead bail handles and lids of metal. Occasionally an additional cupped, lug type handle was applied near

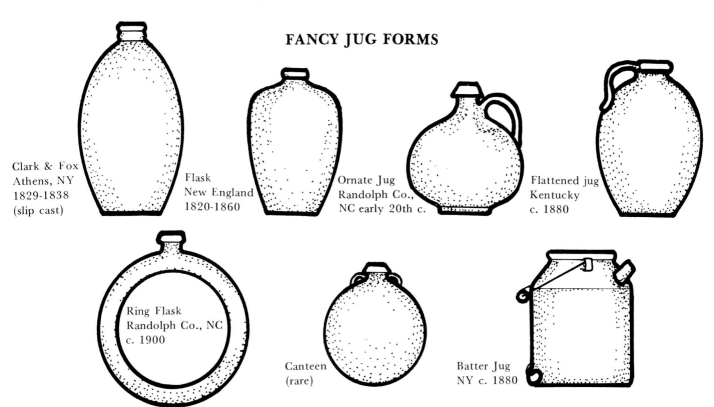

Clark & Fox
Athens, NY
1829-1838
(slip cast)

Flask
New England
1820-1860

Ornate Jug
Randolph Co.,
NC early 20th c.

Flattened jug
Kentucky
c. 1880

Ring Flask
Randolph Co., NC
c. 1900

Canteen
(rare)

Batter Jug
NY c. 1880

the base to assist in pouring. Batter jugs were used primarily for the storage and working of sourdough pancake batter.

Canteen, Costral, or Pilgrim bottles were an old and common European form of container. They were formed differently from a common jug by joining two very shallow, wheel-turned bowl forms together and then adding a separately thrown mouth or spout at the top of these two forms. Tiny loop handles were usually placed on the shoulder near the spout. This was a very rare form in North America in the nineteenth century. Twentieth-century cast jugs of this sort, having somewhat more of a drum or canteen shape, were quite popular. The exterior of this cast type usually had an ornate raised pattern. Capacities are usually from one pint to one quart.

Ring jugs, one of the most unusual forms of fancy jug, appear in both stoneware and earthenware. They are not thrown as a jug, but as a double-walled, low, ring-shaped cylinder form on the wheel. The two walls are then closed over to form a circular tube. A separately thrown spout is added at the top. Some ring jugs are also fitted with a flat base so that they may stand upright. This was definitely an unusual form and not made in large quantities. The ring form, a Germanic inheritance,

was used early but rarely in the northeastern areas of the United States. They were manufactured in larger numbers for the tourist trade in the late nineteenth and early twentieth centuries in the Piedmont region of North Carolina. These late ring jugs are commonly of about three-fourths quart to one quart capacity, but may be large enough to contain two quarts.

Bottle forms are small mouthed forms made to hold liquids, but are generally a quart or less in capacity and without handles. They are cylindrical in form, showing almost no temporal change. Special forms with large and heavy lips or collars were made as containers for effervescent liquids such as beer and ale. The heavy lip allowed a wire to be tightly tied beneath it to hold the cork in under pressure. Some were also made for drinks like Sarsaparilla. These bottles were made by hand on a wheel or in special press molds, most often by large, industrialized potteries. Beer or ale bottles often have a merchant's name impressed upon them.

Ink bottles were produced in both large and small sizes. The smaller sizes are either short, cone-shaped forms or short cylindrical forms holding approximately two to four ounces. Larger ink bottles are commonly up to one quart in size, but may be as large as one gallon capacity. They are cylindrical in form, and usually have a very tiny pouring spout made in the mouth ring. All have small mouth openings. Inkwells are most commonly formed as broad, low cylinders with one or several small openings for the pens and one somewhat larger opening in the center for filling. These are often rather specially decorated with rouletted patterns or other forms of decoration. Rarely an entire stand complete with one or two wells was made using slab techniques hearkening back to European forms of the eighteenth century. More commonly these fancy pieces were cast in molds. Hand formed inkstands are rare in American stoneware.

Other small bottle forms, frequently with larger mouths than those used as ink containers, were made to contain dyes, shoe blackings, and even medicines. These were all uncommon forms in utilitarian stoneware in North America.

A pair of small salt glazed flasks. The flask on the right is 7-1/2 inches tall, was formed in a two part press mold, and is marked "CLARK & FOX / N.Y." Athens, New York 1829 - 1838. The tiny flask on the right was wheel-turned, then flattened on the sides while soft. It is only 5 inches tall and probably held about 6 ounces. New England, 1st half of 19th century. Left to right: $2450, $450

Another fancy form in which small liquor container were made, this pig was formed in a two part mold. Ears, feet, and tail were hand-modeled and added. This pig was dipped in an Albany type slip glaze, then the ears and legs were wiped clean. These were then covered with an uneven transparent glaze — not salt-textured. Hand incised on the reverse "A Democratic Candidate for President," on the front "Sent with full instructions to the Cincinnati convention by Texarkana Pottery." The convention took place in 1880. $2500-3000

A pair of small jugs holding about one quart and one pint. Both are salt glazed and turned in unusual decorative forms. The one and one-half gallon salt glaze pitcher on the right has a very sinuous form with a widely flaring mouth. All seem to have had some influence from the "Art Nouveau" trend and are the forerunners of many artistic vase and jardiniere forms that followed. Seagrove area of North Carolina. Second quarter of 20th century. The small jug is impressed "JUGTOWN POTTERY" in a circle around a jug. Left to right: $475, $450, $795

A salt glazed "ring jug." This form of jug is a very old form produced by a different manner of turning - the potter throws a low, double walled ring and then brings the tops of the walls together, the spout is thrown separately. This form is usually a fancy container for hard liquor, varying from one pint to about one gallon in capacity. This ring is 9-1/2 inches in outer diameter, salt glazed, and impressed "SOUTHERN PINES, N.C." Seagrove area of N.C. 1890-1910. $850

Bottle Forms

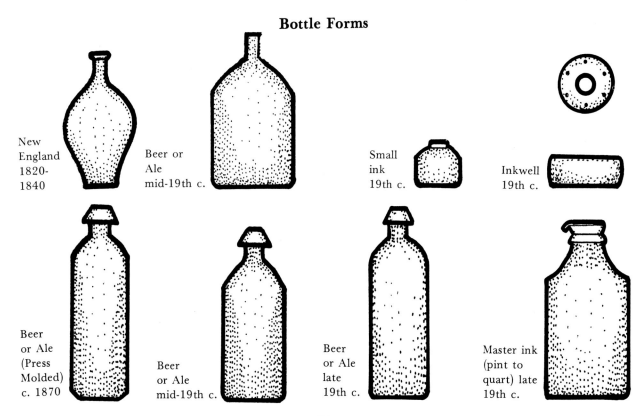

New England 1820-1840

Beer or Ale mid-19th c.

Small ink 19th c.

Inkwell 19th c.

Beer or Ale (Press Molded) c. 1870

Beer or Ale mid-19th c.

Beer or Ale late 19th c.

Master ink (pint to quart) late 19th c.

A group of three typical American beer and ale containers. The quart bottle on the left has a deep tan salt glaze with a top dip and lining of a dark brown Albany type slip glaze. It was made in a patented faceted mold. "DR. CRONK" impressed (this was a brand of sarsaparilla). The central pint bottle was hand turned. It has a salt glaze with cobalt around the mouth ring and brown slip glaze lining. It is impressed "L. WERRBACH /MILWALKEE." The hand-turned quart beer on the right has a thin gray-brown salt glaze and brown slip interior. It is impressed "ROCHESTER." All American, second half of the 19th century. $75-125 ea.

Two hand-turned, salt glazed ink wells. Both have a central opening for filling and smaller openings around the outer edge of the top for dipping the pens. The well on the left is 1-1/2" high and 3-3/4" in diameter and is impressed "C' CROLIUS / STONEWARE MFG. / MANHATTEN WELLS, N.Y." c. 1835. The large well on the right is 2-5/8" high and 6-1/2" in diameter. It is impressed on the base "SATTERLEE AND MORY / FT. EDWARD, N.Y." 1861-1885. L $450; R $975

On the left a dark brown Albany type slip glazed one-gallon jug. It has "S. O. DUNBAR" impressed on the front shoulder and bears a paper label for "Dunbar's Black Ink, Taunton, Mass." The lip is pulled into a tiny pouring spout. The 4-1/8" tall cone shaped jar on the right is salt-glazed with a brown slip glazed lining. "PRATT'S" is impressed near the base and it has a paper label reading "Pratt's Package Marking Fluid." Both from Northeastern U.S.A., mid-19th century. *Courtesy of Bob and Beka Mebane.* L-R: $150, $75

JARS

WIDE-MOUTHED JARS

Wide-mouthed jars are one of the most common and the simplest forms in which stonewares are manufactured. These vessels are usually called "jars," but have also been termed "crocks" over the years. They are designed for the storage of foodstuffs and as containers for the processing of various pickled foods, such as sauerkraut and cucumber pickles. The large jars of this form were used for salted meat and are sometimes listed as "meat jars" by potters. Commonly these jars were made in one-half gallon to ten-gallon capacity sizes by potters who turned on the wheel. As the jigger and press molding processes became popular in industrialized potteries, these vessels were made in even larger sizes -- fifteen, twenty, thirty, and even fifty gallon capacities. Such large vessels were probably for restaurant and industrial use. Most of these very large jars are late jiggered products and are glazed with a white Bristol form of glaze.

In this form of jar, the mouth opening is as large as the base and is generally also the maximum distance between the walls. In earlier jars that show a hint of the ovoid form, the mouth opening may even be larger than the base. In sizes over one gallon capacity there are usually bilateral lug handles to assist in the lifting of the filled jars. The large, late jars often have metal and wood bail type handles in the place of clay lug handles.

The mouth opening is usually encircled with a heavy band or roll rim of some sort to give the vessel stability and durability. These heavy rims assist in keeping the form in the round during drying and firing. The heavy rims are also more durable for the heavy household or restaurant purposes for which these vessels are used.

Wide-mouthed jars and large jars with a slightly smaller mouths were often used interchangeably. In some potteries, especially before 1875, the jar with the slightly smaller mouth was the only one made, but it was intended for the same purposes as the wide-mouthed type. The smaller mouth of these ovoid pots is usually as large as the base, but smaller than the maximum diameter between the walls.

The very wide mouth of this jar form has advantages and disadvantages. In the storage of lard, meat covered by lard, and any form of sugared preserve, the large opening and subsequently large exposed surface allowed more rapid oxidation and contamination of the contents. On the other hand, when pickled foods were placed in these jars, a wide plate or weight could easily be placed over the top of the pickling solution to keep the contents submerged under the solution. This was an advantage. One- to five-gallon jars were also used frequently for short-term storage of milk. Butter was commonly stored in such vessels, frequently in a low, wide form. Wide-mouthed jars in small sizes were also used as containers for salt and baking soda in the kitchen. During the mid-nineteenth century a low lidded form of this jar was termed a "cake pot." Presumably this was for the heavy, long-lasting sort of cake which we now call a fruitcake.

Although the early forms may show some rounding of the sides, wide-mouthed jars became more or less cylindrical in form after the mid-nineteenth century in all parts of this country. They remained more or less the same in form from that period onward. Some are short, but most are relatively tall, full cylinders. They have little grace of form.

Wide-mouthed jars are consistently handled with bilateral, opposite lug handles, usually fixed two to three inches below the rim. Most of these jars were originally topped by some sort of hanging lid. No lid ledge is present on either side of the mouth. The low hanging lid is the most common form, but some vessels have domed hanging lids with a ringed projection on the bottom which fits inside of the jar mouth. The fit of these lids was not tight, and they could not be as completely sealed as a lid which sits upon a lid ledge.

The jar form is still produced for some utilitarian purposes, but is now mainly manufactured by jigger or press methods.

WIDE MOUTHED JARS

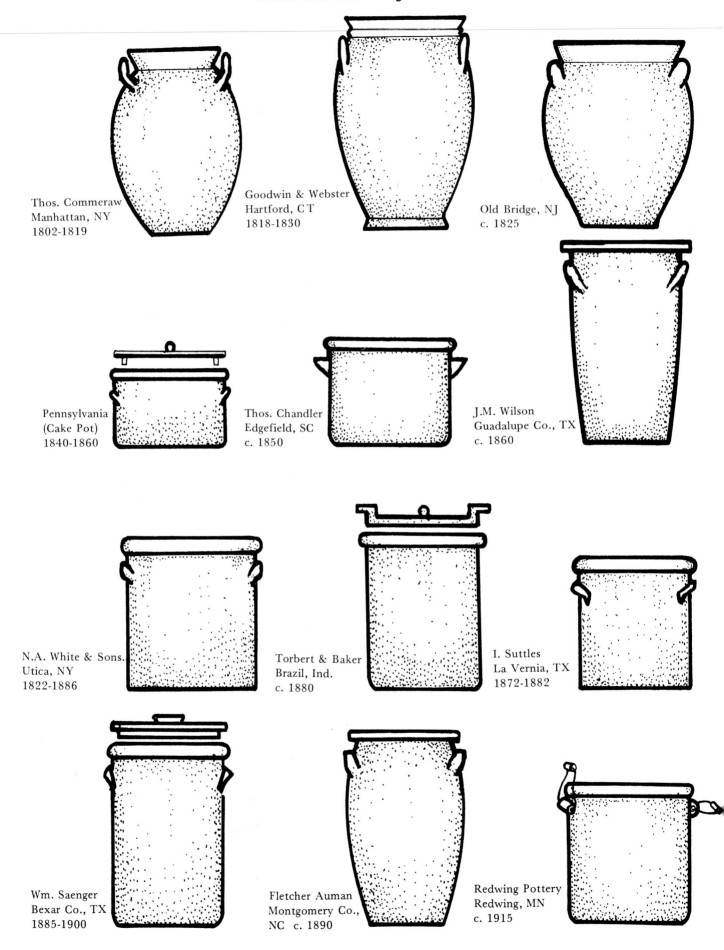

Thos. Commeraw
Manhattan, NY
1802-1819

Goodwin & Webster
Hartford, CT
1818-1830

Old Bridge, NJ
c. 1825

Pennsylvania
(Cake Pot)
1840-1860

Thos. Chandler
Edgefield, SC
c. 1850

J.M. Wilson
Guadalupe Co., TX
c. 1860

N.A. White & Sons.
Utica, NY
1822-1886

Torbert & Baker
Brazil, Ind.
c. 1880

I. Suttles
La Vernia, TX
1872-1882

Wm. Saenger
Bexar Co., TX
1885-1900

Fletcher Auman
Montgomery Co.,
NC c. 1890

Redwing Pottery
Redwing, MN
c. 1915

A pair of wide-mouthed jars from the Seagrove area of North Carolina. Both are cylindrical forms with a wide, flaring, flat rim. The one on the left is unmarked while the jar on the right is impressed "N.FOX." Both are salt glazed with some salt on the interiors. Capacities are about one gallon and 1/2 gallon respectively. These jars were used as household containers, and especially to hold salt and baking soda. About 1870-1900. L $300-375; R $280

A four-gallon wide-mouthed jar with its proper indwelling lid. The tiny jar of the same form and the other made to be fitted with a bail handle were parts of William Meyer's sample set. All three vessels are glazed with the Leon Slip glaze. The large jar is in the cocoa brown color and the small jars are in the mustardy yellow phase. Meyer Pottery, Bexar County, Texas 1890-1930 period. L-R: $200, $375, $350

A low, wide-mouthed jar and its lid. This jar is only 4-1/2 inches in height and 9-1/2 inches in diameter. It fits into the group of vessels of this form which are sometimes called cakepots. They were used to store a moist, longlasting form of cake such as what we call a fruitcake. Salt glazed interior, no interior glaze, and decorated with cobalt painted in an abstracted foliar pattern. Attributed to Central Pennsylvania, mid-19th century. $300

A beautiful large three-gallon preserving jar. It is covered on the exterior with a moderately heavy salt glaze. The broad flattened rim and the beautifully attached broad, flat handles are typical of the potter. A cloth could be tied down over this rim securely to keep insects out of the contents. Impressed "H.FOX/3". Seagrove area of N.C. Third quarter of 19th century. $650

SMALL MOUTHED JARS

Large forms (over 2 gal.)

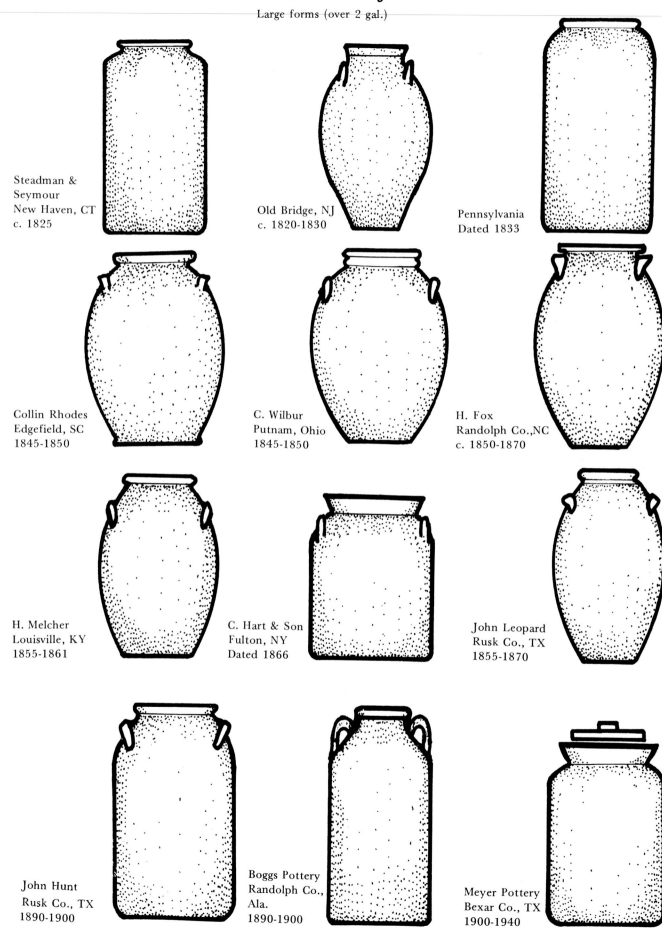

Steadman &
Seymour
New Haven, CT
c. 1825

Old Bridge, NJ
c. 1820-1830

Pennsylvania
Dated 1833

Collin Rhodes
Edgefield, SC
1845-1850

C. Wilbur
Putnam, Ohio
1845-1850

H. Fox
Randolph Co.,NC
c. 1850-1870

H. Melcher
Louisville, KY
1855-1861

C. Hart & Son
Fulton, NY
Dated 1866

John Leopard
Rusk Co., TX
1855-1870

John Hunt
Rusk Co., TX
1890-1900

Boggs Pottery
Randolph Co.,
Ala.
1890-1900

Meyer Pottery
Bexar Co., TX
1900-1940

SMALL-MOUTHED JARS

This jar form in its larger sizes was produced as a container for all sorts of foods that were stored or preserved. Dry ingredients such as flour, sugar, and meal were usually not stored in these vessels, but could have been. They were commonly used for meats preserved in dry salt, lard and meats in lard, pickles of all sorts, apple butter or other fruit butters produced in large quantities, eggs preserved in dry salt or water-glass (a solution of sodium or potassium silicate), butter, and soft soap.

Jars used for the storage of cream also fit into this group. The covered cream pots listed by many potters in their trade lists are this exact form. Cream jars without covers have a full, semi-ovoid body form topped by a wide cylindrical or slightly flaring neck section, making them almost a baluster form, but they fit into the wide-mouthed jar family.

Small-mouthed jars were most common in an ovoid form before and during the third quarter of the nineteenth century, even into the early twentieth century in some remote areas of the deep South. Bilateral lug handles were usually present on all jars over one gallon in size. On very large jars four handles may sometimes be present. Generally made in sizes of from one-gallon to five-gallon capacity, they appear occasionally in six-, eight-, or ten-gallon capacity. A few very large jars of this form were made by the well-known slave potter, Dave, in the Edgefield area of South Carolina. Jars of ten-, fifteen-, twenty-, and even thirty-gallon capacities appear with his signature. They were undoubtedly very useful in the large plantation households of that area and that period. We know that these were primarily used for meat and lard from Dave's inscribed verse on some of the pots. One, now at the University of South Carolina, states that "This jar was made at Stoney Bluff for holding lard enuf." The mouth in these jars is always smaller than the middle of the pot and usually smaller than the base. Many are topped with a heavy rim, and often they have no lid ledges. For those without lid ledges (usually the earlier jars), a tie-down cloth cover must have been the only cover used. Lids to fit these early jars are not seen at the pottery sites. By the mid-nineteenth century most of the jars do have lid ledges present within the mouths, and flat indwelling lids were manufactured to fit them.

Large small-mouthed jars were sometimes still manufactured during the late period. By this period they generally show a cylindrical form with short, rounded shoulders, a fairly heavy rim or collar of some sort around the mouth, and an interior lid ledge. Lids to fit were included when they were sold.

In much of this country the large form of this jar was phased out after 1875 and the wide-mouthed storage jar took its place. The small-mouthed jar remained popular only in the smaller sizes.

A pair of salt glazed, small-mouthed preserve jars made at the Boggs Pottery, Randolph County, Alabama about 1900. The larger jar has bilateral pulled vertical strap handles while the smaller jar has only one such handle. The small jar is about two gallon capacity, the larger four (inscribed). Interior of the large jar is an Albany type slip glaze, but that of the small is probably an alkaline form of glaze - pale green, transparent, and relatively untextured. L-R: $175, $200

A very large jar of twenty gallon capacity made by Dave, slave of Louis Miles of Edgefield, S. C. The jar has a dark brown alkaline glaze inside and out. On the reverse it is inscribed "This noble jar will hold 20 / fill it with silver then you will have plenty." On the front it reads: "L.M. / Dave." "April 8, 1858." The streaks running down the vessel were formed by additional glaze being poured over the surface. These are thickly glazed while the areas between have a thin glaze coating. $26,000

A cookie jar made at the Meyer Potter for use in their home. It has a capacity of about two quarts, a simple domed lid, and handle formed of a roll of clay. Glazed inside and out with a mossy green colored Leon slip glaze. Meyer Pottery, Bexar County, Texas. Probably first quarter of the 20th century. $850

A dark olive green alkaline glazed jar of about three gallon capacity and ovoid form. Projecting knob handles were placed bilaterally just beneath the vessel neck. These knobs appear to have been formed to support the vessel in a rack or by rope so that it could easily be tipped to pour. Probably a household water container. Incised decoration of two encircling straight lines and one wavy line. Attributed to Enoch W. Rheinhardt, Vale, N.C. c. 1930. *Courtesy of The Potter's Museum. Photographer: Bill Jenko.* $1500-2000

SMALL MOUTHED PRESERVE JARS
Small Sizes

Randolph Co.,
Ala. 1840-1860

Collin Rhodes
Edgefield, SC
1845-1850

H.C. Smith
Alexandria, DC
c. 1850

Rusk Co., TX
c. 1850

Lyons, NY
c. 1870

S.H. Sonner
Strasburg, VA
1870-1883

C. Unser
Jeffersonville,
Ind. c. 1870

J. D. Craven
Moore Co., NC
1870-1890

Peoria Pottery
Peoria, Ind.
1864-1889
(Press molds)

? Indiana
c. 1880

Weir Patent
Akron, OH
c. 1900
(jigger molds)

Meyer Pottery
Bexar Co., TX
1900-1940

SMALL-MOUTHED PRESERVE JARS

Small forms of the small-mouthed preserve jar remained popular into the twentieth century, when they were finally eliminated by the glass canning jar. All sorts of patented ceramic forms were tried in an attempt to compete with the glass jar, but they were not successful. Generally made in sizes of from one pint to one gallon in capacity, these vessels were originally intended for use primarily in the storage of sugared or sugared and brandied fruit preserves. Imitations of glass jar sealing devices such as metal lids or patented clamp closures and rubber rings were common after 1875. These sealed jars could be used for the canning of fruits and berries in syrup, tomatoes, or other foods that do not spoil easily.

Early stoneware preserve jars are sometimes cylindrical, although most are ovoid or globular in form, particularly those made before the mid-nineteenth century. The very earliest types had tie down rims or were made with mouths small enough to close with corks. In later jars the lid ledges receiving simple flat lids which could be sealed with grease, wax, or sealing wax were common.

During the later half of the nineteenth century, the imitation of glass fruit jars began and a number of these stoneware jars were manufactured with a specially tooled groove into which the same simple metal dome cap used on glass fruit jars could be fit. This was to be sealed with sealing wax. I presume that these jars were not boiled as the glass jars, but washed and scalded with boiling water to achieve partial sterility. The high sugar content of the preserves ordinarily kept them from spoiling. By the last quarter of the nineteenth century various patented stoneware fruit jars were being manufactured. Some were fancy pressed forms with panels and were made to be sealed by the domed metal lid and sealing wax. Later ones, such as the famous patented WEIR canning jars, were fitted with rubber rings and clamp closures. These forms were produced by the industrialized stoneware factories, mainly in the middlewest. I have even seen twentieth century molded stoneware jars with a white Bristol form of glaze manufactured with a patented screw closure which could be fitted with the same screw metal lid and rubber rings used to seal the glass preserving jars of that period.

Three small preserve jars with different means of sealing. On the left the one gallon Meyer preserve jar has a flat lid fitted on a lid ledge. It has a brown Leon slip glaze inside and out c. 1930. The small pint jar in the foreground is a very pale yellowish alkaline glazed jar with a mouth small enough to be sealed with a cork. Attributed to Randolph County, Alabama c. 1860.
The jar on the right is a salt-glazed jar from central North Carolina. No interior glaze. The jar is fitted with an elegant lid which may be sealed in a special groove with wax. 1875-1900. L-R: $175; $100; $160

A pair of fancy press molded preserve jars with a groove around the mouth formed to receive a dome-shaped metal lid such as was used on glass jars of this type. They were sealed with sealing wax. The one quart jar on the left is covered in a brown Albany type slip glaze. "PEORIA POTTERY" is impressed in the base. The one pint jar on the right has a yellowish heavy salt-glazed exterior and brown Albany type slip glaze interior. "McCOMB STONEWARE CO., McCOMB, ILL." is impressed in the base. Both last quarter of 19th century. L $100; R $45

One gallon preserve jar made by the Meyer Pottery and glazed with the Leon slip glaze inside and out. The glaze is a brownish mustard color. The bail handle represents a modern variation for preserve jars. Bexar County, Texas 1920-1940. $195

A pair of jigger molded preserve jars bearing the pottery mark on the lids and having a patented metal closure. The one quart jar on the left is entirely glazed in a white Bristol form of glaze. The tiny eight-ounce horseradish jar has the lower section of the exterior glazed with a white Bristol form of glaze, but the upper exterior, interior, and lid are all in an Albany type slip glaze. The lids bear the raised words "WEIR PATENT, 92" and "WEIR PATENT, March 1892, Akron O." The original Weir Pottery was in Monmouth, Ill. L $65; R $85

CHURNS

Ceramic churns seem, strangely, to be a form of pottery vessel used mainly during the nineteenth century. Prior to that period this form seldom appears, and most churning of milk was done in a staved wooden churn. Some churns were manufactured in earthenware, but the majority were produced in stoneware. The forceful action of the dasher against the interior bottom of the vessel made the more durable stoneware a distinctly better medium. Stoneware churns could also be much more easily and completely cleaned after being used to make butter.

Churns almost always were made in a tall semi-ovoid or cylindrical form. The sizes are most commonly three-, four-, five-, and six-gallon capacities. Rarely one- and two-gallon churns were made. Most churns have two lug handles affixed bilaterally opposite each other between the mid-point of the body and the neck of the vessel. In the deep South a distinctive variation in handles is often seen. On small churns, only one strap handle, vertically fixed near the top of the vessel, was used. This usually was paired with a lug handle on the opposite side of the vessel, but the additional lug handle sometimes was not used on small churns. Occasionally a second pulled strap handle was applied in the same sort of vertical position beneath the first, near the base of the vessel. This aided in the picking up and tipping of the vessel to pour out the residual buttermilk. This second strap handle was usually added only on five- and six-gallon sizes in the deep South.

The form of churn manufactured at most potteries is distinctive from and a little taller and thinner than large preserving jars from the same shop, although a few potteries appear not to have made churns. The jar form may often mistakenly be called a churn. Although suited for the churning of milk, churns were also often used as preserving jars. I was visiting the Meaders Pottery in Cleveland, Georgia, one summer day a few years ago when a man drove up and asked to buy one of their five-gallon churns. He said that his wife

A churn of two gallon capacity. It is salt glazed outside and has no interior glaze. The proper lid sits on a ledge within the mouth. Seagrove area of North Carolina, probably 1875-1895. $250

CHURNS

C. Croluis Manhattan Wells, NY 1810-1840

Clark & Lundy Troy, NY 1825-1826

Thomas Chandler, Edgefield, SC c. 1850

George Doane Louisville, KY 1840-1860

J.D. Wilbur Boonesboro, AR c. 1885

Joseph Rushton Rusk Co., TX c. 1880

Seagrove area, NC 1875-1900

? Boggs Pottery Randolph Co., AL 1890-1920

C.S. Kline Howells Mills, GA c. 1890

Meyer Pottery Bexar Co., TX 1900-1940

Ideal Pottery Dallas, TX c. 1930

Meaders Pottery Cleveland, GA 1920-1940

used them to pickle beans. At that time the Meaders were not producing a complete line of wares and did not make large preserving jars.

Although churns are generally tall, slightly ovoid or cylindrical forms, some are topped with a straight or flaring neck or collar of several inches in height. This is usually terminated with only a simple finish and no thickened rim. It gives them somewhat the same top form as some open cream jars and pitchers, but most of these wide-collared churns have a lid ledge within the neck to receive a proper lid. This long, gently flaring neck gives the complete churn a slightly different form that resembles a "tulip shape."

The ceramic lids that fit into churns always have a central opening large enough to accomodate the handle of the dasher. This dasher consists of a long handle made from a dowel or rod-shaped piece of wood, generally taller than the churn by about 12 inches. Usually two pieces of flat wood slats about an inch shorter than the inner diameter of the churn are fixed to the bottom of the handle in the form of a cross, but other dasher endings may be found. One somewhat common variation consists of a flat disc of wood with holes drilled through at intervals. A dasher that has been used for some time usually has a distinct line of wear on the handle at the point where it passes through the lid.

All churn lids have a central hole, but there are many variations of the small cup-like form that surrounds the central hole and serves to drain the splashed milk back into the vessel interior. Some are deep cups, others hardly raised rings on the lid. Lids for churns may be glazed or unglazed. Frequently wooden churn lids were employed rather than ceramic ones because they were less noisy and more durable.

A four-gallon alkaline glazed churn made by Cheever Meaders. It shows a single lateral pulled strap handle in the vertical position. This type of handle is frequently seen on southern churns. Meaders Pottery, Cleveland, Ga. c. 1930. T: $325 B: $450

This Strange churn was probably influenced by the "Daisy" churn. This was being produced at that time with a glass jar as the container and a set of egg-beaterlike paddles turned by geared mechanism much like this. White Bristol type glaze inside and out with cobalt lines and stamped cobalt colored mark and "ONE MINUTE CHURN, PAT'D" stencilled in cobalt. The gear mechanism and paddles within the churn are cast and wrought iron. Overall height is 29 inches. Marked: "STAR POTTERY WORKS/ELMENDORF. TEXAS." 1909-1915. $450

95

BOWLS

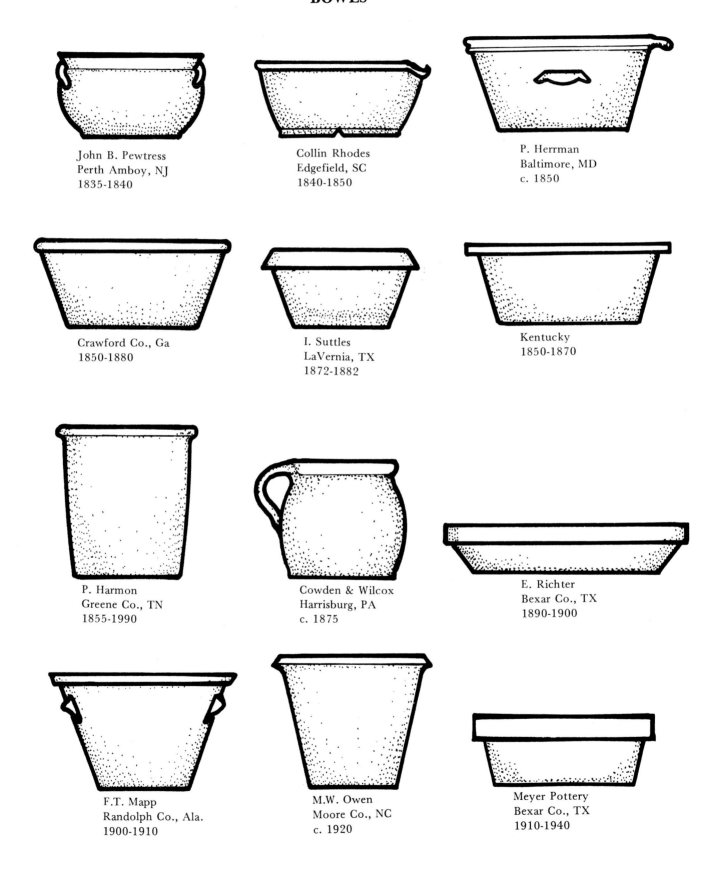

John B. Pewtress
Perth Amboy, NJ
1835-1840

Collin Rhodes
Edgefield, SC
1840-1850

P. Herrman
Baltimore, MD
c. 1850

Crawford Co., Ga
1850-1880

I. Suttles
LaVernia, TX
1872-1882

Kentucky
1850-1870

P. Harmon
Greene Co., TN
1855-1990

Cowden & Wilcox
Harrisburg, PA
c. 1875

E. Richter
Bexar Co., TX
1890-1900

F.T. Mapp
Randolph Co., Ala.
1900-1910

M.W. Owen
Moore Co., NC
c. 1920

Meyer Pottery
Bexar Co., TX
1910-1940

BOWLS AND BOWL VARIATIONS

Stoneware bowls were very popular in some areas and not manufactured at all in others. The reason for this seems to be that in areas where earthenware bowls were manufactured, either in small shops or industrially, stoneware bowls were not commonly produced.

The bowl is an open form, usually with a mouth larger in diameter than the base or any other section of the form. During the early period most bowls were essentially of the pan form with a flat base, sloping sides, and a simple rim finish. Some bowls were deep and rather narrow, others broad and shallow. Some show a roll or band on the rim or sometimes even an everted lip. Bowls of two-gallon or larger capacity often have bilateral handles applied just under the rim. These handles may be open loops or attached lugs in form, but are fixed horizontally on the bowls.

A few bowls were made with a pulled spout on one side to facilitate pouring. Occasionally a small bowl with a pulled spout will have a vertically fixed, pulled strap handle like that of a pitcher, opposite the spout. These were useful for pouring and mixing.

The pan form was the universal form of bowl until after about 1860. It was used for kitchen mixing, milk separation, or any other form of food preparation. They were most commonly one, one and a half and two gallons in size. Variants with capacities as small as a quart and as large as three or four gallons were produced.

The heavily banded bowl became popular after 1860 and was the major form produced after that period. This type is frequently called a milk crock or milk bowl. Such bowls all have a rim with a thick, flattened band finish that served two purposes. First, it was sturdy enough to allow one milk bowl to hang inside another for firing. The bottom and sides of the bowl as well as the interiors were glazed, but an area just beneath the rim as well as the top of the rim were left unglazed and served as the contact points in stacking. This enabled very economical use of the

A two-gallon "cream riser" of the pan form, with a flattened rolled rim, and bilateral wheel turned lug handles. "E. T. MAPP" impressed on front. The glaze is a caramel colored, transparent glaze of the alkaline type. Randolph County, Alabama. First quarter of the 20th century. $650

This one-gallon milk bowl is salt-glazed inside (lightly) and out. It has a pair of lug handles affixed to the sides and a pulled pouring spout between the handles on one side. Brushed with abstract leaf designs in cobalt around the upper area of the body. Impressed: "PETER HERMANN" in a circle around "1 gal." Baltimore, Md. 1850-1872. $475

A two-gallon size milk bowl with a wide banded rim and a deep form. Glazed inside and out with an Albany type slip glaze. Attributed to John Hunt. Rusk County, Texas c. 1900. $275

Two gallon milk pan or pot of the deep form and wide flattened rim preferred in North Carolina. This pan is thinly salt glazed inside and out. Most of the pot is a dark gray-brown color and it was made from a rather dark clay. "M. W. OWEN" impressed and capacity numeral "2" hand inscribed. Seagrove area, N. C. Early 20th c. $225

A deep bowl of two gallon capacity. The form and bilateral horizontal lug handles suggest that it might be a serving bowl. Salt-glazed inside (light toasting) and out. It is decorated in cobalt trailed slip with ferny foliage and a pair of strawberries on the front. Impressed: "JOHN B. PEWTRESS" Perth Amboy, New Jersey, c 1840. $3000-3200.

A milk pan of about 3/4 gallon capacity made of a vitreous deep gray clay and salt glazed on the exterior only. This bowl, found in Kentucky, was probably produced in one of the Kentucky potteries along the Ohio River. Attributed to Kentucky-mid 19th century. $250

A handsome low, wide milkbowl which is 13-1/2 in diameter across the top. it has bilateral lug handles fixed just below the banded rim. Medium gray salt glazed exterior and a shiny brown Albany type slip glazed interior. Impressed: "HARRINGTON & BURGER/ ROCHESTER", N.Y. 1852-1854. *Courtesy of Mr. and Mrs. Ralph Strong. Photographer: William G. Frank, Rochester Museum and Science Center.* $550

A very low one-gallon size milk pan. This form was also often called a "skimmer". It shows the wide banded form of a bowl that became popular in the last quarter of the 19 c. Glazed inside and out and on the bottom with an Albany type brown slip glaze. These bowls hung by the lower edge of the rim in firing, therefore an unglazed band is visible in that area and the bottom is glazed. Bexar County, Texas c. 1890. $375

A very large utilitarian bowl of the pan form having a capacity of about four to five gallons. It is 9 inches high and has a diameter of 17 inches at the top. The interior only is glazed with a Leon slip glaze in a soft cocoa brown. Bilateral pulled open loop handles large enough to admit four fingers are placed horizontally. The eight-ounce mug from the same pottery is included to assist in a concept of size. Meyer Pottery, Bexar County, Texas c. 1900. $475

This is a basal view of a large footed colander. The pierced pattern and the unglazed foot ring may be seen. Glazed in a lustrous brown slip glaze of the Albany type. This is a hand-tooled or cut in foot ring. Probably of New York of Pennsylvania origin. Last quarter of 19th c. $250

space within the kiln, for fifteen or twenty bowls could be placed in the same area that only about four had occupied in the rim to rim and bottom to bottom manner of stacking. Second, this heavy rim kept distortion of the mouth at a minimum during firing. Band-rimmed bowls may be deep with a wide band or shallow with a wide or narrow band. They were commonly produced in the same sizes as the pan form of bowl, mainly one-, one-and-a-half, and two-gallon capacities. They are infrequently seen in the larger range of sizes as well.

Occasionally huge bowls were made for particular functions; for example, meat tubs were produced by the Meyer Pottery for their own use during sausage making. Hand-thrown wash bowls with rolled rims also were produced by some small potteries, but they are usually only about two gallons in capacity. Fancy wash bowl and pitcher sets made in factories were much preferred. Hand-thrown wash bowls are usually a low pan form with an everted rolled rim.

Colanders are often a bowl form with added small feet or a foot ring to provide the slight elevation needed for draining. These vessels were pierced by hand before the clay was hard and dry. Some colanders were not made in bowl form but in the form of a wide-mouthed jar, a straight cylinder. Drainers and presses for cottage cheese also appear in the same forms: a bowl or wide-mouthed jar pierced to allow drainage. Cheese drainers do not usually have feet. A chemical dipping basket consisting of a pierced jar form with a heavy overhead handle was produced by industrialized potteries in the late nineteenth and early twentieth centuries. These are usually of a coarse, thick clay resembling sewer pipe clay and are salt glazed.

Tiny pan-form bowls were made for baked custard cups. Large circular baking molds, with or without a central cone, were a second variation of the pan form. Cake and pudding molds are much less common in stoneware than in earthenware. A lovely fluted cake mold may be made from a pan form by indenting the damp clay in a pattern with the index finger. A central cone may have been thrown originally or added later. Cakes baked in such pans show the Bundt or Turk's Cap form when turned out. The large molds which have no central cone often show a pattern of circular rings on the inner bottom. They were used for steamed and baked puddings of different sorts, the rings producing a decorative pattern when the pudding was turned out. The majority of the stoneware cake and pudding molds seem to be wheel formed. Occasionally press or drape molded ones, so common in earthenware, are seen.

Bowls were often made in Jolly molds during the late nineteenth and twentieth centuries.

This beautiful one gallon capacity milk pan has an interior decoration of a pure white slip trailed over a painted gray brown slip design of swags. It has a smooth light olive green alkaline glaze inside and out. Most interesting is the pulled pouring spout to assist pouring the cream off of the milk. Attributed to Collin Rhodes, Edgefield, S.C. c. 1845. $1400-1800

A pint sized container pierced on the bottom and sides. This was designed to drain cottage cheese and used in the potter's home. Covered with a mossy green Leon slip glaze. Meyer Pottery, Bexar County, Texas c. 1920. $125

A very thick and heavy colander form which was produced industrially as a basket for dipping objects into strong acids. Wheel-turned with a hand-formed handle, is salt glazed. The body is a gritty dark body resembling that of a sewer pipe. "R2133" impressed on front. "No. 5 and a shield for "Knightsware" impressed on the reverse. Maurice A. Knight, Chemical Stoneware, Akron, Ohio. 1911-1915. $300

A wheel-turned cake pan. The deep impressions were made by hand while the pot was still very soft. The center cone and outer walls were thrown in one process. Deep brown Leon Slip glazed, exterior unglazed. Meyer Pottery, Bexar County, Texas c. 1900. These pans also occur in earthenware and are often drape molded. $125

PITCHERS

In North America most spouted vessels are called pitchers. In England this is not true. Most of what we term pitchers are called "jugs," no differentiation being made between the small-mouthed vessels for liquids which are jugs in America and these wider mouthed vessels.

Pitchers were intended for containing and pouring liquids. Although they are a form of tableware, which was not common in stoneware, pitchers were made by many stoneware potteries. Sizes ranged from very large three-gallon pitchers used for milk in farm homes to the tiny six- to eight-ounce pitchers suited for pouring cream at the table. Stoneware pitchers were most common in sizes of from one quart to one-and-a-half gallons. Those larger than this were difficult to handle, while those of the smallest sizes were not usually made as a production item.

Pitchers ordinarily come in three form variations. The Baluster form is the most common and has a full rounded bottom with a cylindrical top section. The top section is usually about one-half to one-third of the total height. There are hundreds of minor variations of this basic form. Globular pitchers are, as the term indicates, full and rounded, and they sometimes have a very short collar or neckband. The third major form is the cylindrical pitcher. It is a straight sided cylinder with the usual pitcher characteristics, a pulled spout on one side of the top rim and a handle affixed to the body on the opposite side. The handle is always a strap handle.

Pitcher spouts are usually pulled in the rim, but added spouts may occasionally be seen on hand-thrown pitchers.

Late industrial stoneware pitchers were most commonly slip cast in a two-or three-part mold. They show all manner of raised decoration on the exterior and are often glazed in color. Many earthenware pitchers were produced industrially in more or less the same forms. The stoneware pitchers were most commonly decorated in blue and gray colors. The main point of differentiation between cast stoneware and earthenware is the vitrification of the body, particularly if the glaze is not a recognizable salt or slip glaze used for stonewares. The Bristol form of glaze was also used, but at times is very difficult to separate from some low temperature glazes on light bodied earthenware.

Wheel-thrown stoneware tea and coffee pots were uncommon, but do occur. Usually a low, full form was made for the tea pot and a tall, rather slender form for the coffee pot. Both had added spouts as well as top openings for filling, and a vertical strap handle commonly occurs opposite the spout. As a rule tea and coffee pots had the same form variations as pitchers.

A huge pitcher with a capacity of three gallons. It has a mottled gray to light brown salt glaze on the exterior and no interior glaze. Cobalt slip was brushed around the handle and in a wavy design on the neck area. It was also used to fill in an incised floral design on the upper front belly. Unmarked. Possibly Norwich, Conn. First Quarter of the 19th century. $3500-4000

PITCHERS

? Norwich, CT
c. 1830

? Ashfield, MS
c. 1850

Thos. Chandler
Edgefield, SC
c. 1950

Prothro Pottery
Rusk Co., TX
c. 1850

J. SWANK & CO.
Johnstown, PA
c. 1870

Crawford Co.,
GA c. 1870

Randolph Co.,
NC 1870-1900

Wm. Saenger
Bexar Co., TX
c. 1880

Meyer Pottery
Bexar Co., TX
1900-1930

Meyer Pottery
Bexar Co., TX
1900-1930

Meyer Pottery
Bexar Co., TX
Dated 1917

Byrd Pottery
Tyler, TX
c. 1930-1940

A small pitcher, 7 1/4 inches tall, which has about one pint capacity. It is completely and beautifully formed having a banded lip and even an added thumb rest on the handle. The incised design of a bird on a fruiting branch and additional free-standing flower with stalk and leaves is filled with vivid cobalt blue. Below the handle it is inscribed "R.C. REMMEY/1872". Salt-glazed inside and out. *Courtesy of Jeremy L. Banta.* $8500-9500

A pitcher in a barrel form emphasized by incised bonds from top to bottom. This pitcher had a spout formed separately and added to the pitcher while it was still damp. Lime green Leon slip glaze inside and out. Meyer Pottery, Bexar County, Texas, probably 1920-1940 period. $400

A two-quart pitcher in a pale yellowish alkaline glaze. Decoration consists of a band of combing or scraffito in a wavy line between two straight combed bands. Also decorated with a dip of the top 1/4 of the pierce in a ferruginous slip prior to glazing. Unmarked but attributed to Joseph Rushton, Rusk County, Texas c. 1980. $700

Pitchers of three forms. The pitcher on the left is cylindrical, the center one a short full form, and the one on the right is a classic baluster form. The sizes vary from one pint capacity to one gallon. All glazed in green and mustard phases of the Leon slip glaze. Meyer Pottery, Bexar County, Texas. 1910-1940. L-R: $450, $175, $550

FANCY WATER AND LIQUOR CONTAINERS

In the pottery price lists these items, particularly the water containers, are almost always mentioned. They may be termed fountains, coolers, and kegs. This last name is very appropriate for many of these vessels, since they were of a keg or barrel form.

CYLINDER SHAPED: Use of this form for large coolers was particularly common after the beginning of the twentieth century. Vessels for iced tea are a late product seen in this form.

KEG: This was the most common of all water cooler forms and was usually made to sit upright on one end, the other (top) being open and fitted with a lid. At the middle of the lower front area, just above the base, there was usually a hole made in the container for the later fitting of some sort of spigot. Many even had "ICE WATER" stamped or inscribed upon the front.

SMALL KEG OR RUNDLET: This is the same thrown form as the large keg except that usually both ends are closed. It was made most commonly in sizes of from one-half to three-gallon capacity. These small kegs may sometimes have been designed to sit upright on one end just as the larger kegs, but more often were made to rest in some sort of a rack on their side. A small opening for a spigot was sometimes made in one sealed end, but an opening was always present in the middle of the full part of the body so that, as the pot sits on its side, this opening is uppermost. The opening was most often made to be fitted with a cork. Brandies of various sorts were usually kept in such containers. The side-resting keg form sometimes had three or four small ball-like (usually hollow and wheel made) feet attached to the bottom. This form had an animal-like appearance and was called a "blind-pig."

This tall, slender jug form with a 12 gallon capacity has an opening for a spigot at the base of the front. It is decorated with cobalt-bearing slip under a salt glaze and has an interior brown slip glaze, probably Albany type. It was probably used as a water or cider container. Impressed "W.J' SCHROP/SPRINGFIELD, OHIO" Summit County, Ohio. Mid 19th century. *Courtesy of the Western Reserve Historical Society.* $2750

An eight-gallon water container of the double-handled jug form. This piece is covered with a transparent, pale gray-green alkaline glaze decorated with a scalloped band around the upper shoulder and a band of flower and foliage elements just beneath this. All trailed in a pure white slip. Impressed: "CHANDLER/MAKER" on the front neck. Thomas Chandler, Edgefield area, South Carolina, 1850-1852. *Courtesy of the Ferrell Collection. Photographer: David Rasberry.* $3500

A coffee pot form in which the end of the spout has been broken. This pot is glazed inside and out with an olive green, runny alkaline glaze. A ledge within the mouth indicates that it originally had a lid. This is probably the form that Cogburne and Massey in Washington County, GA. called a "coffee boiler" in the 1820 manufacturing digest. Attributed to Georgia, first half of 19th century. $750

A tall ovoid jar with a spigot hole near the base made for water or cider. It is 27 inches tall with a cobalt dotted domed lid which may or may not be original. On the center from just below the rim an "All-seeing eye" was drawn in cobalt and just beneath this three links of chain were applied. These may be Masonic symbols. On either side of the chain applied motif's which appear to be shepherd's crocks are present. Beneath all of this what appears to be a multipetalled flower hanging upside down is painted. All are painted with cobalt. Near the footed base a heart was applied with the spigot hole being made in the center and also painted with cobalt. On the reverse "1863" appears in cobalt script. The piece once had bilateral strap handles applied on the upper shoulder and dotted with cobalt. One has been broken. A most unusual mark "BROWN & CROOKS" in the form of an eagle in flight with one name in each wing is impressed on the front and each side of the foot flange. It also is cobalt tinted. Ohio, *Courtesy of the Ohio Historical Society, Ohio Ceramic Center at Roseville.* $8500-9000

An enlargement of the "BROWN & CROOKS" mark.

A "Blind Pig" rundlet or small keg. The "pig" is affixed to these vessels when they have added feet which gives them an animal like appearance. This piece has a one gallon capacity. It stands on three feet and has a central top opening for filling and a bung opening at the base of the front for a small spigot. Heavy light gray salt glaze with abstracted floral and geometric underglaze cobalt decoration. Northeastern U.S., mid 19th century. $450

Small rundlet or keg with a capacity of about two quarts. This small vessel has one added spout at the top center. It is beautifully thrown with incised grooves to resemble banding on a keg at either end. The front side has a finely incised bird on a branch and the date 1846. Elegant incising has been done in a fine design around the spout. A fish is incised on the reverse. The barrel is of a deep brown clay and covered with thin salt glaze on the exterior. The "bird and fish" potter of central North Carolina, possibly a member of the Webster family. *Courtesy of the Potter's Museum. Photograph: Bill Jenko.* $1500-2000

SPIGOTED JUG: The large jug form was the second most common form used for water coolers and vessels for holding large amounts of other beverages, particularly apple cider. These were usually large jugs of five-gallon or more capacity with two handles, their only difference from other large jugs being the presence of a small hole near the base for insertion of a spigot.

URN: Sometimes these containers had very elegant forms, but all had a tulip or urn-shaped body with a fairly wide mouth. They were frequently elevated upon a stand or footing of some sort and this base may be either fused with the body of the cooler or separate. Many such containers were elegantly decorated with cobalt slip trailing or painting. Most have an opening near the base of the main container for the insertion of the spigot.

WATER FILTERS: Water filter forms were very like coolers but usually consisted of two separate vessels. The top vessel was pierced with small holes through its bottom and had space for the insertion of a natural sponge or some prepared filter. It was commonly a keg or urn shape. The lower section, commonly a cylindrical form, was the container into which the filtered water passed. This usually had an opening for a spigot near the base. These were a rare form in American stoneware, but many water filters were shipped to this country from the industrialized British stoneware potteries. These British filters were ornate molded vessels with special patented filters. The filter was useful for the removal of sand and dirt particles from the water, but had no antibacterial function.

A cylindrical water or cider vessel 24 1/2 inches tall and of approximately six gallon capacity. It has a number of ornate press molded designs sprigged on to the front and sides, all of which are colored with cobalt. A banner supported by two eagles and surrounded by rococo floral designs is inscribed "E PLURIBUS UNUM" Dated 1853 in cobalt slip on the back. Attributed to the master potter Franklin Wright at the Hastings and Belding Pottery, Ashfield, Mass. 1850-1854. *Courtesy of Peter E. Schriber. Photographer: Mawson.* $7500-8000

VESSELS FOR BED AND BATH CHAMBERS

A number of vessel types were manufactured for use in the bedroom or bath chamber. Stoneware was a particularly suitable medium because it did not absorb odors and was easily cleaned, and it thus became the primary medium for early sanitary ware.

BEDPANS: The earlier bedpans were wheel-thrown, round forms consisting of a low wide bowl with the top edges curved inward and a short cylindrical spout for emptying attached on one side. They also were produced in earthenware and I have seen them in slip or Bristol glazed stoneware, but not in salt glazed. The industrial product was slip cast, usually in a longer, oval form with a tapered front end, the emptying spout being at the back.

CHAMBERPOTS: The most common sanitary-ware vessel made at utilitarian stoneware potteries was the chamber pot. The form is almost always the same; that of a short, slightly globular bowl, usually with a little inward tapering at the top and a broad flattened rim. The form was fitted with a pulled strap handle beginning just below the rim and inserting vertically near the base. Two sizes, adult and child, were usually manufactured.

A commercially produced bed pan made in at least three press molds and then joined by hand. It is glazed in shiny dark brown slip glaze of the Albany type. Probably from a large Middlewestern pottery in the late 19th c. $250

Chamberpots in adult and children's sizes-the usual two sizes in which these were produced. On the left the adult size is glazed in an olive-brown Leon slip glaze and was made by the Meyer Pottery, Bexar County, Texas 1900-1930. The small pot on the right is from Georgia and covered in a yellowish alkaline glaze. Probably late 19th or early 20th century. L-R: $195, 250

A grease lamp with a double spouted bowl for two wicks. This is a typical form for a grease lamp. It is covered with a thick brown slip glaze which is not typical Albany slip type, probably a local clay. Height: 4 5/8 inches. Attributed to Wayne County, Ohio mid 19th c. $900

A pair of spittoons or cuspidors. One represents the wide open flared mouth form while the other has a downward slanting top section with a central hole well beneath the top rim. This form always has a clean-out opening on the side. The flared mouth form is from the Meyer Pottery and has an olive to brown Leon Slip glaze. The other is stamped "P.C." and came from the Panola County, Texas Courthouse. Dull green unmature glaze, probably alkaline. Texas, c. 1895. $125 ea.

FOOT WARMERS: Wheel-made foot warmers are not common, but were produced. A jug form was thrown and usually closed with a knob at what would have been the mouth. One side of the wall was flattened, and a small opening exactly like those on brandy kegs was made on the middle of the top side and finished off with a thrown ring. These were first corked, but later fitted with a pewter closure having a rubber gasket and screw cap. Cast molded footwarmers were produced in a number of different forms.

GREASE LAMPS AND CANDLE-STICKS: Grease lamps in stoneware are uncommon, but candlesticks are even rarer. Many modern studio potters are now making stoneware candlesticks in a number of forms, but grease lamps are a thing of the past. These lamps burned oil or fat of any sort. They were usually made with a basal saucer form, a stem, and a small cup form at the top having one or two tiny pulled spouts into which a wick, generally only a twist of cotton, was placed. Both candlesticks and grease lamps seem to have been made much more frequently in earthenware than in stoneware.

SLOP JARS: These served the same purpose as chamber pots but were made in a tall ovoid or globular jar form having a bail handle and lid. Uncommon products of small utilitarian potteries, they were manufactured mainly in industrialized shops.

SPITOONS: This item, also termed a cuspidor, was commonly manufactured in large American stoneware potteries. They occur in salt, slip, alkaline, and Bristol glazes. Two different forms were manufactured. One was a low, rounded bowl form with a large flaring lip which extended up and out from the mouth at least two to three inches. The other form was a short cylinder with the top closed in and angled downward to a small opening of two- to three-inch diameter in the center. This form always has an opening about the same size as the mouth cut out of the side to allow emptying and cleaning. Slip cast spitoons in stoneware and earthenware are more common than wheel-made vessels and appear with very ornate exterior relief decoration.

113

URINALS: These were uncommon and made for male use only. The form was that of a jug with a relatively wide mouth. The body of the vessel was flattened to rest on one side at a slight angle. A pulled strap handle was placed on the side opposite the flattened section.

WASHBASIN AND PITCHER SETS: Large thrown bowls accompanied by one-gallon pitchers were produced in small quantities. Industrially cast white earthenware sets are considerably more common.

FLORAL VESSELS

This category includes the fancy vases occasionally made as flower containers at utilitarian stoneware potteries, the simple cylindrical vessels made during the twentieth century as containers for cut flowers in florists shops, and all of the fancy as well as plain flower pots manufactured. The first forms were most commonly glazed since they were to contain water. The flower pots and outside decorative jardinieres and stands were usually unglazed, although at times they were subjected to stoneware temperatures or "hard firing." Occasionally they were nicely browned by salt and wood ash vapor when they were fired in stoneware kilns.

VASES: These were not particularly common in stoneware until the late nineteenth and twentieth centuries, when most potteries began making a larger range of forms to compete with industrialized pottery products in both stoneware and earthenware. The Art Nouveau decorative period and the beginnings of the Studio Pottery Movement also spurred this additional range of forms. Vases were frequently of a curving, ornate form reflective of the Art Nouveau influence. Low, rounded vases of a bowl form were also produced and were useful for bouquets and forcing bulbs. The tall cylindrical vases suitable for storing cut flowers in florist refreigerators were a twentieth-century innovation and were produced in a number of sizes with different rim treatments. These were also produced by slip casting in industrialized potteries.

WHEEL MADE FLOWERPOTS:

Flowerpots were produced in the late nineteenth century by small as well as large potteries and are still being made. The early, simple flowerpots had a number of fancy rim variations, but were usually a variation of the pan form: flat bottom with slightly flared side walls. Some, such as those for large fern plants, were very broad, while others were deep. Fluted rims were common. Saucers, both attached and separate, were produced for most pots that were not meant to hang. Hanging pots usually had holes pierced in the rim or upper area for wire or chain. Many of these had fancy "bottom" terminals (the form is actually thrown upside down). Some had ruffled areas at other points along the pots, and many were also combed. Very large pots of fancy "urn" shapes were made with fluting, combing, fancy handles, loose rings fixed in the handles, and other decoration. These also commonly had stands upon which they sat to make more impressive decorative items. Occasionally smaller fancy pots were raised by an attached foot, or even by a stem and foot. These fancy jardinieres were made as decorative items for porch and garden. Unfortunately, few survive to this day. A good many fancy pots were made in simple press or jigger molds as well.

The strawberry pot is a unique form of flower pot made with small pockets (usually six or nine) cut at two or three different levels along the wall of the pot. A number of small plants can be placed in these openings, and they cover the pot as they grow.

All flower pots have a drainage hole. Some jardinieres, particularly if they were glazed, were made without holes, and a smaller pot was placed within them. Flower pots may vary in size from a capacity of several gallons to that of a few ounces. They are not measured by gallon capacity, but by the diameter of the pot mouth, and the numbers sometimes impressed into these pots and their respective saucers are indicative of that dimension.

Other flower pot oddities may have been produced. One of these which I know of is the thrown seed flat, which was made in the form of a low pan or cylinder with a number of drainage holes pierced through the bottom.

The advent of jigger molds made fancy raised designs possible on the exterior of flower pots, and these are made even today. Now mechanical presses stamp out common flower pots by the thousand. Most of these late flower pots have the heavy banded rim seen in jiggered pots. They are stacked in tall piles for firing.

Three floral vases made especially for florists to use in their refrigerators for storing cut flowers. All were made at the Meyer pottery, but other potteries also made such vessels at times. They are 11 1/2, 9 1/2 and 7 1/2 inches in height respectively. All are covered in a Leon slip glaze being yellow-green, brown, and mustard colored. First half of 20th century. L-R; $110, $150, $100

A pair of ornate floral vases showing some of the movement towards art or studio pottery. The vase on the left is 10 1/4 inches tall and covered with a mossy green Leon slip glaze. Meyer Pottery, 2nd quarter of 20th century. The handled case is salt-glazed with interior and top dipped in an Albany type slip glaze. The decorative handles have free ends turned upward. Attributed to Eli LaFever Pottery, Putnam County, Tennessee, first quarter of 20th century. L $350; R $400

Three unglazed, hand-thrown flower pots made at the Meyer Pottery. The ten inch top diameter pot is a ruddy brown and shows that it was warped in firing. The central pot is the smallest size of hanging pot made. It is 6-1/2 inches in diameter. The pot on the left is a small 4 inch pot with its accompanying saucer. All first third of 20th century. L-R: $125, $65, $50

This is a very curious form produced in unglazed, hard fired ware. The earlier ones are of this low cylinder form while later ones from the pottery are made in the form of a banded milk bowl. All have one or more openings in the base for drainage and they were used as containers for staring seeds. One might call them ceramic seed flats. Height: 4-1/2 inches. Diameter: 12-1/2 inches. Meyer Pottery 1890-1920. $100

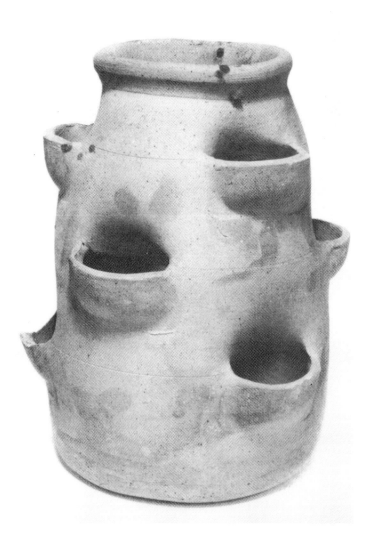

A strawberry pot which is 10 1/2 inches high. Pockets were made in the same manner as the poultry fountain pockets by cutting a slit in the wall and pulling one part out, bending the other in. Such pots were made by many potters and are still being made. Strawberries or any small plant may be grown in the pockets. This one was by the Meyer Pottery, first third of the 20th century. Unglazed. $275

TABLEWARES AND BAKINGWARES

TABLEWARES

All tablewares, with the exception of mugs, were uncommon products of the utilitarian stoneware potter. Sugar bowls and cream pitchers probably follow mugs in popularity. The other forms are rare, but do appear.

MUGS: Made in sizes from one-half to a full pint, these were usually cylindrical in form but may be keg-shaped as well. Many were combed or decorated in other ways.

CUPS AND SAUCERS: Although very rare, these were made by potters upon request, especially when other types of tablewares were not available. I have seen a press molded, handleless cup manufactured at an 1850 period pottery in Texas. Saucers were made at this same site, but are typical, heavy, wheel-turned forms.

PLATES: These were very rarely made, since they are always very heavy when wheel turned and tend to warp in firing. They were made when other tablewares were unavailable and are now a studio pottery product.

GOBLETS: Very rare in early ware, goblets have become a common product of the present-day studio potters.

SUGAR BOWLS AND CREAM PITCHERS: These objects were made, but usually not in sets. Both often imitate cast tableware forms.

TEA POTS AND COFFEE POTS: These two vessels have attached, separately thrown spouts. The tea pot is usually a short, full form, and the coffeepot tall and slender. Both have lids. "Coffee boilers" were advertized by one southern potter, but I judge they were only what we would term a pot.

SOUP AND SERVING BOWLS: These were usually similar to pan-form utilitarian bowls, but smaller in size. A broad flattened rim is sometimes present.

Some examples of stoneware tablewares. A sugar bowl and plate in dark and light green phases of the Leon slip glaze made by the Meyer Pottery in the 20th c. The little salt dish on the right was made in Ohio, probably in the late 19th c. Height: 2 1/10 inches. It is covered with an Albany type slip glaze. Clockwise $125, $90, $100

The mug on the left is a pint sized mug glazed in a dark brown phase of the Leon slip glaze. The central mug is of 8 ounces capacity and has an emblem sprigged on the front which has the initials "KTSA" for Knights Templars of San Antonio and "Comm. No. 7" for Command No. 7. It is of a mossy green color phase of the Leon slip glaze. Both of these mugs were made by Meyer Pottery 1900-1930. The mug on the right is salt glazed on the exterior with the two faint bands colored by cobalt slip. No interior glaze. American, possibly Pennsylvania, mid 19th c. L-R: $375, $70, $100

BAKINGWARES

These wares, with the exception of the bean pot, are uncommon in hand-thrown utilitarian stoneware. Baking vessels frequently needed a modification of the body paste to withstand the thermal shock of oven use properly and therefore were more commonly made by late industrialized potteries. A few utilitarian stoneware potteries made occasional lead-glazed earthenware baking dishes, firing them in the cooler areas of their kilns with the unglazed flowerpots. All bakingwares are much more common in earthenware.

BEAN POTS: These are short ovoid pots with one or two side handles and a lid ledge. The proper lid is a simple flat indwelling lid with a central knob. They usually vary from about one to two gallon capacity in size.

CAKE MOLDS: These are discussed under the bowl forms.

CUSTARD CUPS AND CUP CAKE PANS: Custard cups were very small, rimless, pan-shaped bowls. Cup cake pans usually consisted of six to eight of these cups joined together. Many were formed in a pressed or cast mold. These are more common in earthenware.

PIE PLATES: Always low, saucer-shaped forms, some pie plates are slightly deeper than others. All have a flat bottom and low outwardly slanted walls.

ROASTING OR BAKING PANS: I have seen one such pan which was oval in form (being shaped from a round thrown form by removing a piece of the bottom and pressing the walls together again.) Round or oval, they are very rare in stoneware. Most were originally made with deep matching lids.

STEW POTS: The stew pot was a deep kettle form, usually having lateral pulled strap handles when hand thrown. They were quite common in late, cast or jiggered forms with bail handles. A pie plate to be used as a cover when desired is known to have come with such a pot as a set. These industrial products usually have a trade mark such as "OVEN-SERVE" or "IXL" appearing on the base.

A marked "Boston" bean pot. This low one gallon jar, probably a bean pot, is attributed to Frederick Carpenter's Charleston Pottery about 1804. It shows a brown ferruginous underglaze dip typical of Carpenter. Salt glaze exterior, dry brown interior, possibly a local clay. *Courtesy of Peter Schriber*. $450-500

KITCHEN, YARD, AND BARNYARD ITEMS

A few vessels or other forms of ware were manufactured by utilitarian stoneware potteries to serve a variety of ordinary household or barnyard purposes. The most common of these were various forms of poultry watering and feeding vessels. Feed and water containers for small animals such as rabbits, cats, and dogs were also quite common. Other items, while not so common as feeders, were in general use at various periods.

FEEDERS AND WATERERS

BUTTERMILK FEEDERS: These were usually two-piece forms much like the two-piece water fountains. The reservoir often had a wide, open bottom and sat on three or four tiny raised projections in the saucer. Used for poultry.

DOG, CAT, AND RABBIT FEEDERS: These vessels may be used for both food and water for such animals or even for caged poultry. They are short, cylindrical, wide-mouthed forms. Some are about four inches deep, some only two, and they are five or six inches in diameter.

POULTRY FOUNTAINS: These vessels occured in several different forms, but all operated on the same principle. A full vessel standing upside down in a shallow bowl of water created a vacuum in the top of the closed vessel. This vacuum suction allowed the water to rise only to the level of the low opening into the bowl, refilling as it was consumed.

The one-piece vessels were usually a jug form closed at the top and having a hand-modeled, small, dishlike opening "near the base" on one side. The two-piece ones usually were composed of a jug or bottle form without a top opening that rested in a shallow dish. Such a mouthless jug may have a hole near the base or a completely open base with a notch in one side. Sizes from one-half to two-gallon capacity are common, but they were sometimes as large as five gallons in capacity.

WESTKO BUTTER MILK FEEDER and POULTRY WATERER
This Fountain is made for a Butter Milk Feeder or Waterer. Acid in Butter Milk will not effect the glazing, therefore no Poultry will be poisoned. ALWAYS SANITARY

A one-gallon capacity buttermilk feeder or poultry waterer. This consists of a low saucer form and a bottomless container which sits in this saucer. A small opening near the container's base allows the liquid to fill the saucer. The curious statement stamped on the front refers the fact that this stoneware glaze contains no lead. Lead glazed earthenware vessels could not be safely used for buttermilk. Bristol white glaze. Mid 20th c. $250

Small poultry fountain of the "hooded" form. One jug form was made and closed at the top, having an opening about the size of a quarter near the base. A second jug form was made and cut in two. One half was joined to the side of the original container and an opening about two inches in diameter cut out of it so that the head of the bird could enter to drink. One quart capacity. Exterior salt glaze with cobalt band decoration, no interior glaze. Attributed to Pennsylvania, third quarter of 19th c. $325

Simple cylindrical vessels which were used for the feeding of small animals. Suitable for cats, small dogs, and rabbits, these vessels hold about one quart and one pint respectively. Such vessels were produced, many by press molding or jiggering, all over the United States. These are from the Meyer Pottery and have mustard and yellow-green phases of the Leon slip glaze. Early to mid 20th century. L-R: $60, $50

Three poultry fountains. All work on the vacuum principle. They are filled upside down and then inverted. Since the tops are closed, the water rises only to the top of the tray or opening. The one on the right is one gallon capacity and from central Alabama, early 20th century, and glazed in an Albany type glaze. The central one-half gallon size is from Meyer Pottery and has a yellow-green Leon slip glaze. The "indented" jug form is a very common early form of water vessel for poultry. A slit is cut near the base and the area above the slit is pushed in so that a small cuplike area remains at the base to allow drinking. The lip of this area sometimes has a roll of clay added to make it a little higher that the slit edge. The tall two-part fountain is also from the Meyer Pottery, but hard fired and not glazed. Both early to mid 20th c. L-R: $125, $90, $175

DRAINPIPES AND OTHER TUBULAR ITEMS

DRAINPIPES: Short drainpipes for attaching to a kitchen sink to drain water outside of the house were fairly commonly manufactured by small potteries before the advent of sewage systems.

SEWER PIPES: Salt-glazed, vitrified sewer pipe was also a stoneware product. This heavy, thick form of pipe may have been made in small amounts at potteries during the early period of its use, but it was later manufactured in huge plants making only this form of ware. The clay is coarse and thick, frequently having a heavy greenish coat of salt glaze over the exterior. Salt has only recently been discontinued as a glaze for this type of ware. The so-called sewer pipe whimseys were made by workers in these specific plants and fired in the salt glaze kilns.

STOVE COLLARS: Stove collars are short tubes of fired clay with a flange around the top opening. They were used as insulators around a stove pipe as it passed through a wall, and were thus slightly larger in diameter than standard metal stove pipe.

WATER PUMPS: Stoneware tubes made in the form of a water pump and greatly resembling a metal pump were an unusual stoneware form sometimes manufactured in the middlewest. Like a metal pump, they have the long tube that sits over the mouth of the water well, a place for the handle to operate the pumping mechanism on the interior, and a spout for the water to flow out of.

WATER TANK FLOATS: One very unusual stoneware form made by a few potteries was the water tank float. I have never seen this on a list from a pottery and have only seen them in Texas. The form varied somewhat in shape, but was a substitute for the large copper float used for turning on and shutting off the water flow into a tank for livestock.

Stoneware floats were made in a modified jug form, sometimes with handles at the top to attach to a rod that was connected to the lever arm of the water cut-off valve. The jug mouth was sometimes sealed in the manufacture and a small opening made in the base for a vent during firing. This base remained above water as the vessel floated. A second form was a modified, short, full jug form with an ordinary mouth, sealed by a cork when used as a float. They range between one and two gallons in capacity.

Two water tank floats of stoneware. The one on the left is low and fat and has an opening in the top that must be corked. The wire bail allows attachment to the water cutoff arm. Dark mossy green Leon slip glaze. Meyer Pottery, early 20th century. The tall float on the right has a small hole in the bottom and no opening in the top. It was used upside down. It is covered with a very thin white Bristol form of glaze and the iron in the body clay burned through this in firing, so it has a rusty color in patches. Rusk County, Texas Early 20th c. L-R: $100, $150

On the right a bucket with a heavy wire handle was made of a section of sewer pipe clay. Greenish heavily salt-glazed exterior. Capacity about one gallon, Bexar County, Texas, probably early 20th c. The piece on the left is a bank fashioned of sewer pipe clay. The top, if not all of the piece, was fashioned in a press mold and raised name **"T. SUTTLES"** can be seen on the top. Dark brown salt-exterior. Ohio. Late 19th c. L-R: $125, $200

OTHER USEFUL ITEMS

WATER BUCKETS: Wheel-thrown water buckets were manufactured in a few areas. They generally imitate the metal bucket form and have a bail handle. Enthusiasts say the water flavor was sweeter and purer than when metal or wooden buckets were used. These are usually about like a metal bucket in size—one to two and one-half gallons in capacity.

FUNNELS: This common, useful item was manufactured on the wheel as well as in molds during the late period. They are uncommon but are seen in both forms, thrown and cast.

BIRDHOUSES: Birdhouses were often made and decorated in various manners but were usually left unglazed. They were sometimes ornately combed to resemble tree bark. Most have an opening for the bird on the side and a small opening in the bottom for drainage.

A pair of stoneware funnels. The larger one on the left has a diameter of 6 inches at the top. It is salt glazed and attributed to Denton County, Texas c. 1900. The smaller funnel on the right was made at the Meyer Pottery. It measures 3 1/4 inches across the top and is glazed in a yellow-green Leon slip glaze. Probably early 20th c. $350-400

A fairly large, ornate bird house. A loose ring has been put in the top for hanging. The lower part of the house is combed and has little stoops over the entrances which are also combed. Height: 9 1/2 inches. Attributed to G.W. Suttles, Wilson County, Texas c. 1890-1900. $900

A birdhouse fashioned from a one-quart jug form. It has a hole for drainage pierced through the underside. Dark brown with small patches of gray salt glaze. Meyer Pottery, Bexar County, Texas. Probably late 19th century. $650

PORTABLE FURNACES: These furnaces were more of a yard fixture than an interior object. They are of earthenware, but were produced by many stoneware factories and are listed in price lists from 1870 onward. They are more a matter of curiosity than a vessel, but since they are not described in any place that I know of, I thought it best to include them here. They have very thick walls (one inch or over) of a soft, open clay body, sometimes white and sometimes pink in color. Some contain coarse particles of previously fired clay ground and placed in the body to make it more heat resistant.

The form is that of a wide-mouth jar with a very slight taper in toward the base. Within the interior of this jar a heavy slab of the same clay, which has a number of holes of about one inch in diameter cut through it, was fixed across the whole jar, about half way between top and bottom, forming a sort of grate. On one side near the base there is a rectangular opening of some two inches in height. The pots appear to have been crudely press-molded in most cases. They were covered, when new, with a thin metal jacket up to within one inch of the top. A wire bail handle was fixed into this jacket. The small opening in the jacket over the hole near the base of the pot had a sliding metal closure that was used to control the air intake.

Portable furnaces burned charcoal and, while they may have been used in homes for interior heating, were dangerous for home use because they were unvented. They usually were used in the yard or wash-house for heating water or boiling clothes and also for heating irons before automatically heated irons were available. Smoke or smudge pots to discourage mosquitoes in the yard were made of the furnaces by placing green wood and leaves on top of the charcoal. I also have fond memories of toasting weiner and marshmallows over these furnaces in my youth.

A portable furnace in which charcoal was burned to heat water or to make a smudge pot. Although this is not really stoneware, having a heavily grogged soft body to withstand heat, these furnaces were made in many stonewares potteries. They were very popular in the lower South during the first third of the 20th century. This one still has its bail handle, galvanized sheet metal jacket and remains of a paper label indicating that it came from the McDade Pottery. Height: 9 inches; Diameter: 12 inches. Bastrop County, Texas, first third of the 20th century.

CEMETERY VESSELS: The stoneware potter was ever ready to try his medium for the production of useful or necessary articles. In a number of areas, particularly in the South, where small pottery shops were present, stoneware head markers as well as foot and corner markers for graves may be found. This was an inexpensive, but relatively permanent method of marking a grave. Many of these markers were made for members of potters' families. They were generally cylindrical in form with an open base and a closed top. The top may have been finished with some sort of fancy terminal and might even have areas of fancy throwing in between the top and base. These markers are seen in salt, slip, and Bristol forms of glaze. Many are unglazed but hard-fired. The name of the individual resting in the grave as well as certain vital statistics such as age and date of birth and death are usually inscribed by hand on the marker or stamped with impressed letters. A small amount of cobalt was used at times to make the name and other lettering more pronounced. I have also seen one with the molded bas-relief of a lamb sprigged on to the marker. Foot or corner markers used with these pieces are usually smaller cylindrical forms with a less ornate top. Other markers were made by joining slabs of clay in a form not unlike a tombstone, but these are less common than the cylindrical forms.

Large, fancy jardinieres and flower pots were also very commonly placed upon graves. Another form of cemetery vessel, rarely seen, was a cylindrical or slightly ovoid vessel with an open mouth and a cone-like form tapering to a closed, pointed, bottom end. These vessels were used as vases for placing fresh flowers on graves. The point of the vase was pushed into the soft earth on top of the grave to hold it upright.

Cemetery marker placed at the head of a grave. This is a typical form for such markers which were made in many areas where there were potteries from the mid 19th century to the mid 20th century. This one is an Upshur County, Texas cemetery and was made by Abe Byrd for a small daughter. Impressed "Our Little Darling/Died Nove. 14, 1916." Unglazed. $1250-1500

Grave headstone made of unglazed, hard-fired stoneware in Putnam County, Tenn. This is considerably more ornate than most ceramic headstones. It bears the inscription "W.C. Hedgecough/Born February 10, 1815 and Died April 14, 1903." He was a member of a well known Tennessee family of potters. *(Courtesy of Tennessee Department of Conservation, Archeology Division.)* $2200

A pair of vases of the form made to place flowers upon a grave. The point is inserted into the soft soil of the grave. The one on the left is 9 1/4 inches high and has a brown Leon slip glaze, having been made at the Meyer Pottery during the first half of the twentieth century. The vase on the right is thirteen inches high. It has a lightly salt-glazed exterior and was probably made at the Saenger Pottery, also Bexar County, Texas, about 1890-1900. $300, pr.

TOYS AND WHIMSEYS

Many toys and whimseys were manufactured by stoneware potters as odd items. They are not listed in price lists, but were made in small numbers, often as special presentation pieces for friends and members of the potter's family. During the mid-twentieth century they became more common as souvenier items made in some quantity.

A tiny wheel-made whistle in the form of a chicken(beak broken) which was made at the Meyer Pottery, Bexar County, Texas between 1890 and 1920. These whistles were made as gifts for children by many German potters, but few survive. Green Leon glaze. Height 3 1/4 inches. *(Courtesy of Joanne G. Wells.)* $2500-3500

BANKS: During the early nineteenth century small banks were sometimes finished on the top with bird finials in the Rhenish manner. Early banks were often made as special presentation pieces. Later banks are simpler and not commonly marked or decorated. All have the traditional slit through which to insert coins.

Three small stoneware banks. The bank on the left is very small measuring only 2 7/8 inches in total height. It has an Albany slip glazed base and Bristol white top. Attributed to the Macdade Pottery, Bastrop County, Texas c. 1920. The center bank is also glazed in a white Bristol glaze, maker unknown, early twentieth century. The bank on the right is a small bottle form turned on its side and modified to resemble a pig. Is covered in an Albany slip glaze, but was made about 1977 by Norman Smith, a traditional stoneware potter in Alabama. L-R: $50, $90, $395

DOORSTOPS, FIGURES, AND FIGURINES: These items were made from time to time by stoneware potteries all over the country. They usually appeared in larger numbers when there were a number of potteries in the area or during the mid-twentieth century when the demand for ordinary wares was diminishing and all sorts of odd decorative and souvenir items were being manufactured. The imitation Staffordshire Spaniels are one of the commonest of these forms. They were made in earthenwares and stonewares, including sewer pipe clays. Most of these various figural forms were made in simple press molds or formed by hand. The Mexican Sombrero, popular (at least in Texas) during the early and mid-twentieth century, was a wheel-made form. It appears in sizes from two inches across the base to sixteen inches across the base. There is hardly a limit to the forms which may be seen. I have seen a stamp moistener in the form of a miniature grindstone, as well as molded picture frames. The characteristics of the glaze and the clay body, thick and coarse in nature when made by utilitarian stoneware potters, sometimes allow us to identify the oddities and whimseys made by these men.

A small pig bottle with an opening at the rear and formed in a mold. This pig has a few details added by hand, but no inscription. It is sewer pipe clay and was made in a sewer pipe plant. Area unknown. Late nineteenth or early twentieth century. Shiny transparent glaze, probably salt but showing little texture. Length: 8 1/4 inches. $350

A small pig figurine which was probably slip cast since it is very light in weight. It has no openings and appears to have been an advertising piece. The raised letters "Monmouth Pottery Co., Monmouth, Ill." are on one side only. Albany slip glaze in a rich, shiny chocolate brown. Monmouth, Illinois, last decade of nineteenth century. Length: 7 1/2 inches. $650-850

MATCH HOLDERS, STRIKERS, AND TOOTHPICK HOLDERS: All of these small forms were made occasionally in stoneware. They were both glazed and unglazed. Toothpick holders usually were glazed.

MINIATURES: Smaller versions of large standard forms of ware such as jugs and pitchers were one of the most common forms of toys. Jugs in particular were made from as small as a half an inch high to those holding one to four ounces and being two to three inches tall. Many of these were not toys but advertising items, particularly for vinegar and whiskey. Tiny pitchers, jars, churns, bowls, and even chamberpots were made.

PIG BOTTLES: The Kirkpatrick Pottery at Anna, Illinois, is the only pottery known positively by me to have made pig-shaped bottles by modeling and adding clay onto wheel-made forms. There are many other pig vessel forms, usually whiskey containers with the opening at the rear, which were cast in molds and finished by hand. Many of these pig whimseys have inscribed legends and even crude maps on them.

STRING HOLDERS: Seen upon occasion, these are usually a simple cylindrical form closed on the top, open on the base, and having a tiny hole in the lower wall for the string to pass through.

An unusual stoneware form made to hold a ball of string upon a store counter. The string passes through the hole made near the base without tangling. Albany type slip glazed interior and lower section, Bristol white glazed top. Attributed to Macdade Pottery, Bastrop County, Texas 1900-1920. $200

Two match holders with striking areas of hard fired, unglazed clay. There are examples of small items made in many stoneware potteries. The coggling used as decoration as well as to form the striking area in the free-standing examples is very fine and was possibly made with a wheel from a clock. Meyer Pottery, Bexar County, Texas. 1900-1920. L-R: $300, $100

WHISTLES AND PIE BIRDS: A wheel-made form resembling a bird with an opening in the base and in the beak was made to use in the tops of large pies, allowing the steam and juice to rise in this vessel rather than through splits in the crust. Whistles and water flutes were also commonly made in this shape. The whistles and flutes had a closed base and openings in the tail and beak. Other forms of whistles were made at times. One that I have seen is in the form of a small jug with an opening near the base for blowing into.

SHORT-STEMMED TOBACCO PIPES: Short-stemmed tobacco pipes were made by quite a few small nineteenth-century potteries in both earthenware and stoneware. During the later period, machines to press the pipes became more common and finally special establishments manufactured nothing but pipes. The pottery at Point Pleasant, Ohio, has been studied in the past few years because of the great number of different pipes manufactured at that site. The main period of operation appears to have been the period between 1849 and 1854 when Cornwall Kirkpatrick was one of the owners. There were many different molds, probably all produced by Kirkpatrick. Even the later Pampillon pipe factory did not use as large a number of different molds.

Only one or two different pipe molds were used at most small nineteenth-century potteries, and only a few pipes were produced in each firing. An old story is that the wives of the potters formed the pipes in molds and that when the potter fired he put them in the kiln for her. Her bit of pin money was derived from the sale of these pipes.

All of these pipes are of the short-stem form that was fitted with a reed for smoking. Stoneware pipes are not usually obviously glazed, but many have a sheen and even small deposits of salt from being within a salt glaze or wood firing. Rarely, they have been dipped into a brown slip glaze. The pipes made in small numbers at local shops were never shipped far distances, but were intended for local consumption. Some are plain or grooved, while others have intricate anthropomorphic designs with Roman and Turks' heads in the pattern. Since there are a number of excellent articles on American tobacco pipes, I shall not go into detail describing them.

Unglazed, hard-fired pipes. The pipe on the right is stoneware and had a very thin salt glaze. The pipe on the right is a smooth unglazed terra cotta and is of earthenware. American, second half of the nineteenth century. L-R: $150, $190-225

The tremendous range of possibilities of form available to knowledgeable potters makes knowledge of all the oddities produced impossible. Some objects I have seen or heard of, and others I may not even have dreamed of. Oddities were manufactured by the potter for reasons usually now unknown. Some oddities known to me are discussed here primarily to provide an idea of the range of items that might be included in this category.

ANT TRAPS: Low cylindrical forms with an inner wall separating a central ring from an outer circle, these were made so that a table or food safe leg could be placed in the inner ring and the outer filled with water. Ants could not pass over the water and get into the food. Only persons brought up in the deep southern states before insecticides were commonly available can understand their great value. They are usually about one to two inches high and six to ten inches in diameter.

CERAMIC INSULATORS: For use in household electric wiring, telephone wiring, and other types of wiring, insulators were manufactured in large numbers in late industrialized potteries. These are still an important ceramic product. During the late nineteenth and early twentieth centuries a few of these were produced in very small quatities by utilitarian stoneware shops.

These low cylindrical forms were produced in sets of four to be used under table and foot safe legs. They are traps designed to keep ants from crawling up the legs of furniture to reach foods. The leg of the piece of furniture was placed in the central area and water or kerosene in the outer ring to furnish a barrier. This custom was common in the deep South. The one to the left has an Albany slip glazed interior and salt-glazed exterior and is attributed to Richter's Pottery in Bexar County, Texas. The piece standing on edge is from the Meyer Pottery and has a brown and green mottled Leon slip glaze. Both are very late nineteenth or early twentieth century. $125, set.

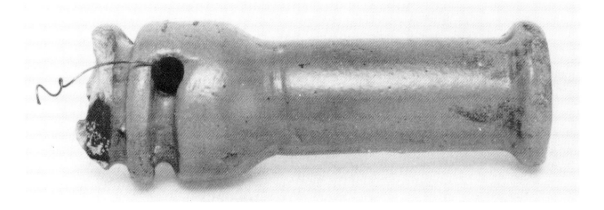

The fragment an insulator made at the Meyer Pottery. Other electrical insulators were produced in stoneware or a laboratory grade of porcelain by potteries, but usually in plants designed to produce only this form. Length: 5-1/8 inches. First half of the twentieth century. $150

FIRESTARTERS: I have heard that some small utilitarian potteries produced objects called firestarters (to soak in kerosene) as well as some sort of railroad "bullseye" (to spread oil for rapid burning), but I have not seen these items and do not know how to describe them. I am sure that other oddities were manufactured in stoneware, but they are all exceptionally rare and will seldom be encountered by the average collector or student of American stoneware.

ROACH TRAPS AND BEEHIVES: I have not seen these objects except in earthenware, but they very possibly may have been made in stoneware. The roach trap is a small vessel with an incurving top and small central opening. They were filled with water and the roaches were inquisitive enough to fall through the opening into the water.

SAUERKRAUT PRESS: This very unusual form was made in Bexar County, Texas, by two German potters. It consists of a round, very thick (1½ to 2 inches), solid clay disc, pierced at intervals with holes about the diameter of a common pencil. This disc is topped by a central, short cylinder with a strap handle inside of the cylinder. This item was set in a barrel or crock on top of the kraut to keep the kraut under the brine pickling solution. These could also have been used for holding pickles under brine in a large crock.

This unusual and extremely heavy piece of stoneware was designed to be used as a weight over sauerkraut or pickles. The solid bottom disc was pierced to allow the gases produced in fermentation to escape. The cylindrical form added to the top has a heavy strap handle within an everted broad lip. The lip was to enable the weight to be hung on the crock or barrel rim after it was lifted. Salt-glazed. Impressed: "WM. SAENGER/ELMENDORF, TEXAS." c. 1900. Basal diameter: 12 inches. $350

TREE RINGS: Double-walled, circular vessels of unglazed clay, about eighteen inches in diameter, were used around the base of a young tree. The ring could hold water for seepage on the tree as well as offer protection with its small wall. Tree rings were made in the Bexar County, Texas, area. I have not seen these in any other area, and old automotive tires were more commonly used for this purpose, even in the area in which these were manufactured.

A curious item of unglazed ware burned in a stoneware kiln. This ring form was used as were old automobile tires around a small tree to protect it from mowing or trampling. Diameter: 13 1/2 inches. Meyer Pottery, Bexar County, Texas about 1920-1930. $350

Three sizes of molds made to forms cones of brown sugar. The tallest is 6 1/2 inches tall, while the small one is only two inches high. Rims of the two larger have been dipped in the Leon slip glaze, but they are otherwise unglazed. These are an imitation of the much larger cones in which sugar from the West Indies was shipped to Europe in the seventeenth and eighteenth centuries. Brown sugar produced in Mexico today is marketed in small cones. These are said to have been used by candy companies in San Antonio. $350

SUGAR CONES: Large, coneshaped forms, probably of earthenware, were made by British potters during the eighteenth and nineteenth centuries and shipped to the colonies. They were filled with a boiling sugar solution that crystallized within the cones and was taken out of the molds as a solid cone of what we call brown sugar. It is still the custom in Mexico to make small cones of brown sugar in this manner for marketing. Cones for molding sugar such as those used in Mexico were manufactured in Bexar County, Texas, for some of the local candy companies during the first and second decades of the twentieth century.

The sizes range from two inches to about eight inches in height. These were used for the production of large and small cones of brown sugar, mainly for consumption as candy.

A heavy stoneware bowl which is in imitation of the usual lava rock "mocahere" used to grind peppers and spices for Mexican cuisine. The "mano or pestle" is also an important part. Both pieces show a heavy salt glaze, almost greenish on the mortar, and are of a coarse sewer pipe clay. The inner section of the bowl has an incised pattern to aid the grinding and the glaze has been worn away. Top diameter: 6-1/2 inches. Attributed to one of several sewer pipe companies near San Antonio, Texas. Twentieth century c. first quarter. $200

These slip cast cylinders were produced by some of the large industrialized potteries in the twentieth century. They were fitted with a wooden rod to become rolling pins. Merchant's names are often stamped on them and they were probably used as advertising gifts. Length: 7-1/2 and 7-3/4 inches. First half of the twentieth century. $200

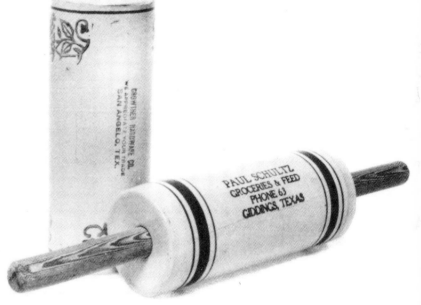

A hunting horn—one of the most curious pieces of American stoneware that I have ever seen. Horns are known to have been made of earthenware in Aachen, Germany in the late medieval period, but otherwise they are a rare item. This horn has a dark gray, salt-glazed exterior and is known to have been made by William Grindstaff, probably at his pottery in Knox County, Tennessee about 1900. Length: 16 inches. (*Courtesy of the Tennessee Department of Conservation, Division of Archeology.*) $500

The numeral three inscribed by hand to indicate the gallon capacity. Alkaline glaze, Texas 1860-1880.

A hand-inscribed Roman numeral, III, to indicate gallon capacity. Alkaline glaze, Alabama, c. 1840.

The numeral "2" impressed in the rim of the wide-mouthed jar with a metal stamp. This is not a common position for the capacity mark, but is seen at times. Salt glaze with interior slip glaze. Texas. 1875-1900.

A two gallon capacity indication impressed with a hand carved wooden stamp. The notching within the numeral seen in this example is characteristic of such stamps. Salt glaze. Texas, 1870-1880.

Chapter 4
Names, Numbers, and Embellishments

THE EVOLUTION OF DECORATION

Both the manner of marking and the manner of decorating American stoneware vary greatly. Marking and decoration appear to proliferate in those areas in which a number of different potteries were active during the same period. These techniques most certainly proliferated during the first half of the nineteenth century among stoneware potters in the easternmost states, such as New York and New Jersey. As potters moved into the states west of the Allegheny and Appalachian mountains, marking as well as decoration declined greatly. Between 1840 and 1860 the pots being manufactured in Indiana, Illinois, and Kentucky in the Middlewest, as well as in Alabama, Mississippi, and Texas in the deep South, showed little, if any, decoration. Marks begin to appear on these pots most often after several potteries were functioning simultaneously in the same local area. At about this same period, pots in New York, New Jersey, and New England were being vividly decorated with all manner of slip brushed and trailed decoration, and unique slip decorated, alkaline glazed pots were being produced around Edgefield, South Carolina. After 1860 decoration was still very popular in the mid-Atlantic and New England states, but minimal to absent in most of the more westward states. It was obviously not necessary as a means of attracting customers in the pioneering areas of the nation.

Decoration may appear at times on early pots from some of these central areas of the country, usually special, rare, presentation pieces. The production of special pieces became even less frequent in the late nineteenth century, especially in potteries producing in the far west. Stamped and stencilled names of merchants, however, became rather common in many areas during the last quarter of the nineteenth century, especially in the central states and some of the western states.

The decorative and stamped or stencilled features were almost always added to a pot upon the very same day that the pot was thrown on the wheel. Any sort of encircling banding was done by incising into the soft clay of the pot as it remained on the wheel. The clay was most receptive to any sort of impressing or incising just as it was ready to be removed from the wheel or soon thereafter. Handles and knobs were added as soon as the pots were dry enough to be slightly firm. The numerals indicating gallon capacity were also impressed or incised by hand at this stage. Any other inscription was also performed while the clay was fairly soft. Names were incised by hand or stamped with some sort of metal, clay, or wooden stamp during this still slightly soft stage of the pot's existence. Any other manner of decoration such as the incision of a design to be filled in by brushing with cobalt or some other ceramic coloring oxide, the addition of applied decoration, or modelling to change the form of the vessel also had to be accomplished while the vessel was still damp and relatively soft. Stencilling could be applied upon a relatively dry pot and was usually done later, after the day of turning, during the "leather-hard" to dry stages.

The most common mark found upon American stoneware is the capacity

137

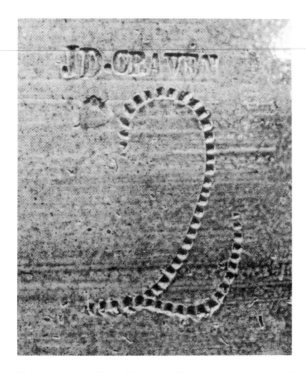

The capacity mark on this two gallon jug was incised with a "penny roulette wheel" - a penny was noticed around the edge with a knife, then pierced and, with a nail as the axle rolled to form numbers and decoration. Salt glaze, Impressed: "J.D. CRAVEN" Moore County, N.C. 1860-1890.

A stenciled star with the gallon capacity stenciled within it. This was the mark of the Star Pottery, Elmendorf, Texas from about 1895 to 1909. Bristol white glaze.

numeral. It is usually on the front or side of the vessel. These numbers may be produced by almost any of the general methods of decoration and are intended to clearly show the gallon capacity of each particular vessel. One-gallon and smaller capacity vessels were frequently not marked as to capacity or even with a maker's mark.

After capacity marks, maker's marks are the most common feature seen on old stoneware vessels. Unfortunately many old potters felt that their work spoke for itself and that there was no need to mark their names upon the pots. In the backwoods and pioneering areas this was true, for there were rarely more than one or two potters who supplied the needs of a small local community. On wheel-thrown pots the maker's marks appear, as do most of the capacity marks, on the front face of the vessel. Many present-day dealers and collectors of old pottery use the term "signed" for impressed or stenciled maker's marks. This term should only be used when the potter's mark is a hand written inscription of his name. All other impressions or stamps of the potter's name are properly called marks. These marks may or may not indicate that the person whose name is present actually made the pot. The name is most often indicative of the name of the owner of the pottery or of the pottery itself.

Maker's marks were most commonly made by impression of a metal, hand carved wooden, plaster of paris, or biscuit fired clay stamp. Rarely they were produced with a roulette wheel. Such marks may consist of nothing more than initials, but often include the full name of the shop and also the city and state in which it was located. Stencilled and stamped marks using a coloring oxide such as cobalt are most common on late salt-glazed vessels and Bristol glazed pots. Marks on ware made in a jolly mold wiith the "jigger machine" are often different. Since the base of the vessel was in this instance made in a mold, a maker's mark was often incorporated in this mold. This produces an impressed or a raised mark on the bottom of the vessel.

The inscription upon this jar gives us the potter's name, "Dave;" the master's initials. "I.M.;" and the date, "January 22, 1859." This unusual method of signing and dating his pots was typical of Dave, the Negro slave of Louis Miles of Edgefield, South Carolina. Alkaline glaze.

The capacity numeral encircled by a ring of dots is often seen in mid-nineteenth century pots. This stamp is also said to have been carved of wood. The maker's name appears to have been a metal stamp. Salt glaze exterior. It reads "W. H. CRISMAN/STRASBURG, VA." Mid 19th century.

This impressed maker's mark was probably made with a metal stamp. An extra wavy circle of cobalt blue decoration around it emphasizes the mark: "C. CROLIUS/ MANUFACTURER/MANHATTAN-WELLS/NEW YORK" Salt glazed exterior, probably 1820-1835.

An unusual one gallon capacity mark and a bordered rectangular maker's mark stand out on the front of this pot. The mark reads "I. SUTTLES/LA VERNIA/TEX." Salt glazed exterior, Albany type slip glazed interior.

Masonic emblems, frequently appear as decorative devices on stoneware pieces. This potter, however, combined his maker's mark, and Masonic emblem of square and compasses all within one circle. The capacity was probably impressed with another stamp. "J. F. BROWER," Randolph County, North Carolina c. 1875. Heavy salt-glazed exterior.

The potters of central Georgia used initials rather than full name stamps and frequently placed them on the handles rather than on the body of the pot. "J.H.L.," the impressed initial stamp, suggests that this potter may have been a member of the Long family. Crawford County, Georgia. Alkaline glaze. 1890-1915.

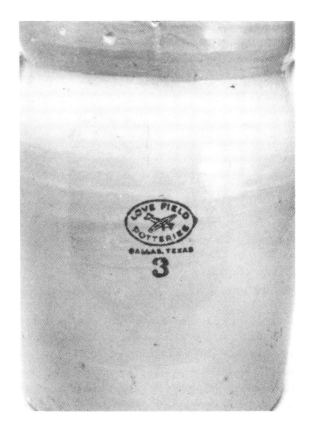

A World War I monoplate became the symbol of the Love Field Potteries of Dallas, Texas when the plant was built at Love Field after the airfield was closed in the 1920s. A rubber stamp and cobalt ink were used for this mark under a Bristol glaze. 1925-1935. $150-200

The mark of the Star Pottery Works at Elmendorf, Texas between 1909 and 1915 was this star within a circle. It was produced by a rubber stamp using a special cobalt-containing ink pad. This is a white Bristol type of glaze.

The relief lettering on the base of this bowl indicates that the maker's mark was carved within the plaster mold used in a jigger machine to form the bowl. The foot ring is also typical of this form of manufacture. Black-brown Albany type slip glaze. "HENDERSON POTTERY/ HENDERSON, TEXAS" c. 1880.

This fired clay capacity marker was made and used by the D.L. Atcheson Pottery, Annapolis, Indiana. It appears to have been hand constructed and carved. Unglazed except for fly ash and salt vapor, c. 1845. *Courtesy of Indianapolis Museum of Art. Photographer: Robert Wallace.* $225

A potter's stamp for the numeral 8 made of hand-carved applewood. This is one of a set of such stamps. *Courtesy of the Conner Prarie Pioneer Village. Photographer: Robert Wallace. Indianapolis Museum of Art.* $250

Two small preserving jars which are covered with the buttery, yellowish alkaline glaze typical of the Pottersville Community near Edgefield, South Carolina. They exhibit small marks impressed near the base — an inverted "V" in the pint jar and a very tiny "C" near the base of the gallon jar. These marks are thought to be those of individual potters employed at this pottery. 1820-1840. L-R: $400, $575

Impressions, inscriptions, stamps, or stencils bearing the names of merchants who had vessels made to order for them at a pottery are rather frequently seen on pots of the late nineteenth and early twentieth centuries. These names may be confusing and may be mistaken for maker's marks. Many of these pots are without maker's marks, adding to the confusion. The most frequently occuring vessels with merchants names were jugs. These were often produced for general merchandising stores as well as for dealers in hard liquor, especially bourbon whiskey. Jugs were, however, frequently used for the storage of other liquids and vinegar advertising is not uncommon. Jars, butter pots, and even mixing bowls as well as miniature jugs frequently were made with the name of a merchant on them and were given away as a sort of premium when a customer's bill was paid. The merchants ordering these special pots were usually in the close proximity of the pottery. However, some of the potteries in western Pennsylvania and along the Ohio River shipped special marked pieces made for merchants down the rivers as far as Vicksburg, Mississippi, and New Orleans, Louisiana.

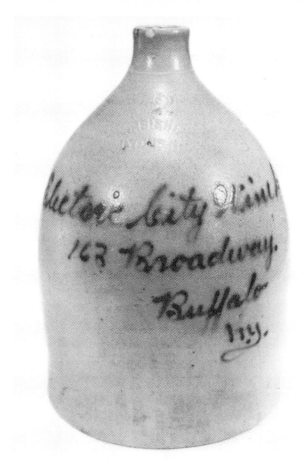

An excellent example of a pot showing an impressed maker's mark: "J. FISHER/LYONS, N.Y." and a blue slip trailed merchant's name and address. Salt glaze with Albany type slip glaze lining; last quarter of 19th century. $450

These foot warmers show flattening of one side of a closed jug form after it was turned. A mouth was then created by making a hole in the new top of the vessel. One mouth has an added turned opening, while the other if fitted with a pewter closure. The warmer on the right is salt glazed. American, no maker's mark and mid to late 19th century. The "Henderson" is Bristol glazed and probably early 20th century. It is impressed "DORCHESTER POTTERY WORKS/ BOSTON/MASS." $250

A one-gallon capacity shouldered jug glazed in an Albany type brown slip glaze inside and out. It is inscribed "FROM/WALLACE & GREGORY BROS./SPRIT, ESSIG/ PADUCAH, KY./SOLD BY KNOCKE & EIBAND/NEW BRAUNFELS, TEX." The miniature two-ounce jugs were probably also made in the Paducah area. One is inscribed "COMPLIMENTS OF JOSEPH COURAND, CASTROVILLE, TEX." while the other has a Bristol white glazed lower section and a stamped Kentucky vinegar label. The two all brown jugs probably date 1890-1900, the brown and white 1900-1920. $500

143

The discussion of the actual decoration of certain pots is the feature which takes us out of the simple craft tradition and into a discussion of folk art and individual expression. The number of well-decorated pieces is actually not large when the total numbers of utilitarian pots manufactured by American stoneware potters is considered. Even in potteries in which decoration was not habitually added, occasional pieces were made by potters for special presentation or expression. This expression may be in the form of actual artistic decoration or no more than an inscription expressing some particular feeling of the potter at the time that the pot was made. **Without a doubt there is a higher survival** rate for pieces with any form of inscription or decoration. They were treasured by the recipient or purchaser somewhat more than plain pots.

Most makers of utilitarian stonewares in this country regarded themselves as craftsmen working to produce ware of sufficiently good quality to supply the local demand for these utilitarian vessels. Few regarded themselves as artists, although historians and collectors now view some of the early ovoid forms, the natural variations of the glazes, and even some of the defects or "misfires" as unusual, beautiful, or artistic. This aspect is in the eyes of the beholder, not the eyes of the maker. American utilitarian stoneware production was indeed an expression of a folk craft, but some of the additional decoration, particularly the more intricate painting done on the exterior surfaces of utilitarian pots, was at times not even done by the potter himself but by artists hired to paint the pots. These artists were as a rule untrained individuals with some drawing abilities.

On the other hand, true artists in clay such as Cornwall and Wallace Kirkpatrick of the Anna Pottery in Illinois produced a line of absolutely plain utilitarian wares at their pottery. A sideline of unique special pieces which they produced allowed them to express their artistic feelings in all manner of decoration. This decoration is, however, not an expression of conscious formal art, but most often constructed to express humorous and caustically witty

A 38 inch high decorative water or punch container which was formed by uniting a separately turned base and an urn-shaped vessel. It has incised floral designs filled with cobalt as an enhancing decoration under a salt glaze. This is one of two such pieces found in Ohio. No other history. Probably second quarter of the 19th century. *Courtesy of The Ohio Historical Society, Ohio Ceramic Center at Roseville.* $9500

144

thoughts. I feel that these pots as well as the occasional pots with cartoon-like incising, special presentation pieces, and hand-modeled clay figures are the truest expressions of folk art by American potters.

A handsome pitcher made from two colors of clay which swirl as the clay is turned on the wheel. It is covered with a light, transparent glass form of alkaline glaze, Impressed: "REINHARDT BROS./VALE, N.C." c. 1934. *Courtesy of the Mint Museum of History. Photographer: The Mint Museum.* $1500-2000

THE MAJOR METHODS OF DECORATION

Decoration may be accomplished by several different methods. The essential character of damp clay and the fact that these pieces must pass through a high temperature firing before they are finished articles are factors that influence the manner in which decoration may be produced.

Initially decorative forms may be produced during the throwing of the pot by the execution of fancy finials or a fanciful rather than straightforward form in the throwing. One example of this is the fluting of the edges of flower pots and saucers. At times two or more pieces thrown separately may be joined while damp to produce tall "fancy" pots, usually in the form of elegant water coolers and jardinieres. Vessels were also sometimes thrown upon the wheel and then modeled by hand to produce such forms as foot warmers and flattened bottles that resemble flasks. A second distinctive type of modification for decorative purposes accomplished during the turning process was produced by the preparation of balls with different colored clays which were then arranged in one ball in a particular manner. This produced an artistic swirled pattern demarcated by the contrast between the different clays in the thrown **piece. This method was most often used by** utilitarian potters to produce decorative vases and pitchers.

The second major method of decoration was achieved by making an impression in the soft clay. This was accomplished while the pot was still on the wheel, and single, multiple, or groups of multiple incised encircling lines were produced. Any sort of drawing, impression, or inscription was done on the pot within a few hours after it was removed from the wheel — at a moderately soft to "leather-hard" stage of drying.

The technique of incising into the damp clay with a sharp tool is termed **scraffito,** or **sgraffiato.** The term comes from the Italian word meaning "to scratch" and is the proper name for any sort of decoration accomplished by scratching into the clay.

Although we now use an Italian word to describe this process, the technique has been in use ever since man first discovered the properties of clay in a moist state. Inscription is a form of scraffito, but when letters and numerals are written in script to form names, comments, capacity numerals, and dates, I prefer the term "inscription."

This three-gallon storage jar is decorated with five bands each consisting of a number of incised lines. It has a flat, outward extending tie down rim and bilateral broad pulled lug handles. Salt glaze with no interior glaze. Stamped: "N.H. NIXON" Almance County, N.C. 1860-1880. *Courtesy of the Potter's Museum. Photographer: Bill Jenko.* $700

This one-half gallon preserve jar was found in Lauderdale County, Mississippi. It has a pale yellowish alkaline glaze inside and out and is decorated with a number of incised, encircling lines at the midsection and at the shoulder. Probably c. 1860. $450

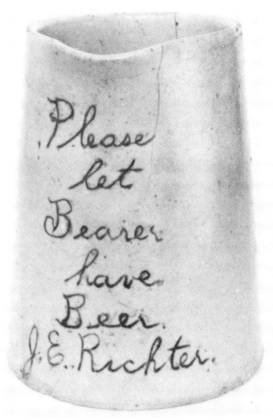

A one-quart pitcher made by E.J. Richter at the Star Pottery, Elmendorf, Texas about 1900. The white Bristol glaze was incised, possibly with a cobalt pencil. The inscription "Please let bearer have beer, J.E. Richter" was made so that his children could be sent to the local saloon to have the pitcher filled for the potter. (Gift of J.E. Richter, Jr.) $650

A third form of decoration employed by American stoneware potters was accomplished by the production of raised decorative designs on the exterior surface of a pot. This was done by the addition of clay. Many of these decorative designs were accomplished by freehand modeling of additional clay, while others were formed by pressing small bits of clay into press molds made of plaster of paris or biscuit-fired clay. These small molded forms were then added to the surface by sticking them on with a small amount of thick clay slip. The term "sprigging" is used for this method of decoration.

An exceedingly ornate one pint mug made at Saenger's Pottery, Elmendorf, Texas c. 1890. The wheel-made cup was hand-modeled with additional clay to resemble a tree trunk and then incised to resemble tree bark. The handle was artfully worked to resemble a branch with a fork in it. On the front face a shield pattern was incised and the initials "J.B.N," are incised within the shield. They are said to have been the initials of the brewmaster at one of the local breweries. It is covered with an Albany type slip glaze which has small areas of yellow on the exterior where fly ash or salt vapor reached the pot during firing. $1400-1800

An ovoid two-gallon jug in a deep green alkaline glaze. It is inscribed by hand "August the 30/1864/maid and sold at/ a low price for confederat/money by me/Thomas Ownby." Thomas Ownby was working in Union County, South Carolina at that period. $16,500-18,500

A fourth method of decoration was immensely popular for the decoration of stoneware vessels, especially salt-glazed ware. Primarily it consisted of the application over the surface of the pot of a solution of clay slip containing a metallic oxide. This produced a contrasting color in the area of application after firing. This application could also be accomplished by the dipping of a portion of the pot into such a solution or the painting of such a solution in a design pattern on the surface of the vessel. The painting was accomplished either by the use of small brushes or a goose-quill-spouted slip-trailing cup. During the latter portion of the nineteenth century, potters also began to use stencils for the application of colored slips in decorative patterns as well as in letters for marks.

The oxides that are useful in high temperature ceramics for this form of decoration are somewhat limited. Cobalt, which produces blue, is one of the strongest and most commonly used. Iron and manganese both produce browns, but iron is not strong and must be used in some quantity. Copper, producing greens in oxidation, is also a good coloring oxide for high temperatures but was seldom used on utilitarian stonewares. Other oxides tend to burn out at high temperatures. Pure white clay, often termed "pipe clay," china clay, or Kaolin, was also used at times when the clay body was dark enough to produce good contrast.

Another decorative technique seen in American utilitarian stonewares is rare and was used in a limited area over a limited period of time. It is decoration with bits of glass, which melt down over the pot during the firing.

This handsome dark brownish salt-glazed water cooler is attributed to Wingender's pottery in Haddenfield, New Jersey. It is rouletted, cobalt decorated, hand incised, and has a sprigged on grotesque face around the spigot opening near the base. The decoration is Germanic in type, for these men continued to employ the techniques of decoration learned in their youth for some years after they came to America. c. 1885. Albany type glazed interior. $2500

A five-gallon churn showing the numeral 5, five number signs, and a very simple decorative device, all trailed in cobalt slip. It was made in Denton County, Texas about 1870 to 1880. The exterior surface was supposed to be salt glazed but no true glaze developed, only slight browning of the body. The interior has a rich brown slip glaze, probably Albany type clay. $975-1200

A two-gallon salt glazed jug with an Albany-type slip-glazed interior. This jug has a fantastic decoration which resembles an abstract human face trailed in cobalt slip on the front of the jug. At first glance this decoration appears to be floral, but eyes, eyebrows, nose, and mouth can then be seen. Impressed: "Ottman Bros. & Co./Ft. Edward, N.Y." Third quarter of the nineteenth century. *Courtesy of Albert C. Revi.* $5500

Decorative forms of all sorts may be produced by the use of molds, particularly slip casting and simple press molds. The latter were used by utilitarian stoneware potters to make such crude decorative figures as the imitation Staffordshire dogs so beloved by all American potters. These dogs occur in a wide range of sizes, shapes, and mediums. More complicated exterior patterns on milk bowls and flower pots were accomplished in molds used on the jigger machine, mainly in industrialized potteries late in the nineteenth century or in the early twentieth century. These same potteries also produced pitchers, salt jars, tobacco jars, butter crocks, and a like range of ornately formed vessels by slip casting with a stoneware casting slip.

Pipes made by hand pressing in molds are another form of commonly produced molded wares. They were frequently manufactured by small folk potteries in the southern United States. Although somewhat ornate molded forms were produced in stoneware, they sprang from more industrialized ceramic roots and are not considered folk pottery.

Very rarely, totally hand-formed or modeled whimseys were made by folk potters or workers in sewer pipe factories. Upon other occasions "folk" decorated pots were formed of wheel-turned vessels with added, hand-modeled forms. Grotesque jugs and jars as well as "snake" jugs (in which a hand-formed snake is coiled around a wheel-thrown jug) are examples of the modification of thrown forms with additional clay for decorative effect. The very fantastic pig bottles, snake jugs, and mugs with tiny molded frogs in the interior produced by the Kirkpatricks at the Anna Pottery all fall into this category. Most other pig bottles were produced in simple molds.

A charming American variation of the Staffordshire spaniel, this little unglazed dog figurine is attributed to the Newcomerstown area of Ohio. It was made in a press mold and is of reddish buff clay, but seems somewhat vitrified and may be stoneware. It is 9-1/2 inches tall on a 4 by 5 inch base. c. 1860. *Courtesy of Nancy and Bob Treichler. Photograph by Doug Moore.* $5800

A two-quart pitcher formed by slip casting and exhibiting the relief decoration on both pitcher and handle which this method of forming ceramic wares allows. The "Flat Iron Building" in New York is part of the decoration. Glazed inside and out with a white Bristol glaze and hand tinted with cobalt in areas of the design. Stamped on the bottom "THE ROBINSON CLAY PRODUCTS, AKRON." Early 20th century. $1600-1800

A grotesque jug made in upper Mississippi probably in the last quarter of the nineteenth century. It is covered with a light straw colored, transparent glaze, probably an alkaline glaze with added ground glass. The thrown form has been altered by slight modeling and the addition of bits of clay for the features. The pupils are colored blue with cobalt and broken bits of ironstone represent teeth. $5500

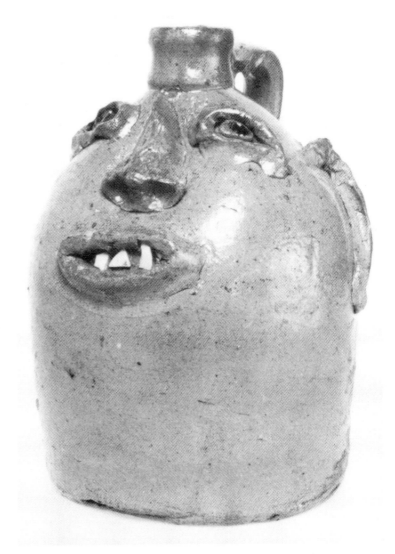

Three pipes from the site at Point Pleasant, Ohio. These pipes represent only a few of the designs produced at this site during the period of Cornwall Kirkpatrick's ownership, about 1850. They were made in simple press molds and fired in saggers within a salt glazing kiln. Few show any salt deposits. Each pipe is about 1-1/2 inches long. Top left-$250, Top right-$350-400, Bottom-$350-400

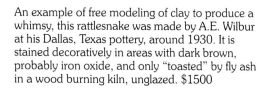

An example of free modeling of clay to produce a whimsy, this rattlesnake was made by A.E. Wilbur at his Dallas, Texas pottery, around 1930. It is stained decoratively in areas with dark brown, probably iron oxide, and only "toasted" by fly ash in a wood burning kiln, unglazed. $1500

This hand-modeled frog sits perkily atop a scallop shell formed in a press mold. The shell has had a base added and top opening cut to form an ink well. It is decorated with cobalt spots in areas and salt glazed. The base is inscribed "Anna Pottery, 1882." The inkwell on the right is a small turned well decorated with cobalt and has initials which appear to be S.J. in cobalt. Salt glazed exterior, probably from New York or Pennsylvania, mid 19th century. *Courtesy of Bob and Beka Mebane.* L-R: $1800, $850

VARIATIONS IN METHODS

Simple incising or impression into the soft clay may be used as a decorative device on stoneware vessels in a number of different ways. Very commonly, one incised band was made around the pot while it was still on the wheel. The band served as a minor sort of decoration and deliniation, but it was also helpful in pots on which bilateral lug handles were to be attached. The line frequently served as a mark for the positioning of these handles. Such a line may appear at the level of the top, bottom, or mid-section of the handle. Two or more lines were often incised around the shoulder and neck of a jug. Multiple rings around a jug neck form a decoration which is sometimes termed "reeded." The use of bands of multiple incised lines encircling a pot produced a very effective decoration, especially in salt or alkaline glazed pots.

A one-half pint container made in the form of a pig. This is one of the wheel-formed pigs made at the Anna Pottery, Anna, Illinois, by the Kirkpatricks. It is Albany slip glazed and on the back an incised map of the Mississippi River and various Illinois railroads may be seen, while the inscription on the presenting side reads "Safest & Most Reliable R.R. and R. Guide, from Anna Pottery to S.V. Quenner with a little good old rye in a ®," c. 1880. Length: 6-3/4 inches. $2000

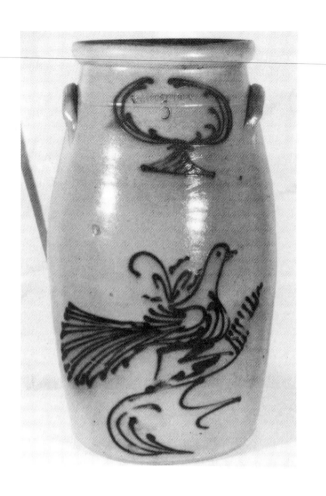

This six-gallon salt-glazed churn is beautifully decorated with a wreath motif encircling the impressed name and a large bird on the lower front face trailed in cobalt slip. It also shows an incised line at the shoulder area which was made to assure even placement of the bilateral lug handles. Impressed: "WHITE'S UTICA/NEW YORK" 1865-1877. *Courtesy of Robert C. Vose III.* $2500-3000

A pair of mugs combed and decorated to resemble tree stumps. The mug on the left is covered inside and out with an Albany type brown slip glaze. The one on the left is in a white Bristol type of glaze with a heart-shaped medallion on the front outlined in cobalt blue. The initials "R.S.," and "1903" appear trailed in cobalt inside this heart. Hand-inscribed on the bottom of this mug is "From G. Richter, Elmendorf, Tex." Star Pottery, Elmendorf, Texas c. 1900 and 1903. L-R: $300, $275

Incising may be limited to a single area and a simple design, such as that of a flower on the front of the pot. Many incised pieces had cobalt painted within the design after incising to produce an incised and colored decoration. Few American utilitarian pots have other than simple incised bands used as decoration entirely around the pots. At times decoration may appear on both front and back or around the pot, but it is most common only on the front face of the pot. Incised decoration was also frequently achieved by potters with a simple multi-pointed tool called a comb. This may have been an ordinary, rather finely toothed hair comb or such a simple object as a table fork with its three or four prongs. Design may be achieved by waving or rotating this tool as it is drawn over the clay surface.

In more ornate and decorative pottery, roulette wheels—small rolling cylinders may be rolled along the surface of soft clay pots to impress designs in bands around the pot. These were very commonly used before slip casting techniques were well developed. Utilitarian stoneware potters used them upon occasion to decorate pots. Potters also frequently used a simple cog wheel constructed of a notched coin or an old clock wheel. The New Jersey potters around South Amboy during the first quarter of the nineteenth century employed both these tools frequently on stonewares. Their use was, however, rare in most other parts of the country. Occasionally the maker's mark was carved into a roulette wheel. The same name repeats in the same form around the pot when this is the manner in which it was impressed.

The use of various stamps for decoration was not uncommon. Sometimes one single stamp (such as the "man-in-the-moon" impressed on Old Bridge, New Jersey, pots) was all that appeared. At other times stamps in the form of crescents and leaves were used in multiple combination to produce designs. Thomas Commeraw of Manhattan used a cookie cutter like crescent combined with a small stamp in the form of an abstracted tassel to make a swag and tassel decoration around the

necks of many of his pots. The crescents and swags were then colored with cobalt paint to produce an attractive decoration. Stamps which look like bow knots as well as others shaped like holly leaves were used by Warne and Letts of South Amboy, New Jersey. These potters also used roulette wheels to produce additional impressed decoration on many of their pots.

A two-gallon jug which has a nicely incised or "reeded" neck and decoration over the shoulder and upper body produced by multiple rollings of a roulette wheel over this area. Additional circles of cobalt (blue) were painted within this area. Salt glazed without interior glaze. Attributed to Old Bridge, New Jersey, first quarter of 19th century. $2500-3000

A one-half gallon jug attributed to early Manhattan potters, possibly the Crolius family. It is salt-glazed without an interior glaze. A beautifully incised multiple petalled flower with stem and leaves have also been painted with cobalt. Very late 18th or early 19th century. $3800

A globular bodied pitcher with a thin yellow-brown alkaline glaze. Two incised and scalloped rows of decoration made with the use of a "comb" of some sort encircle the shoulder. The initials "J.R." are those of the potter Joseph Rushton, Rusk County, Texas c. 1880. $1700

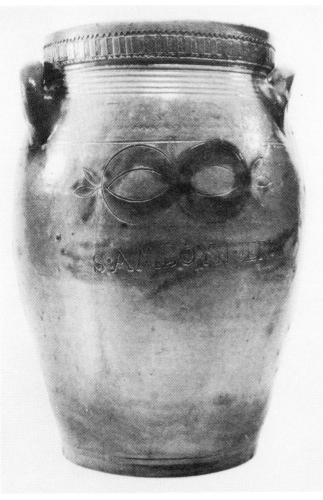

A one-gallon jar marked "S. Amboy, N. Jersey" shows a rouletted decoration impressed around the upper rim and again faintly beneath a group of incised lines on the shoulder area. The bilateral handles are of the early open loop type bent upward toward the pot to make them less easily broken. The bow-knot impressed design is filled with cobalt. Salt-glazed. South Amboy, J.J. 1800-1810. $2400

A two-gallon salt-glazed jar attributed to the Old Bridge pottery in New Jersey. The circular stamp seen on the front of the jar is one of the so-called "Man in the Moon" stamps attributed to this pottery. The center of the stamp has been painted with cobalt. No interior glaze. First quarter of 19th century. $1200

A three-gallon capacity jug impressed "CHARLESTOWN" and having an eagle sitting upon a cannon as a decorative stamp impressed just below the mark. Salt-glazed with a ferruginous top dip. Charlestown, Mass. c. 1805-1810. $1750

157

Paul Cushman, on the other hand, produced decoration by freehand incising, often without added color, but used a roulette wheel to produce his "PAUL: CUSHMAN'S: STONEWARE FACTORY 1809/HALF-A-MILE-WEST-OF AL-BANY GOAL" mark.

Occasionally small stamps not containing a numeral were used to denote capacity. Two hearts or three hearts may be seen on Charlestown pots to denote two-or three-gallon capacity. Three small circles are impressed upon the upper front of a jug marked "M. TYLER & CO./ALBANY" (N.Y.) to denote three-gallon capacity. Small circles, square grids, rosettes and other tiny stamps were often impressed into the pot to form a decorative pattern. These may have been used singly by shop employees to indicate pots which they had made but we are not absolutely sure that this was their purpose.

A different form of scraffito decoration may often be seen on pots glazed with a deep brown slip glaze, usually the Albany type. Inscriptions or designs were made into the surface of the pot soon after it had been dipped into the slip glaze solution. The clay was still soft enough that the slip glaze could be scratched through or cut away to reveal the contrasting light body beneath the glaze clay. This technique was very commonly used to produce jugs and sample jugs or souvenirs with merchant's names upon them by potters around Paducah, Kentucky, during the last quarter of the nineteenth century. It was also effectively used for decoration of special pieces by potters such as those of Cannelton, Indiana, to produce the "Welcome, Cannelton String Band" pitcher. Rarely, coggling or rouletting was done for decorative effect through a slip clay.

A small one-half gallon jug in salt-glazed stoneware. It shows a ringed neck and the potter's mark was made by passing a roulette wheel around the middle of the jug. It reads: "PAUL: CUSHMAN'S: STONEWARE-FACTORY: 1809/ HALF-A-MILE-WEST-OF-ALBANY GOAL." $795

A "CHARLESTOWN" jug with decorative incised lines just below the neck and two hearts impressed with a metal stamp to indicate gallon capacity. Salt-glazed exterior. Charlestown, Mass. c. 1805-1810.

A fully ovoid three-gallon jug with an exterior salt-glaze and interior Albany type slip glaze. A floral design on the front is executed in grayish cobalt slip. The three little impressed circles indicating the gallon capacity are unusual. Impressed: "M. TYLER & CO./ALBANY" New York c. 1830. $1200

A curious stamp which is one of several seen upon pots marked J.D. CRAVEN. Their significance is unknown. J.D. Craven, Moore Co., N.C. 1860-1890.

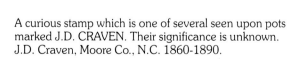

An unusual stamp used, usually with the date of 1807, upon their pot by Warne and Letts of South Amboy, New Jersey. It reads; "LIBERTY FOR EV./WARNE & LETTS - 1807."

A one-half gallon Albany type slip glazed poultry fountain made by George W. Suttles at his pottery in LaVernia, Texas between 1880 and 1910. The cartoonlike decoration was incised through the glaze while it was still damp and is undoubtedly the potter's sentiment upon that day. $6500

This very large pitcher is between two and three-gallons in capacity. It is attributed to the R. Clark & Co. pottery at Cannelton, Indiana, 1860-1890. The scraffito technique is unusual in that broad areas of letters were deeply cut in and removed. The underlying clay body was then pricked so that it appears stippled. Albany type slip glaze. $8500

Decoration achieved by adding hand modeled or molded clay decoration on the exterior surface of the pot may be very, very simple (such as the small sprigged emblems and initialled plaques placed on mugs by the Meyer pottery of Texas) or very complex, as when a great deal of ornamentation was added in applied clay decoration (such as the presentation field jugs made in central Ohio). The Ohio jugs frequently had twisted handles resembling vines and added grape leaves in an extensive design. The Kirkpatrick snake jugs from Anna, Illinois, are outstanding examples of this manner of decoration with all sorts of added clay forms.

An ornately decorated harvest or field jug of 1-1/2 gallon capacity. It is glazed inside and out with a shiny dark brown slip glaze of the Albany type. Applied or sprigged-on molded relief decoration appears on all sides. Grapes and leaves on the front, floral designs on either side and under the handle, and a female figure beneath the filling spout. Tuscarawas County, Ohio. 1860-1870. *Courtesy of Nancy and Bob Treichler. Photographer: Doug Moore.* $1800

One of the fantastic "snake jugs" attributed to Wallace Kirkpatrick of the Anna Pottery. This jug is only 11 inches tall and of about one-gallon capacity, and has a light tan salt-glazed exterior. Various inscriptions identify some of the figures. They are "A.G. Berner going in," "Capt. Watson at Camp Dubois," "Capt. Davidson," and "Liut. Short." Inscribed on the bottom "Kirkpatrick Anna Pottery/Anna, Union Co./ Illinois/Jan. 17th 1862/Camp Dubois." Over glaze blue, red, and gold colors painted on the exterior. *Courtesy of Barry Cohen. Photographer: Henry Cox.* $7500-8500

Decoration with color produced by adding coloring oxides to a clay slip or solution and using this to paint design patterns upon vessels was one of the most frequently used methods of decoration in the United States and Canada. The use of iron, manganese, and cobalt coloring oxides with salt glazing dates back to the use of these oxides by Rhenish potters as early as the sixteenth century. The dipping of the pot into an engobe or clay solution containing iron became a common practice during that period. It was this ferruginous dip that produced the famous mottled "Tiger" glaze of Cologne and Frechen. Apparently the engobe was prepared from high temperature clays and iron or a naturally high iron bearing clay and did not melt and run when the pots were salted. During the late sixteenth century, cobalt oxide and in the seventeenth century, manganese oxide, were added to their decorative palette by the Rhenish potters. In this instance the oxides were painted on in particular areas, producing a different form of decoration. They were usually applied within scraffito or incised designs on the surface of the pot. The same technique was used by early American stoneware potters.

British potters further developed the use of a ferruginous engobe dip as they began to salt glaze in the mid-seventeenth century. They used these dips in bands at the tops and bottoms of vessels as well as over the entire surface. The use of a brown ferruginous dip persisted in England through the next century, and we see this form of decoration at the earliest stoneware pottery so far excavated in this country, that of William Rogers at Yorktown. German potters seem to have abandoned the use of brown dips as they moved out of the early stoneware centers along the Rhein and into the Westerwald area in the late seventeenth and early eighteenth centuries. They did, however, continue to use a large amount of cobalt for decoration, and they sometimes used manganese as well on the same vessel. German potters migrated into the New York - New Jersey coastal areas as early as the seventeenth century. We have no documented extremely early stoneware potteries in the area, but by the second half of the eighteenth century one Colonel Morgan is known to have had a pottery at Cheesequake, New Jersey. The ware produced at that pottery was decorated with cobalt, and both the forms of the decoration and of the wares are very reminiscent of Rhenish salt-glazed stonewares. The major workmen at the factory may well have been German in background. The Crolius and Remmey families of Manhattan Island were certainly producing cobalt decorated, salt-glazed stonewares, manifestations of their Rhenish background, by 1775.

An enlargement of the finely incised fully rigged ship upon the front of a four-gallon churn manufactured by "GEORGE W. DOANE/LOUISVILLE, KY." Probably about 1860. The inscription reads "Homeward Bound." Exterior salt-glazed, interior Albany type slip glaze.

A beautiful two-gallon salt-glazed jug attributed to Fredrick Carpenter of Charlestown, "BOSTON" and the capacity numeral are impressed on the front just below the mouth ring. Carpenter's customary brown colored dips are seen on the top and bottom of the vessel. Some form of ochre or ferric oxide was used to make the dipping solution. Exterior only salt-glazed. Stacking scars are visible here also. c. 1805 to 1810. *Courtesy of Professor Emeritus F.H. Norton and the Department of Metallurgy and Materials Science at the Massachusetts Institute of Technology, Museum of Fine Arts, Boston, 1971.* $1200

By the early nineteenth century this manner of decoration had been absorbed into the mainstream of the American stoneware pottery tradition. Although the painting is much more limited in its scope than that of the Rhenish potters, free designs, most often of faunal or floral derivation, were used on American vessels by potters of both German and British descent. During the earlier period various designs were generally incised into the clay and then filled by brushing in a cobalt containing slip. Some students of stoneware feel that this incised and colored decoration was always early, but this is not true. Special pieces were made as far west as Louisville, Kentucky, and as late as the mid-nineteenth century. Incised decoration was more common during the earlier years of the nineteenth century, but occasional use of the technique persists until much later.

Free surface painting without the use of incised design then became very common. It was the primary type of painted slip decoration and was always underglaze in application. An ordinary artist's type of painting brush or a slip cup was used. Designs trailed with a slip cup usually show a cordlike line of deeply colored slip over the surface of the pot, while brushed decoration is not so intense and the edges usually fade into the surface of the pot in a manner typical of brush painting. There was no particular preferred manner of cobalt decoration. Slip trailing was an old earthenware decorative technique transferred to stoneware decoration. It was a little more difficult to learn than the slip painting technique.

Free painting was done mainly on the front face of the vessel, as was incised design decoration. The back of the vessel might also have some lesser design or a date. At times the painting consisted of no more than single brush strokes sweeping around the handles and over the impressed mark. Early pots from the Pennsylvania area frequently had encircling painted designs, a closer tie to Westerwald decorative techniques. Usually these patterns were simpler and less extensive than the German ones. The height of American cobalt painted decoration was probably achieved during the third quarter of the nineteenth century in New York and New England. It is known that some of the larger potteries had painters who were employed for this specific work. At this period there was a large concentration of somewhat industrialized potteries functioning in these areas. Competition obviously fostered the development of decoration. Rarely, a decoration of a brown color is seen painted upon a pot. The Bennington Potteries did more of this than most, but brown, so-called ochre, decoration is seen on a small percentage of American pieces. The use of other colorant oxides is rare.

A two-gallon preserve jar showing the capacity numeral as well as a simple calligraphic decoration trailed in cobalt-containing slip before firing. Salt glazed exterior, interior brown slip glaze of the Albany type. Attributed to Denton County, Texas 1860-1970. $600

A cylindrical jar dated 1833 in cobalt slip. It has four groups of floral spray decoration around it and so is decorated on all sides. A "3 CNS" in cobalt slip probably indicates three-gallon capacity. Salt glazed exterior, tie down rim. Attributed to Eastern Pennsylvania. $550

The side of this wide-mouthed jar with the impressed mark "C. CROLIUS/MANUFACTURER/MANHATTAN WELLS/NEW YORK" exhibits an excellent example of the custom of encircling handles with brushed-on cobalt slip. This is very commonly seen in early stoneware from the Northeastern United States. Salt-glazed exterior, brown slip glazed interior, c. 1820-1835. $495

167

A beautifully decorated six-gallon churn made in Ontario, Canada and showing close relationship in both form and decoration to New York State potters of the period. The flower and bird design was trailed onto the raw pot with cobalt-containing slip. It is impressed: "S. SKINNER & CO./ PICTON, C.W." Salt-glazed, 1855-1864. *Courtesy of David L. Newlands.* $2500-3000

A two-quart pitcher impressed "J. SWANK & CO./ JOHNSTOWN." It shows brushed cobalt designs on the front and sides in an abstracted floral pattern. Salt-glazed exterior only. Johnstown, Pa. c. 1860. $895

An example of the use of a cobalt-containing slip to decorate beneath a light tan, glass containing alkaline glaze. A broad band of blue from under-glaze cobalt may be seen just as the neck begins to swell outward to form the belly of the pot. Hilton Pottery Co., Hickory, N.C. c. 1925. $1200

An example of a brown slip decoratively trailed beneath a light, straw colored alkaline glaze. Impressed: "CHAN-DLER" beneath the handle. Thomas Chandler, Edgefield, S.C., c. 1850. $9250

Another form of free painted and slip trailed decoration developed during the late 1830s and persisted through the 1840s around the Edgefield area of South Carolina. A ferruginous slip and a pure white kaolin slip were used for the decoration of alkaline glazed pottery. Although both of these forms of slip were used separately at times, they were also combined at other times. When combined, the brown slip was brushed on, and a slip cup was used to trail the white slip over the brown. Many of these patterns are executed in simple loops and swags, others are floral. One or both slips may be employed. A few pots with human figures executed in both colors of slip have been found. The most ornate of these designs are thought to have been done by colored female slaves owned by Collin Rhodes. All traditional stoneware decorative painting was done prior to the application of the glaze if it was a salt or an alkaline type. Cobalt was not frequently used in the decoration of alkaline-glazed vessels until the late nineteenth century development, in the **Catawba Valley of North Carolina**, of the very light colored glaze incorporating ground glass. The natural iron in most slip or alkaline glazes discolors the usual blues of cobalt, producing deep browns and blacks.

Two curious forms of slip decoration incorporating the use of an Albany slip type glaze are seen in specific regional areas. During the late nineteenth century a ware of somewhat different type than the routine salt-glazed, blue decorated ware was produced in limited quantities in the Greensboro - New Geneva area of Pennsylvania. Although this ware is referred to as "Tanware," it is reported to have been made with exactly the same clay as the salt-glazed pieces. It is also said to have been fired at a different temperature from the salt-glazed wares. The body is vitrified, however, and it properly falls into the stoneware classification. A dark brown colored glaze was used on the interiors of the vessels as well as being used for brush- and occasionally stencil- painted decorations on the exteriors of the vessels. This glaze does not appear to be a lead glaze,

but more of a dark slip glaze resembling the Albany types. It is probable that Albany clay was used or that additional iron oxide was mixed with the normal slip glaze to produce more intense color. If Albany slip clay is used in a very heavy suspension with water, it may be painted on to produce the same sort of decorative patterns on the exterior of stoneware vessels. The actual unglazed body clay was used as the base for the exterior decorative painting, and the result is deep brown patterns on a dry, pink-toned beige or tan surface. No other exterior glaze is present. I have seen one or two pots with merchant's names stencilled on an unglazed exterior in what appears to be a thick, Albany type slip glaze, but do not know if they were made in this same area.

An interesting example of the use of pure white clay slip trailed on a pot to form a decorative mark and capacity numeral. This white slip was used under an alkaline glaze in the Edgefield area of South Carolina. Light olive green alkaline glaze inside and out. "C. RHODES/MAKER" Collin Rhodes c. 1850. $5000

A one-quart pitcher of the special decorated stoneware produced at New Geneva, Pa. It is called New Geneva "Tanware." It was made of the same body clay as was used in their salt-glazed stoneware. The pieces usually have an opaque brown slip glazed interior. The exterior is unglazed except for painted or stenciled decoration in the same dark brown slip glaze which appears to be an Albany type. These were frequently presentation pieces and bear names such as "Anna M. Shaw" on this piece. Probably 1860-1870. *Courtesy of Nancy and Bob Treicher. Photographer: Doug Moore.* $8500-9000

The second form of slip decoration incorporating the use of an Albany type slip glaze seems to have been limited to the areas around Ripley and Moline, Illinois, and Davenport, Iowa. In this instance a white slip was used over an Albany type slip glaze prior to firing, making it an overglaze application. Most of the decoration was trailed in this dry white slip over the usual complete coating of slip glaze, mainly in calligraphic designs accompanying capacity numerals. Occasionally simple, abstract floral patterns were brush painted by hand, and I have seen one piece with a stencilled maker's mark. The white slip was prepared from a dry, refractory clay, probably kaolin or china clay. It did not melt and combine with the slip glaze during firing, and therefore the decoration remained distinct and was a true overglaze decoration on utilitarian stoneware.

Maker's marks also were occasionally stamped or stencilled with a cobalt-containing ink or slip over the Albany types of glaze during the late nineteenth and early twentieth centuries. The resultant mark is usually black in appearance from the combination of the cobalt with the iron coloring agents in the slip glaze. This method of stamping or stencilling marks was also occasionally done with some alkaline forms of glaze during the very late nineteenth century or early twentieth centuries. Here again the marks appear deep brown or black in color.

In all American stoneware decoration the use of two colors of slip decoration on one pot is rare. We have already spoken of the Edgefield, South Carolina two-color slip decoration. Cobalt was the preferred coloring oxide, especially for salt-glazed pots. Iron and possibly manganese were used considerably less frequently and copper was very rarely used for decoration on any utilitarian stoneware until the twentieth century. At this late period, green from copper as well as occasional red and yellow stains are seen on some jigger-molded milk bowls and on other such industrially produced stonewares employing a Bristol form of glaze.

Although cobalt painted bands were occasionally used on salt-glazed vessels, they were most commonly incorporated into some design such as the imitation banding of a keg-shaped water cooler. Something about the pure white of the Bristol glaze promoted the use of one or two painted bands of cobalt encircling the wares. This decorative blue banding accompanied by a mark which used a cobalt stamp of some sort is being used today by one of the potteries still producing hand-turned utilitarian wares, the Marshall Pottery in Marshall, Texas. Free brush-painted designs with cobalt in a slip suspension were very uncommon in early twentieth century wares, but patterns made by the use of a small sponge dipped in coloring mixtures were frequently used for decoration under a Bristol form of white glaze in the very late nineteenth and early twentieth centuries.

An example of the application of a dry white slip (probably china clay) over an Albany type slip glaze. This unusual decoration has only been seen around Ripley, Illinois and Des Moines, Iowa, mid to late 19th century. *Courtesy of Robert Sherman.* $750

This white Bristol glazed pitcher had a cobalt and glaze mixture applied by a sponge in a criss-cross pattern to form a decoration before it was fired. Attributed to Byrd Pottery, Tyler, Texas c. 1935. $495

A water or cider container of three-gallon capacity made in the keg shape so popular for these vessels. The bands in imitation of metal hoops are colored blue with cobalt as are the impressed doves used as decoration. Light gray salt glaze with no interior glaze. No cover. Impressed "L.& B.G. CHASE/SOMERSET." Somerset, Mass. c. 1845. $1800

This three-gallon jug has a design painted under the glaze in which two colors of decorative slip, brown and pure white, were used. The brown slip was painted on the pot, then the white slip used in a trailer to outline and enhance the decoration. All is under a light olive green alkaline glaze. The reverse shows a flower resembling a tulip in the position that the numeral "3" bears on this side. Attributed to Collin Rhodes, Edgefield, S.C., c. 1845-1850. *Courtesy of the Ferrell Collection. Photographer: David Rasberry.* $1800-2000

173

This blue speckled pitcher was decorated by applying cobalt sprayed with an airbrush over a white Bristol glaze. San Antonio Pottery, San Antonio, Texas c. 1930. $300

Air brushes have also been used to apply a thin spattered decoration, usually colored by cobalt, over the surface or a portion of the surface of Bristol glazed pots in the twentieth century.

Stencils were very frequently used to produce gallon capacity and makers marks on salt and Bristol glazed utilitarian wares after the mid-nineteenth century. They were also used for marking merchant's names upon pots. The western Pennsylvania and West Virginia stoneware potteries changed from hand-painting cobalt designs on pots to stencilling rather ornate patterns shortly after the mid-nineteenth century. The Eagle Pottery of Greensboro, Pennsylvania, even used a large and ornate stencilled eagle as their mark. Other potters throughout the country used stencils but never to such an extent as those in the areas previously spoken of. Flowers, grapes, and various geometric patterns were used for this stencilling. Occasional pots are seen with hand-painted and stencilled combinations for decoration.

A three-gallon preserve jar which had the maker's name and location as well as a foliate decoration applied by painting a cobalt colored slip over a stencil pattern is typical of the New Geneva-Greensboro area of Pennsylvania. Deep gray salt glaze with brown slip glaze lining of the Albany type. Stenciled "JAS. HAMILTON CO./GREENSBORO," 1850-1880. $2200

Stamps using a coloring oxide or decalcomania transfer prints were not commonly used on utilitarian stonewares until the beginning of the twentieth century. These designs were mainly employed on jugs used by distilleries for packaging whiskeys. At the present time jugs made in industrialized potteries as containers for honey and various forms of syrups are labelled with rather ornate decalcomania prints.

The fresh and warm appearance of folk painting or decoration is no longer seen on utilitarian vessels. A few years ago the Marshall Pottery of Marshall, Texas, which still employs eight men to turn pitchers, jars, and water coolers by hand, tried a resurrection of hand painting upon these vessels. One artist produced very attractive pots with small intricate paintings on them. These paintings were not excecuted in the manner of early cobalt decoration and could not be mistaken for such. The woman who did the painting is no longer able to work, and the present artists do little more than handpaint given names on pots and mugs to be used as presents. All of the pieces are glazed with a modern, formulated, semitransparent feldspathic glaze.

Decoration with two colors of glaze is very rare in slip or alkaline-glazed stonewares. I have seen a very few examples of a dark alkaline glaze obviously applied decoratively over a light form of an alkaline glaze.

A one-gallon jug of the "shouldered" form. The handle projects at the back so that I do not think it was used for stacking. A San Antonio merchant's name, "L. KUNKEL" is stenciled on the front face. Pale gray salt glaze, Albany type glazed interior. Star Pottery, Elmendorf, Texas c. 1900. $500

An ornate water cooler of the urn form shows a twentieth century stamped pottery mark and "Water Cooler" in cobalt blue. The trademark, a wing, is stamped in red. Blue bands encircle the vessel top and bottom. The spigot is a replacement. White Bristol glaze. "RED WING UNION STONEWARE CO." Red Wing, Minnesota c. 1920. $650

A twenty-gallon storage jar with a stenciled eagle as the pottery mark and "WILLIAM COMPTON, NASHVILLE, TENN." stenciled on the front in cobalt for that merchant. Deep gray salt-glaze and brownish-black. Albany type slip glaze lining. "EAGLE POTTERY/GREENSBORO, PA" 1850-1880. $4500-5000

Whether or not the use of Albany types of slip glaze in combination with salt glazes and later Bristol white glazes was intended decoratively is difficult to say. Shouldered "stacking" jugs and milk bowls with wide rims were habitually glazed with a slip glaze in the areas that would be sheltered from salt vapor in salt kilns. It was a natural extension of the use of slip glazes as interior liners for salt-glazed vessels. Only the milk bowl rims and the body below the shoulder in the case of shouldered jugs and preserve jars were exposed to the salt. As the Bristol form of glaze became popular, this old manner of glazing jugs with the interior and upper shoulder and neck glazed in a slip glaze and the cylindrical lower body section in white continued to be popular. During the very late nineteenth century and first quarter of the twentieth century, this bi-colored glazing technique was then transferred to large jars and churns as well as ordinary jugs. These pieces were assuredly using two contrasting glazes for decorative effect. British vessels with the same sort of color contrast — brown tops with white middles and lower section — may have influenced this combination of glazes. American potters may have been hesitant to stop using the Albany form of slip glaze that had been such a tried and true interior glaze for many years, and so combined it with a new Bristol glaze as they had used it in salt-glazing.

The use of bits of glass placed upon pots as they were loaded into the kiln is a rare form of decoration on stoneware. It was employed only over an alkaline form of glaze in the Catawba Valley of North Carolina. Pale, transparent streaks of melted glass produced patterns as they ran down the sides of the pots during firing. The streaks are generally a transparent, pale blue-green color which contrasts well against the deep olive or brown color usual in the alkaline glaze type common in that area.

This two-gallon open jar was made in a jigger machine. The black stamped mark, trade mark, and gallon capacity show the decadent decoration of the second quarter of the 20th century. This is a representative piece from a highly industrialized modern pottery. The glaze is a semi-transparent, whitish glaze, probably a Bristol variation. Stamped: "WESTERN STONEWARE COMPANY, MONMOUTH, ILL" c. 1930. $200

A one-half gallon whiskey jug glazed with both an Albany type brown slip glaze and a white Bristol glaze. The liquor company name is stamped in black. The "Motto" jug is an eight-ounce size, also in both glazes, while the "Palmer" two-ounce sample jug is completely glazed in white with black stamping. All U.S.A. early 20th century. Left to Right $125, $250, $75

An eight-ounce pitcher with a semi-transparent Bristol type glaze. It shows the unique form of hand-painted cobalt decoration done by Kay Butler at the Marshall Pottery in the 1970s. Marshall Pottery, Marshall, Texas. $300-400

A six-gallon jug with an olive green alkaline glaze and decorated by stricking transparent, colorless "runs" down one side. This decoration was created by placing small pieces of window pane glass on the handles or shoulders of the jug as it was placed in the kiln for firing. The glass melts and leaves the streaks as it runs during firing. c. 1900 *Courtesy of the Mint Museum of History. Photographer: The Mint Museum.* $900

Chapter 5
Glass, Gloss, and Glaze

THE NATURE OF GLAZE

Glaze, as applied to ceramics, is nothing more than a coating of a glasslike compound over the surface of a vessel that has been formed of clay. The glaze must melt at a lower temperature than the clay of which the vessel is composed so that the vessel will retain its form while the glaze covers the surfaces desired. Lead, sodium, potassium, and some other strong alkaline compounds are used to "flux" or produce melting of the silica base in both glass and ceramic glazes. Just as there are lead glasses and soda glasses, there are lead glazes for use in lower temperatures ranges and alkaline types of glaze for both high and low temperature ranges. Feldspar glazes, which are in the high temperature range, require additional fluxes, usually alkaline earths.

The purpose of a glaze is multifold. First of all, it smoothes over and gives a gloss to what would otherwise be a rather rough and dry surface of fired clay. This quality makes glazed wares easier to clean and more pleasant to handle.

Whether transparent or opaque, glazes enhance the appearance of vessels by providing glosses of varying intensity. The gloss can vary from that of the very smooth, highly glossy surfaces to the soft stony surfaces of matte glazes. This is true of utilitarian glazes, but much more so of artistic glazes. Both transparent and opaque glazes can also provide color if desired.

The ability of glaze mixtures to form a coat of a sort of glass during firing seals over the surfaces to which they are applied. In earthenwares and also in incompletely vitrified stonewares this was their most important function insofar as utilitarian potters were concerned.

Only five different types of glazes were employed in the production of American stoneware vessels throughout the period of popularity of utilitarian stoneware from the beginning of its manufacture on this continent through the first half of the twentieth century. Salt glazes, slip or loam glazes, southern alkaline variations, volcanic ash, and the Bristol type of feldspathic glase are the types used. However, true, completely vitrified stoneware does not need a glaze to seal the body of the pot properly. Unglazed, vitrified, high temperature wares, produced in the valley of the Rhein River as well as in northern France, were the predecessors of salt-glazed wares. These wares were developed during the late Medieval period (thirteenth to fourteenth centuries) and persisted until the nineteenth century at the stoneware centers around Beauvais and LaBorne in France.

All of the glazes employed for utilitarian stonewares in the United States shared the following common properties:

1. The ingredients were inexpensive.
2. They could be employed in a single firing process, being applied to the raw clay pot rather than a bisqued pot. This was considerably less expensive than the double or multiple firing necessary for finer wares. All but one of these glazes were prepared as dipping mixtures and, therefore, had a high clay content so that they would adhere to the raw clay pot.
3. The glazes after firing were durable, easy to clean, and acid proof. Being acid proof made stoneware vessels coated with these glazes superior to lead-glazed earthenware vessels for the storage of acidic foods and beverages as well as acid chemical compounds.

179

THE SALT GLAZE

During the fifteenth century, salt glaze appeared for the first time in the great stoneware centers along the German Rhein. No documentatin exists of just how it was discovered that salt thrown into a kiln at a high temperature would react chemically with the fluid surface of the clay and develop a hard, transparent glaze, enhancing the appearance and durability of the vessel. The sodium reacts with the silica and alumina compounds to form a soda glass or glaze. Since such wares were completely vitrified, use of a glaze was not necessary to seal the interior of the pots. Salt vapor usually does not reach the interior of the vessels in enough concentration to form a true glaze.

From these German roots sprang the development of European salt-glazed utilitarian stoneware. The salt-glaze stoneware potters manufactured common vessels such as jars, bottles, and jugs, as well as ornate and highly decorative drinking, storage, and serving vessels.

During the seventeenth century, the manufacture of salt-glazed stonewares began in England. By the eighteenth century, salt-glazed stonewares in Great Britain had lost their essential Germanic characteristics and had developed into a special British tradition, having some unique characteristics such as top and bottom dips in a ferruginous solution. As ceramic technology improved and European fine stonewares and porcelains were developed during the eighteenth century, the period of popularity of decorative salt-glazed wares waned. The glaze was used more commonly in the nineteenth century in Europe for coarse household vessels necessary for the preparation, storage, and preservation of foods.

The earliest stonewares produced in North America during the mid-eighteenth century still included decorative drinking vessels, although these show considerable regression of decoration when compared with the Rhenish vessels of the sixteenth and seventeenth centuries and the fine British salt-glazed table and decorative wares of the eighteenth century.

Eighteenth-century American utilitarian stonewares are generally salt glazed and without interior lining glazes. Few documented examples exist, but some, such as the pieces from Yorktown, show very definite British patterning of form and decoration. Those of the New York - New Jersey area were quite Germanic in form and decoration. Immigrant German potters were prevalent in that area during the late eighteenth century.

During the last decade of the eighteenth century, these two influences had already spread, as shown by the pots from the Boston factory of Carpenter and Fenton, operating between 1793 and 1787. Some pots, attributed to Johnathan Fenton are of very Germanic ovoid form with incised designs and cobalt used for decoration, while those attributed to Frederick Carpenter often reflect British styling. These latter pots have underglaze dips of top and bottom in ferruginous mixtures, and their shapes echo the British straight-sided forms. Melding of the two salt-glazed stoneware traditions first brought to America by immigrants from Germany and the British Isles had already begun, and a separate American tradition can be identified at the beginning of the nineteenth century. Salt glazing was one important phase of the American pottery tradition and was the most commonly used utilitarian stoneware glaze throughout the nineteenth century.

The method of glazing with common table salt, or sodium chloride, is an entirely different process from that by which most ceramic glazes are prepared. Generally ceramic glazes are prepared in a suspension with water, and the vessels are then painted with, sprayed with, or immersed in the solution. Salt glazes are produced by the vapor method. Common salt is introduced into the hot kiln, where it immediately vaporizes. Historically, in North America it was either dropped into the kiln through holes with moveable covers, "saltports," in the vault of the kiln or thrown with a shovel into the fireboxes. Salt vaporizes at the relatively low temperature of 800 degrees C, but the exterior surface of the clay body must be in a state of surface melt, approaching the maturation or vitrification point, for the reaction producing the glaze to take place. There must also be sufficient silica free in this melted surface to combine with the sodium of the salt to produce sodium silicate, the chemical name of the salt glaze.

The usual temperature range employed for salt glazing stoneware is between 1200 degrees C and 1260 degrees C. Experimental bodies have been prepared with sufficient silica and lower melting points for a salt glaze to be produced at earthenware temperature ranges as low as 1050 degrees C., but this has not been done as a routine process for the production of salt glazes. Other chemical salts such as barium and borox which will combine with silica to form a glassy compound, have also been tried, but mainly on an experimental basis.

In spite of the very undesirable emission of chlorine gas or hydrochloric acid vapor from the kiln at the time that the glazing reaction is taking place, salt glazing remained a relatively unadulterated method of glazing for over four centuries. Its use for utilitarian stoneware in the United States faded out at the beginning of the twentieth century. Now even its use for the production of glazed sewer pipe is being supplanted by other forms of glaze as air pollution control has become necessary.

Production of a salt glaze is relatively simple. Dry, unglazed, raw pots are loaded into the kiln, which is then fired to high stoneware temperatures. The process of introduction of the salt into the kiln then takes place and is usually repeated three times to assure an adequate coating. Since the reaction cools the kiln considerably, it must be brought back up to a high heat before the next salting can take place. In the past, small pieces of clay, commonly small rings and triangles or rectangles with a pierced hole at one end, were often placed inside of the salt glaze kiln, close to a spy hole. These could be fished out with a long metal rod during the firing period. They are called "draw trials" and were examined after the second salting and any

subsequent salting to assure that a glaze had developed.

The amount of salt used during the process varied somewhat with the potter and the size of the kiln. At times the salt was measured by weight, as it is at the present time, at others by volume. One old North Carolina potter told me that a five-gallon churn full of salt was enough to completely glaze an average-sized ground hog kiln containing about 240 gallons of ware. For approximately the same size kiln at the Jugtown Pottery today thirty to thirty-five pounds of salt are used. Large, upright kilns undoubtedly used one hundred or more pounds for one firing.

The use of salt in a kiln more or less destroys its usefulness for the firing of other high-temperature glazes. All exposed surfaces, by they of pots, kilns, or kiln furiture, become salt glazed. The entire inner kiln surface becomes covered with a glassy deposit, produced by the reaction of the salt with the brick. This may become very thick in time, with drips resembling stalactites hanging from the ceiling.

This depositing of salt on all clay surfaces in the kiln made the method of stacking salt kilns somewhat different, for shelves were not used. In upright kilns the pottery was arranged in tall stacks with the assistance of various forms of kiln furniture to hold the stacks in place. The majority of this kiln furniture was discarded after the firing, since it also was salt glazed.

The texture of the glaze that results from the salting process is generally described as resembling orange peel. This slightly textured surface may be seen if the pot is held so that light is reflected off of the surface. The glaze itself is most often transparent, being colored by the amount of iron present in the clay body itself. The surface of a good salt glaze may show a texture varying from that of the finely pitted surface of a tangerine skin to the coarse roughness of a navel orange or grapefruit. The optimal surface is also very glossy. In the case of a medium to heavy salt glaze, deposit droplets appear to center around a tiny nucleus and to coalesce at their margins with other droplets. The very

An ovoid one-gallon capacity jug in a medium brown salt glaze. A band of coggling in a pattern of alternating large ovals and small circles runs around the shoulder beneath two simple grooves. There are grooves around the neck also and one just above the base. Attributed to Joshua Letts, between 1813 and 1815 because of similarity to a marked Letts jug. *Courtesy of the New Jersey State Museum. Photographer: Joseph Crilley.* $1200

A pint mug of a banded form, somewhat Rhenish in character, which is salt-glazed inside and out. It has two cobalt bands at the top and at the bottom with "1773" and a whirled design trailed in cobalt around the center of the mug. Attributed to Abraham Mead of Greenwich, Connecticut. The Remensnyder Collection. *Courtesy of The National Museum of History and Technology, Smithsonian Institution.* $950

Three pieces of salt-glazed ware showing different colors and degrees of salt texture. Left: a medium gray, vitreous, unlined one-gallon preserve jar bearing the impressed stamp "I. THOMAS," Maysville, Ky. c. 1850. Center: a greenish-gray salt glaze with a very heavy texture from overhead salting. Impressed "J.D. CRAVEN," Moore County, N.C. c. 1875. Right: one-half gallon preserve jar with a very pale gray, moderately developed salt glazed texture and an interior glaze of Albany type brown slip. Saenger Pottery, Elmendorf, Texas c. 1895. L-R: $150, $220, $100

A very fine salt texture and relatively thin glaze deposit. (I. Thomas pot in photograph above.)

A heavy salt texture showing increased thickness and coarser surface pitting.

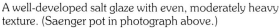

A well-developed salt glaze with even, moderately heavy texture. (Saenger pot in photograph above.)

An extremely heavy salt texture with areas beginning to run and agglutinate. (J.D. CRAVEN pot in photograph above.)

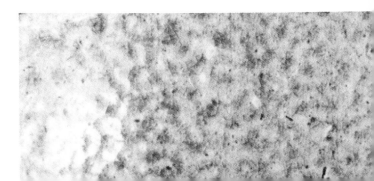

finely textured surfaces have thin glaze deposits, the heavily textured surfaces thicker glazes.

The extremes from optimum salt glazing are a little difficult to describe. A pot that has been exposed to a minimal amount of salt vapor will generally show a rather dry browning or "toasting" of the surface with no development of a glossy coat. No glaze deposit or texture may be discerned. Wood-ash deposits may also give this effect when present in the kiln in small amounts. These pots are really defective in that they are insufficiently glazed, but they were frequently sold and used. It was the custom to put flower pots, birdhouses, and other objects for which a glazed surface was not essential in the portions of the kiln that were known to receive less heat as well as less salt vapor. Rounded or elongated areas of the same toasted appearance may also be seen on pots that have been stacked so that adequate concentrations of the salt vapors were not able to reach some areas of the pots.

This very ordinary flower pot demonstrates some of the color changes produced by so-called "toasting" by light salt vapor, and the bleaching effect of a heavy salt glaze. I assume that it was the top pot in a stack in the kiln, therefore receiving more salt than usual. It also shows the rather ornate rim very often seen on hand-turned flower pots. Lower section: Dry, pinkish tan, fired, unglazed clay. Upper mid section: Brown color from salt and ash "toasting." Top sections: Deposits of a heavy, pale blue gray salt glaze. Texas late 19th century. $125

On the other hand, pots with so heavy a salt glaze that it runs in some areas and the texture is obliterated are occasionally seen. These pots usually are those burned in low, rectangular kilns in which the salt was introduced through ports directly over the pots. Any pot fired in a salt-glaze kiln may also show glassy drops, generally blue green in color, which have dripped from the glazed surface on the interior of the kiln vault during the firing process. These drops are large blobs, while those of excess salt on the pot are more often smaller runs and dribbles.

The glaze is essentially transparent. At times some opacity due to crystal formation may be seen within the glaze matrix. Salt glazes have some tendency to crackle and therefore to stain if the vessel body is not completely vitreous. The color appearing in the glaze is produced by the iron present in that portion of the body which is reacting to form the glaze. Other chemical compounds present in the body clay in small amounts may influence the color shades produced by the iron. Fine English salt-glazed tableware was made from refined, iron-free clays and the glaze is colorless, with the white of the body clay visible through the glaze. Some stoneware clays are almost free of iron and the vessels appear white, but most often a pale creamy beige or pearl gray color is typical of pots with this glaze. Calcium influences the color towards greenish hues. As the amount of iron present in the body increases it inhibits the development of the glaze somewhat, so that in pots in which the deepest body colors develop, the glaze coating is often thin and sometimes lacks gloss or texture. The glaze also has a bleaching effect especially when the deposits are heavy. Thinly glazed body clay of a vessel will appear darker in color than areas that are heavily glazed.

A handsome salt-glazed churn with a swan surrounded by a partial wreath of what appear to be laurel branches. The churn is a light buff to beige color, indicating a slightly oxidizing kiln, and has a medium textured salt glaze evenly deposited. The interior as well as the churn lid have been glazed in an Albany type slip glaze. Impressed: "HART'S/FULTON" Fulton, N.Y. 1840-1876. $2400

A very large early jar having about a five-gallon capacity. It has a brown and gray mottled salt glazed exterior and no interior glaze. Bilateral open loop lug handles have been bent upward to almost touch the banded collar. A single stem with one flower and several leaves has been incised on both front and back and painted with cobalt to produce a deep blue. Attributed to Crolius family, New York, N.Y. probably late 18th century. $2800-3000

Aside from the fact that the composition of the body clay of the pot, the temperature of the kiln, and the amount of salt must all be adequate, the timing of the salting must be correct for proper development of a salt glaze. The atmosphere of the kiln at that time also influences the color of the resultant glaze. Almost everyone knows that sufficient oxygen must be present for the proper combustion of fuel. At times the air entering the kiln is not sufficient to maintain this amount of **oxygen** within the firing chamber in which the vessels have been stacked. When such a condition is present, the fire will rob oxygen available in the chamber itself from both the air and the surfaces of the pots. The iron compounds present on the pot surface will be robbed of oxygen and converted from ferrous oxide (Fe 2 03) to Ferric Oxide (Fe 3 04). Ferrous oxide is the common compound resulting from the oxidation of metallic iron—rust. This oxygen-consuming process is termed reduction, and a kiln in which this reaction is taking place is called a reducing kiln. It is also a smoky kiln.

Iron and copper are two common ceramic colorants in which the reduction process can take place in a hot kiln. The colors of the reduced compounds are markedly different from those of the fully oxidized compounds. This reaction is not so important in the production of salt-

A churn with unusual bilateral projecting knob handles and a thin gray to dark brown salt glaze inside and out. The salt has no well-developed texture on this dark body. "W. GRINDSTAFF 1841" is impressed in very large letters across the upper front. William Grindstaff. Blount County, Tennessee, 1871. *Courtesy of the Tennessee Department of Conservation, Archeology Division.* $750

A handsome double-handled four gallon jug. The salt glaze is a deep gray color and it is lined with a brown slip glaze of the Albany type. Both handles were colored with Cobalt and a large floral spray adorns the upper front in dark cobalt blue. Impressed: "J.C. SMITH/MOGADORE," Ohio. *Courtesy of the Ohio Historical Society Ceramic Center at Roseville.* Mid-nineteenth century. $4200

This tremendous jar stands 27 inches high and probably has a capacity of about twenty-four gallons. The heavy texture of the salt glaze on the shoulder of the pot may be distinguished in this photograph. It is inscribed "JOHN A. CRAVEN, 1855" and a square and compass in cobalt on the reverse and "J.A.C." and a masonic emblem of square and compasses were trailed on with cobalt-containing slip on the front. No interior glaze. *Courtesy of The Potter's Museum. Photographer: Bill Jenko.* $975

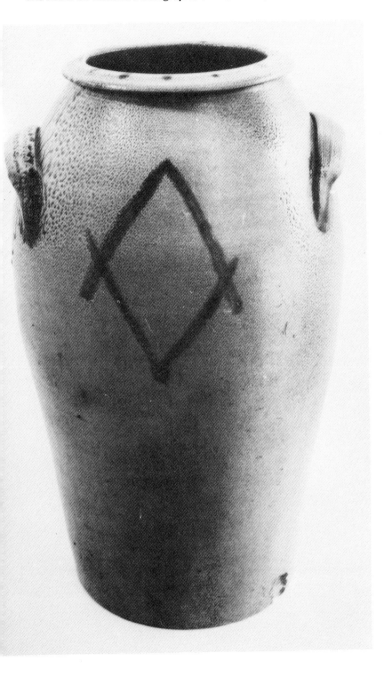

A pitcher of about eight-ounce capacity with a deep brown and gray mottled salt-glazed exterior. Salt toasted interior. It is inscribed "M. LOY/N.C./1874." Seagrove area of North Carolina. This shows the brown mottled agglutination seen in a salt glaze over a dark clay or a dry ferruginous dip. The extreme of this agglutination resulted in the spotted looking "tiger glaze" of the early Rhenish potters at Frechen and Cologne. $1500

This jug shows a dry, gray-white chalky deposit over the surface which should be a salt glaze. The salt glaze in this instance I would call "scummy" since it is dry and thin. This is probably due to the fact that the clay used in this jug has a particularly high ratio of aluminum to silica, thereby being unable to develop a good salt glaze. William Saenger, St. Hedwig, Texas c. 1884. $195

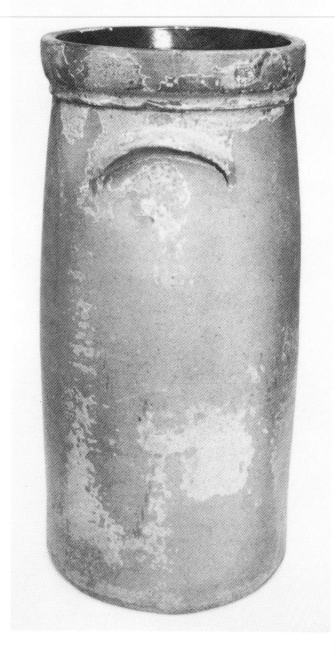

A tall, six-gallon capacity churn which had large amounts of salt dropped upon it, but which must not have been sufficiently hot for the salt to fuse with the body. Thick deposits hand in a few places, but most has flaked off. Albany type slip glaze interior. Bexar County, Texas c. 1880. $400

A low, wide-mouthed jar of one-gallon capacity. It has small lug handles fixed just below the rim. The salt glaze is exceedingly heavy, especially over the cobalt leaf and has run down the front, smearing the decoration. Shiny brown interior glaze, probably an Albany slip. Impressed: (mark cannot be read.) Attributed to Pennsylvania, mid 19th century. $450

A beautiful five-gallon salt-glazed churn adorned with a large peacock on top of a tree branch. This decoration is trailed in a deep cobalt blue. The interior is lined with an Albany type slip glaze. Impressed: "J. & E. NORTON/ BENNINGTON, VT." 1851-1859. *Courtesy of Robert C. Vose III*. $4500

A pair of batter jugs of 1-1/2 and 2 gallon capacities. Both are of the usual form of this vessel with a wide, heavy spout, bail handle, and single lug handle at the base opposite the spout. Light gray salt-glazed exteriors decorated by a simple cobalt floral spray and Albany type brown slip glazed interiors. Both impressed "EVAN JONES/PITTSTON, PA." Second half of the 19th century. *Courtesy of Jack Troy*. $1500

Salt-glazed pots with varying amounts of iron present in the clay, but fired in a more oxidizing kiln, will have colors ranging from creamy beiges through fairly deep browns. The pots fired in a mainly reducing atmosphere will show gray and gray-green to deep muddy gray and olive colors on their surfaces. The presence of some calcium in the clay usually promotes more development of the greenishgray colors rather than bluegrays. My reason for being reserved about pure oxidation or pure reduction is that these conditions are variable within a hightly heated kiln fired by wood, coal, or gas, and therefore the pure states rarely exist. These reactions are also important in the explanation of the colors produced in the Southern alkaline forms of glaze. The slip glazes are only slightly influenced, and the Bristol family of glazes even less.

The salt glaze, aside from the fact that the fumes of chlorine and hydrochloric acid released during the salting are most objectionable, has some defects. Because of their dull color over light clays, salt glazes were frequently used over engobes or coloring washes applied to the surface of the pot. A dry iron wash, or engobe, was used by the Rhenish potters as early as 1500 A. D. to produce a brown or richer color upon the whole pot. The result was the famous "Tiger Glaze" of Rhenish wares. The British followed this method of using an iron wash before salt glazing to enhance the color of a pot. They also were fond of dipping only the top of a vessel or top and bottom into iron solutions, and this preference in decoration was employed with Bristol as well as salt glazes. The use of salt glazes over a dry engobe was purposeful, but its use over a slip glaze was purposeful by utilitarian potters only in a few instances. One is the production of the "Frogskin" glaze by North Carolina potters. These uses, as well as defects resulting in slip glazes when salt vapor accidently contacts them, will be discussed under slip glazes.

Another defect of salt glazes results from the fact that a high silica clay is necessary for the production of a salt glaze. However, if the potter understands his clay properly, silica, in the form of fine sand, can be added to a deficient clay. A defect can result from use of clays in which the alumina content is very high. Salt-glazed vessels made of such clay usually show a very thin, scummy sort of glaze that does not adhere to the pot well, since the sodium does not combine with aluminum to form a glaze.

One defect easily seen in some old salt-glazed pots results from the addition of the salt before the surface of the pot has become fluid and able to react. This may involve an entire kiln of pots or just pots in a cool area of one kiln. The salt does not combine with the pot surface and, therefore, it separates or powders off, and large areas of the pot show a dry, unglazed condition. Such areas do not show the toasted finish that areas receiving too light an application of salt usually present.

The fact that the interior surfaces of salt-glazed pots are poorly glazed, if they show any salt glaze at all, results from stacking the pots one upon the other in the kiln or, in the case of jugs, from the very small opening left in the pot. The salt vapor is unable to get down into the partially blocked areas, so little if any glaze is formed, but, if the clay vitrifies completely, the pot is sufficiently sealed. It became the custom in the United States, especially after 1850, to pour a glaze solution into the interior of the pot to ensure proper sealing. This was done at the time when any ordinary glaze is applied before firing. In a few areas of the country, low rectangular kilns were used in which the pots were not stacked; rather, each pot sat separately upon the floor of the kiln. When salt glazing was done in these kilns by pouring salt through openings in the top of the kiln, all of the vessels, with the exception of those with very small mouths (i.e. jugs), were glazed on the interior as well as the exterior. These potters had little need for accessory glazes to line the pot interiors.

One other defect of salt glazes is their tendency to "craze" or crackle, making them undesirable, particularly on vessel interiors since they may stain or leak. Rarely do they shiver or blister.

A fully ovoid, salt-glazed two-gallon jug bears the impressed mark "I. SEYMOUR/TROY FAC-TORY." A dynamic Indian Chief with feather head-dress and decorated clothing is incised on the mid-front. In his right hand he holds a drawn sword, with the left a Christian banner. The design is colored with cobalt. This is thought to be the legendary Chief Handsome Lake. I. Seymour, Troy, N.Y. 1824-1850. *Courtesy of Jeremy L. Banta.* $10,000-15,000

A handsome ovoid two-gallon jug in a tan to buff salt glaze and decorated with a brown flower, leaves, and stem on the front surface. Some form of iron was probably added to the decorating slip. Impressed: "LYMAN & CLARK/GARDINER" just beneath the neck. Maine, 1837-1841. *Courtesy of M. Lelyn Branin.* $975

NATURAL CLAY OR SLIP GLAZES

By the beginning of the nineteenth century, a second class of stoneware glazes, called slip or loam glazes, was being used in America. These were prepared from natural clays, which were usually strained and made into a watery suspension into which the pots were dipped. Earthenware glazes were commonly prepared in this manner, and stoneware slip glazes had already been in use in Europe prior to this period. Clays of contrasting colors thinned with water to form a slip had been used decoratively for centuries on earthenwares. It did not represent a great development in technology, after the development of high temperature kilns, to discover that certain clays would melt to form a glaze at the same temperature that the body or clay of which the pot was formed became mature or hardened. Thus, slip clay glazes began to be employed by stoneware potters. The pots produced by "Swan & States" of Stonington, Connecticut, about 1825 are covered with a deep brown exterior glaze, probably produced by this method. Many common brick clays may also be used for preparing suitable slip glazes for stoneware.

It has been said that Paul Cushman was responsible for the discovery of the very well known clay at Albany, New York, that had the ability to melt and cover the surface of a stoneware pot as a glaze. This may well be an old wives' tale, but nevertheless, the clay was discovered and began to be used by potters of the Albany area as a glaze during the first quarter of the nineteenth century. Local slip clays dug and prepared by the potter himself were also employed by American potters. Albany clay became the most popular glaze of this type and was shipped all over the United States as railroad expansion took place, particularly during the last quarter of the nineteenth century and the early twentieth century. Clays of much the same type were later mined commercially at Elkhart, Indiana, and Rowley, Michigan. It is almost impossible at times to distinguish which of these clays, local or commercial, was actually used upon an old pot. Because of this difficulty it has become acceptable, unless the clay is known to be local, to call these glazes Albany Type slip glazes. A few local slip glazes used by some potters may be distinguished by their heavy coat and texture, thin coating, or color.

One major example of this latter type is the Leon Slip Glaze clay dug in Bexar County, Texas, by a family of German potters. The colors produced by this calcareous clay range from a light greenish yellow through greens, golds, and speckled browns. Some of the color variations of this glaze were probably caused by varying amounts of iron in different batches of clay. Others were produced by atmospheric variations in the kiln during firing.

A two-gallon jug and a pint jar covered with a shiny brown slip glaze of the Albany type. The light haloed areas represent areas of the glaze influenced by fly ash and salt vapor during firing. William Saenger, Elmendorf, Texas c. 1890. L-R: $250, $150

These two one-pint preserve jars were made by the same pottery for a nearby merchant. Although both were glazed with the same Leon slip glaze inside and out, the jar on the right received a heavy deposit of salt over the slip glaze. This salt melded with the fluid slip glaze surface in the kiln and the resultant covering mimics an alkaline glaze. Since one small area on the back and interior show a normal slip glaze, identical with that of the other pot, we know that salt was the reason for the difference. Meyer Pottery, Bexar County, Texas c. 1900. L-R: $100, $150

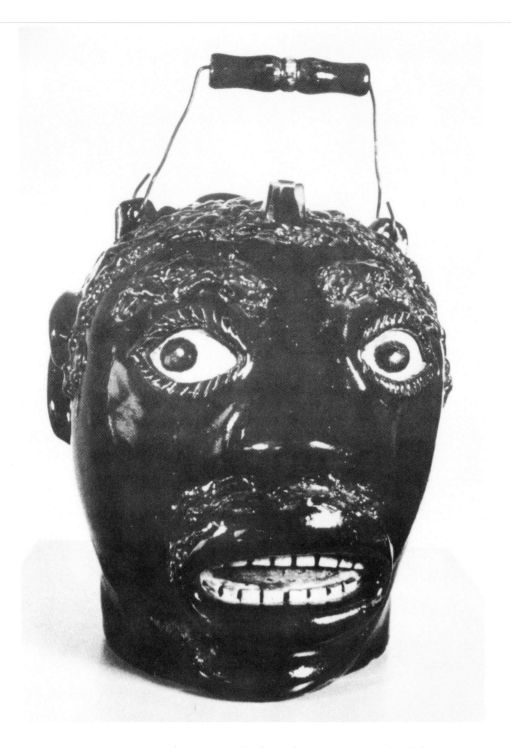

A spectacular stoneware harvest jug in the form of a grotesque negro head. It is approximately one-gallon in capacity and glazed inside and out with a shiny dark brown slip glaze of the Albany type. The eyeballs and teeth are covered with a white glaze, but each iris of the eyes is brown, giving a lifelike appearance. Considerable clay was added to the original pot to produce the features. A large filling spout is fixed in upper center shoulder of the back and a small pouring spout is just within the hairline on the front. Ohio, late 19th century. *Courtesy of the Zanesville Art Center.* $5200

A nine inch diameter pie plate of a coarse clay made to withstand baking temperatures. Covered on the interior with a shiny brown Albany type slip glaze. The lower exterior and bottom are unglazed pinkish-tan clay with an illegible mark. Made in a jigger mold. Probably midwestern U.S.A., early 20th century. $65

Clay from the area of the Alazan Creek in the same county produces a shiny chocolate-brown glaze, visually indistinguishable from Albany types. It was employed briefly by local potters about 1900. Natural clay glazes, "slip glazes" in potter's terminology, were the second most common glaze used for utilitarian stoneware in this country. They were frequently used as an interior glaze on vessels with a salt-glazed exterior to give an impermeable coating to the interior of the vessel. This use of an interior slip glaze with an exterior salt glaze became neary ubiquitous with salt-glazing potters after 1850. The fact that many American stoneware clays did not vitrify completely at stoneware temperatures, and therefore liquids seeped into and through the vessel walls, made a sealing form of glaze necessary in many parts of the country. It was for this reason that Albany type slip glazes came to be commonly used on the interior of vessels that were glazed on the exterior with a salt vapor glaze. Slip glazes were also used on the exteriors of pots when the clays available to the potter did not take a salt glaze well. During the last quarter of the nineteenth century, the use of this form of glazing on both interior and exterior became especially popular.

Before the advent of compressed air spray guns in this century, all stoneware glazes of the liquid form were applied by a dipping or pouring process. The suspension of glaze ingredients was placed in a large vat of some sort, usually a half of a barrel or hogshead of staved wood. Small vessels were quickly filled with glaze, swirled to coat the interior, and then dipped to cover the exterior. The vessels were then inverted over a couple of wooden slats across one side of the vat so that the excess glaze dripped out and off. The glaze suspension was stirred from time to time since it had a tendency to settle. Large vessels were often filled partially with glaze suspension, swirled to coat the interior, and turned upside down. Glaze solution was then poured over the exterior as the pot sat on slats over the vat. Any glaze material remaining on the base of the vessel was usually sponged off before it was turned upright to dry. As vessels were turned upright glaze was also cleaned from the upper rims of those that were to be stacked up in the kiln. This prevented the adhesion of the vessels during the firing. Slip glazes, alkaline glazes, and Bristol glazes were all applied in this manner.
The fact that a slip is nothing more than a mixture of clay with water thinned to a more or less creamy suspension has been discussed. In earlier periods slips were used on the surfaces of pots decoratively and therefore were, as a rule, of a color contrasting with that of the main body clay. Slip glazes are generally not purpose-

A decorative one-pint jug which was evenly glazed inside and out with an Albany type brown slip glaze. The slip was inscribed while still damp with the name of a merchant "C.F. Schultz/Seguin/Tex." Bexar County, Texas c. 1895. $550

A small jug of 9-5/8 inch height and a capacity of about one-half gallon. The natural beige salt-glazed surface is pricked all over. A total of six snakes accented with dark brown wind in and out and around the jug. A man's face is applied just below the jug neck in the front. A final snake head decorates the stopper. Attributed to Crooksville, Ohio. Mid to late 19th century. *Courtesy of the Zanesville Art Center.* $7500-8000

fully colored; they are natural clays, containing varying amounts of iron, that melt at the maturation temperature of stoneware pottery and are used as inexpensive glazes for stonewares. The fact that these clays contain iron compounds along with small amounts of other color influencing oxides makes the colors of the glazes produced by these clays most commonly in the brown range.

Occasionally, as in the instance of the Leon Slip Clay, lesser amounts of iron, reducing firings, and possibly a higher or varying calcium content produced colors in the gold and green range as well as browns on fully mature pots.

The methods of preparation of these glazes may vary. Commonly Albany type clays are fine and clean enough in their packaged form to be diluted with water to the proper consistency and then strained through a sieve or cloth. This mixture is then ready for the pots. Pottery that is leather hard (that is, partially dry) can be quickly dipped into this suspension. The excess is poured out of the interior back into the vat, and the pot is wiped clean on the bottom and the upper rim. All surfaces that touch other pots in the kiln should be free of glaze or they will adhere during the firing.

A second method of preparation is termed the "Terra Sigallata" method. It is the same method by which Roman potters prepared the fine slips used on their vessel surfaces to produce a lusterous finish. These were forerunners of slip glazes. In this method the clay is dissolved in a large amount of water and each day the suspension is stirred very well and, immediately, the top poured off and retained. The coarser ingredients of the clay settle to the bottom first and are discarded. This process is continued for several days until the clays in the retained portion feel very fine, smooth, and "silky." This method is most often used with local slip-glaze clays because they frequently have a much larger content of coarse particles than commercial clays. Any excess water may be decanted and discarded, and the suspension is ready to be used in the same manner as the commercial slip glazes. These local clays must be tested by the potter to be certain that they will adhere well to the body clay and melt at the desired temperature. At times we find other stoneware glazes being erroneously termed slips by potters because of their high clay content. The hickory ash and clay alkaline form of glaze was sometimes called "Hickory slip," and I have heard several old potters refer to the Bristol form of glaze as "Bristol slip."

Slip glazes have defects, but in general they have attributes that overshadow the defects. The Albany and other commercial types, which shall be classed as Albany types for convenience, all have a particul-

Two pieces of Albany type slip-glazed stoneware showing dipping lines where the slip is thick or thin. The two-gallon jar on the left shows a thick band of slip in the middle from dipping bottom and then top. The jar on the right appears to have been rolled around in the glaze solution. The line of dark slip running down the front face overlaps a very thin section which was probably the starting point. Both Texas c. 1890. L-R: $150, $275

199

A planter made by slab technique. The slabs for the sides were pressed into a mold with grooves resembling tree bark before being combined with the ends and bottom. Pierced for hanging. Green to yellow Leon slip glazed exterior. Meyer Pottery, Bexar County, Texas. Second quarter of the 20th century. $100

arly long firing range. This means that they will melt to form a suitable glaze over a range of temperatures. This range covers the maturation range of most stoneware clays, making the glaze useful to both potters using different clays, and those using kilns which heat rather unevenly. A second attribute is that these clays will adhere to most stoneware clays. If a slip adheres poorly, it may dry and flake off before firing, which is a serious defect. The great resistance of these slip glazes to crackling after firing is most important, since a glaze that cracks or crackles will allow liquids to seep into the body of a vessel, making it unsatisfactory for utilitarian uses. Last of all, when properly fired, slip-glazed vessels are resistant to strongly acidic or alkaline compounds, so may be used as storage vessels for such compounds. These attributes are undoubtedly those which made this form of glaze exceedingly popular. Slip glazes may also be fired in a kiln in which salt has been or is concurrently used. Salt within the kiln has a deleterious influence on the proper maturation and development of most other glazes, including the Bristol form.

Although local clays for slip glazes may have almost the same attributes as Albany clay, they must first be located and then thoroughly tested. Potters commonly used local clays for slips during the earlier periods of the nineteenth century when commercial slips were not available at any distance from Albany, New York. As the industry expanded, commercial slip glazes became inexpensive and easily obtainable, and therefore immensely popular for use both as an interior glaze accompanying exterior salt glazing and as a glaze for both surfaces of the pot.

The main defects of slip glazes are that they will peel off when placed in areas of the kiln in which they may be licked by the direct flame prior to melting, that they may be highly influenced by sulfur fumes in the kiln and fail to mature with a proper sheen, and that they have a dark color. During the "hygienic revolution" of the late nineteenth and early twentieth centuries, light colors, especially white, became associated with cleanliness in the kitchen as well as other areas of the home. This diminished the popularity of the naturally dark slip glazes.

Slip clay glazes are smooth, untextured, opaque glazes. The color range manifest in slip glazes depends upon their iron content along with other oxides in small amounts which may affect color. The brown tones prevail, chocolate browns with a rather shiny, opaque, textureless surface being most typical. Ruddy brown tones also are not unusual, and occasionally a rusty or mahogany color with a glistening, almost crystalline, surface results when the firing temperature has been very high and the atmosphere reducing. Albany slip, according to Parmelee, develops a dark, glossy brown color at 1,170 degrees C., a brilliant blackish brown at 1,210 degrees to 1,250 degrees C., and a yellowish brown at 1,290 degrees C. These colors all develop in a generally reducing firing. Shiny blacks are infrequently seen but do occasionally occur when the firing is completely oxidizing. Rusty overtones are generally also present in the black glaze. The dull, muddy green occasionally seen is most commonly the result of underfiring or sulfur fumes within the kiln. Potters have also upon occasion mixed another ingredient, such as whiting, with their Albany slip to produce a lightening of the color. This results in a mustardy yellow or green, shiny, opaque glaze. Such a modification may have been used by the Stark pottery of Orange, Georgia, to produce its ruddy, mustard colored pots. The same combination has been used in the past few decades to produce a green glaze in poor imitation of old southern alkaline glazes.

When pieces with an exterior slip glaze were fired in a kiln which was salted some protection was required if the pots were to remain an even brown color. During firing, slip glazes are affected by both salt in the kiln and fine wood ash (called fly ash), as well as by direct flames. Since both salt vapors and ash may be circulating in the kiln during the firing, the effects frequently seen on some slip-glazed pots may be the results of both as well as the licking of flames after the glaze has melted. Fairly large or very small areas that appear yellow and greenish may be seen on slip-glazed exteriors which have received salt or fly ash deposits. They may be small, half-moon shaped areas near the base or large irregular areas over a large surface of the pot. This effect is called "flashing." Direct flame will also bleach glazes at times. Both ash and salt also have the ability to bleach the iron color to yellow or green. Frequently the shoulders of slip glazed pots show speckled, partially bleached areas from such deposits. If a very large amount of salt happens to be deposited over a slip glaze, the salt reacts with the surface of the slip, and an area greatly resembling an alkaline form of stoneware glaze appears. The slip in this area becomes more fluid during firing, and combines with the salt glaze also being produced, resulting in a very shiny, semitransparent surface without salt glaze texture and with yellow or greenish colors. Truly it not only mimics the alkaline glazes, but is more or less the same sort of compound, since the sodium in the salt fluxes the clay of the slip. The point of differentiation for purposes of identification depends on the presence of an interior or base which shows a typical slip glaze appearance.

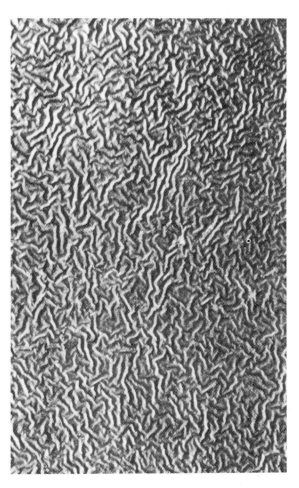

A close-up of the glaze of an underfired one-gallon preserve jar showing an Albany type glaze in an underfired state—dull and heavily wrinkled. Bexar County, Texas c. 1890.

I have been told that one Texas potter added a small amount of salt to his hot kiln full of slip glazed ware to make the "rattlesnake" pattern of greenish runs. This practice was carried out by other potters in the deep South. It was thought to help mature the slip glaze and make the ware more durable. However, use of salt over a slip glaze is well known in another area. The potters of the "Jugtown" area of North Carolina add a very small amount of salt to a kiln containing Albany slip-glazed wares to produce the rather muddy yellow-green, semi-mat glaze which they call "Frogskin." This, I am sure, is practiced more by the artist potters of this century than it was by the utilitarian potters of the past. Only about four pounds of salt are used in the firebox to produce this color change, whereas it would take approximately thirty pounds to produce a good salt glaze in the same kiln.

A baluster shaped pitcher of one gallon capacity covered inside and out with a dark brown slip glaze of the Albany type. It has a broad collar around the mouth and a band of simple rouletting was done just below this. Four more decorative bands of rouletting encircle the full midsection of the pot. Of Ohio origin, mid to late 19th century. *Courtesy of the Western Reserve Historical Society.* $650

SOUTHERN ALKALINE GLAZES

The third type of glaze commonly employed by American stoneware potters developed peculiarly without any definite European traditional background around the beginning of the nineteenth century. This was the alkaline dipped type of glaze originally employing wood ash, clay, and sand. Although this type of glaze was used in China from the Han period (206B.C.-A.D.220) onward, no reason for its development around a focus in the Edgefield area of South Carolina can be directly associated with Oriental potters.

A possible, but remote, link may be found in the letters of a French Jesuit, Pere D'Entrecolles, describing the manner of preparation of true porcelain in China. The letters had been published and even translated into English before the mid-eighteenth century. In England, William Cookworthy obtained a patent to prepare true porcelain "after the Chinese method" in his Bristol factory in 1768. He describes the use of fern ash in combination with Cornish stone, a form of feldspar, in the preparation of his glaze. Whether this rather remote link spurred the development of a stoneware glaze employing wood ash in South Carolina is still a matter of conjecture. At any rate, this form of glaze was employed at the Pottersville site just out of Edgefield. This particular village is described in the 1820 U.S. Manufacturing Census as a busy pottery-producing center. There must, therefore, have been previous development of this type of glaze within that area for at least a decade, probably longer.

The use of this unique stoneware glaze and its ramifications spread regionally during the next half-century, not only northward as far as the western section of North Carolina but southward through the entire lower row of states into Texas. No European counterpart of this type of glaze for stonewares has been found. Potters of this tradition, mainly of American birth with British surnames, spread this glaze from the Edgefield focus across the entire southernmost portion of the United States during the period of westward expansion between 1810 and 1860.

One reason for the glaze's popularity and persistence into the twentieth century in rural areas of the southern United States was that all of the ingredients necessary were easily available and cost almost nothing. Salt for glazing was at times scarce and very expensive. The alkaline glaze mixture, with wood ash as a flux, formed a considerably harder and more durable glaze than most of the local slip-glaze clays. Improtation of special glaze clays, such as the Albany type or commercially prepared glaze ingredients, from distant urban areas into the southern backwoods was almost prohibitive in cost. Production cost was always important to the utilitarian potter, whose vessels were designed for ordinary household use. During the second half of the nineteenth century, the southern states remained poverty stricken and remote from the great industrialization taking place in other parts of this country. The alkaline glaze was perfectly suited to the needs of the small pottery shops and the still agrarian population in the deep South.

A number of common names have been applied to the many variations of the southern alkaline type of glaze. Most of them give an indication of the particular variation of the glaze used. Generally the name "sand and ash" was applied to the early, basic form containing wood ash, sand and clay. The sand may sometimes only be the mixture of sand and clay found in the clay seams. The name "Rattle-snake" was applied to the heavily textured forms of this basic glaze. "Tobacco Spit" has been used by some persons, but is a poor term since the iron colored, transparent brown lead glaze used on many utilitarian earthenwares is "Tobacco Spit" in some southern states. The latter is a smooth, transparent brown glaze without texture. "Flint" is a name applied by some potters to the hard-fired, smooth basic mixture probably containing some added calcium. "Lime" is used when the wood ash is reduced or eliminated and slaked lime is substituted. "Glass" is the name applied when a large amount of ground glass is used as a fluxing component (this may have wood ash in the mixture as well).

"Iron Cinder" was the name used by potters in the Catawba Valley of North Carolina for their version containing ground cinder from old iron foundry waste piles. "Hickory Slip" was the name applied to their mixture of clay and hickory ash by some workers. Cheever Meaders of Cleveland, Georgia, termed his own basic wood ash and clay glaze, which was very runny and textured, his "Shanghai" glaze.

Some of the history of this unique glaze used on American stoneware by a small number of potters in the states of North Carolina, South Carolina, Florida, Georgia, Alabama, Mississippi, Louisiana (possibly), Texas, and Arkansas has already been discussed. Smith and Rogers found only one site in which this glaze was used in Tennessee, and that was near the southern border. Salt and slip glazes were used contemporaneously with southern alkaline glazes in some areas of the southern states and Bristol forms of glaze were employed by a number of semi—industrialized southern potters early in the twentieth century. The popularity of the alkaline glazes waned as the South became more urban and the need for any form of utilitarian stoneware decreased during the first half of the twentieth century. Only two strongholds remain today, one in White County, Georgia, and the other in Lincoln County, North Carolina. The two potters who have continued to use this type of glaze have, undoubtedly for "economic reasons," modified their production so that more decorative or unique vessels are produced rather than purely utilitarian vessels.

The alkaline glaze would probably never have become so widely used if the South had not been separated from industrialized northern areas of this country during the Civil War and so economically depressed after that war that it remained rural and remote for several decades. During the early westward expansion period and the Civil War, salt was frequently a scarce and expensive item, and salt glazing therefore became at that time a relatively expensive form of glazing in the deep South. The development of the wood ash, sand, and clay mixture produced an excellent substitute glaze. All of the ingredients were readily available in the backwoods with little monetary outlay.

The glaze is very durable and hard. The one drawback for the early potter was that it necessitated a little more labor in preparation. The wood ash could be varied and could be produced from both hard and soft woods. Although hickory ash was preferred by many potters, pine was preferred by others, and oak could be substituted. The ash was frequently not washed, but added directly to the clay and sand. The clay used was often the same clay as was used for the body of the pot, and the sand varied from pure fine sands to sandy clay deposits found in digging the body clay. The mixture of wood ash, clay, and sand, usually measured by volume rather than weight, was mixed with water and then ground. The grinding most often was done by hand in a large stone quern or glaze mill. (See discussion in Chapter II.) The ground glaze suspension was placed in a glaze vat and the leather-hard pots dipped into it, or glaze was poured over large pots in the same manner that other dipping glazes were used. After this the pots were completely dried to ready them for firing. Bottoms and any other areas that might contact other pots or the kiln in firing were wiped clean of glaze.

Since this glaze type contained natural local ingredients, its variations are multi-ple. It was also used by many very small potteries, and the individual potters often varied the formula to suit their needs or desires. During the second half of the nineteenth century a number of specific variants of this glaze developed in certain local areas. In western North Carolina, potters found that the "cinders" from local iron foundries assisted the fluxing of the glaze, and these were added to the mix. In several areas the addition of ground glass was found to aid in the melting and formation of the glaze, and therefore this was added to the glaze. Salt was sometimes added to the mixture and the resulting glazes were somewhat lighter in color. Although I have been told that the addition of salt made the glaze less hard on the hands of the dipper, I can see no reason for this statement, since salt surely did not acidify the glaze. It was the tremendously alkaline sodium solution from the wood ash which made the glaze a weak lye water suspension. At any rate, the addition of salt was one of the variations. Certain central Georgia potters found that they could replace the wood ash with slaked lime and prepare a suitable glaze, and this variant was the glaze of choice in that area during the early twentieth century.

Three alkaline glazed pots showing differences in color and texture in the glaze. On the left the one-half gallon jar marked "T.R." has a heavily mottled and textured deep olive green glaze (Catawba Valley, N.C. c. 1860.) The tall central jar has a pale yellowish glaze which has agglutinated and run in long riverlets down the pot (Rusk County, Texas c. 1850.) The full two-gallon jug on the right has a relatively untextured grassy green glaze which is dry and underfired near the base (Edgefield S.C. c. 1830) L-R: $125, $200, $275

The textured, alkaline glaze on the "T.R." jug showing large particles of white rock (quartz) remaining with the matrix. (See photograph on page 204.)

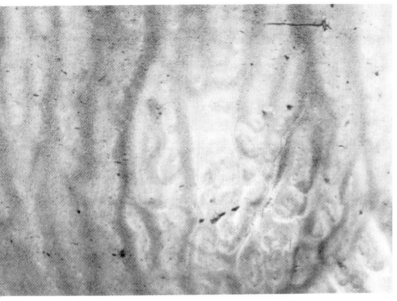

The separated, agglutinated alkaline glaze on the Texas jar. (See photograph on page 204.)

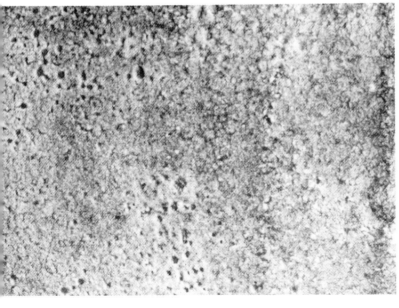

The glaze on the two-gallon jug showing a fairly even lightly mottled, mature glaze at the top and a dry, underfired area of glaze at the base. (See photograph on page 204.)

A beautiful six-gallon jar bearing the impressed initials "D.S." on one handle. This is a medium olive green alkaline glaze inside and out. "D.S." (Daniel Seagle) Lincoln County, N.C. c. 1840. *Courtesy of the Mint Museum of History. Gift of Daisy Wade Bridges. Photographer: The Mint Museum.* $675

A small puzzle jug (also called a "monkey jug" in North Carolina) standing only seven inches tall. It consists of two separate chambers, one having an opening at the top and the lower one having a spout at one side. It is decorated with plain and scalloped incised, encircling lines. Dark brown semi-transparent alkaline glaze. Attributed to Sylvanus Hartsoe, Lincoln County, N.C., second half of the nineteenth century. (Photographer: Rob Hicklin.) $450

This tall five to six-gallon capacity churn has a dark olive green alkaline glaze inside and out. It shows a pulled vertical strap handle on one side and a cupped, wheel-turned, horizontal lug type handle opposite. There are several incised lines just below the neck. Central Georgia c. 1890-1900. $450

The character of alkaline stoneware glazes may vary immensely. Mainly they are shiny, transparent glazes colored by iron compounds. The amount of iron determines the depth of color, but the atmosphere of the kiln has a vast effect on these glazes. The range of resultant glaze colors extends from cream or straw colors to deep browns in the oxidation-fired pots, and from pale bluegreens and yellowgreens through deep olive to black tones in the reduction-fired pots. Even white and sky blue shades, which are produced by iron in association with titanium and calcium, appear in scattered surface areas on pots from western North Carolina. Occasional glints of iron reds, which are nearly as rich as the blood reds produced by copper in reduction, may appear within the variegated texture of a brown to olive glaze.

The texture within the glaze is one of its most noticable features. Some of the most finely prepared alkaline glazes, such as those produced at Pottersville and by Thomas Chandler in Edgefield, South Carolina, show almost no texture. They closely resemble Oriental celadon glazes. These are, however, unusual and possibly the result of finer grinding or superior natural ingredients. Almost all of the other combinations seen across the South are variegated and show streaks and runs of color within the glaze. The glaze itself sometimes seems to separate and agglutinate in runs, adding to the textured quality. This is a characteristic of wood ash glazes. Occasionally fairly large bits of sand and rock can be seen within the matrix of the glaze, unmelted. Finer grinding probably would have eliminated this defect. The almost exclusive use of these glazes in the typical rectangular cross-draft groundhog type of kiln is probably responsible for the large number of pots that exhibit reduction-fired iron colors. These kilns had a tendency to produce smoky reducing firings because of the poor draft.

The defects of the alkaline glazes are much the same as those of the slip glazes. They were often blistered off before melting by direct flames. Large quantities of sherds from underfired glazes which appear rough and dry are seen at kiln sites. The temperature necessary to melt these

A two-quart pitcher attributed to the Meaders Pottery, Mossy Creek, Georgia, probably 1915-1930 period. It has a black and olive green streaked alkaline glaze. This agglutinated melted, and ran in streaks which are so decorative that they appear purposeful. $400

Alkaline glazed jars attributed to John Leopard, Rusk County, Texas. 1856-1879. The one gallon preserve jar on the left shows a light olive to brown alkaline glaze which has separated and run in areas. The three gallon jar on the right shows a light olive green alkaline glaze with a fairly even texture and no running. This variation may normally be seen in different batches or different firings of the same glaze formula. L-R: $200, $175

A one-gallon alkaline glazed pitcher from the Catawba Valley area of North Carolina. It has been decorated with crossing wavy lines within straight incised lines on the shoulder. Glass was also placed along the rim before firing and melted, giving this additional decorative effect. Yellowish olive alkaline glaze inside and out. Western N.C. Probably 1890-1900. $750

A globular storage jar of about 5 gallon capacity. Covered inside and out with a brownish olive alkaline glaze, it has a branching floral design trailed in a white slip on the front face. A nice tie-down rim and bilateral flaring lug handles are present. Attributed to Collin Rhodes, Edgefield, S.C. about 1850. *Courtesy of The Ferrell Collection. Photographer: David Rasberry.* $1550

glazes was almost always over 1200 degrees C, therefore underfiring was common. The problem of a cool floor in groundhog kilns also led to the frequently seen underfiring near the base of a vessel. Where the glaze is too thin the areas are brownish and show no depth. A deep transparent or translucent glaze coat is chacteristic of this thickly applied glaze. Opacity, when it occurs, usually is due to underfiring. Alkaline glazes crackle at times, but this is a minor defect. Little variation produced by fly-ash deposits is noticable in these glazes.

Salt vapor glazing was seldom used in combination with these glazes, but I do know of one particular kiln in which salt-glazed wares were first produced, and then the potters changed to alkaline glazing. Large drips of salt from the kiln roof appear on these particular alkaline glazed pots and are an uncommon defect. Large concentrations of salt vapor in the kiln with firing alkaline glazed vessels would undoubtedly distort the normal appearance of the glaze.

One of the major characteristics of alkaline-glazed pots is that the same glaze is seen on the interior as on the exterior, although the color may vary slightly. A rare decoration or dip into a brown slip or engobe is seen, but there are almost no combinations of this glaze with others. I have seen a very few late nineteenth-or early twentieth--century pots from Alabama that appear to have interiors lined with an alkaline glaze mix and salt-glazed exterior. It is possible, however, that this was the effect of salt fumes entering the open mouth to influence a slip-glaze lining. It is also possible that an alkaline-glazed interior was being used with a salt-glazed exterior. Since these pots were fired in a low kiln, often in a single layer, salt vapor could easily have influenced the interior glaze, making absolute identification difficult.

VOLCANIC ASH GLAZES

The ingenious use by potters of clays and minerals available in their local area is evident in the use of volcanic ash for the preparation of a stoneware glaze in the far west. During the second half of the nineteenth century potters spread with other pioneers into the states of Idaho, Washington, and Oregon. Here they found excellent clay deposits, especially in some areas along the common border between Idaho and Oregon. Volcanic ash deposits were also common in the area and some of the early potters devised a glaze for their stoneware pots using this ash. It was probably mixed with a certain proportion of the body clay of the pots and made into a dipping solution. Volcanic ash usually contains some compounds resembling feldspars and these acted as a strong alkaline earth flux in the glaze. Considerable experimentation and testing had to take place before the proper formula could be derived. The glaze resembles some of the southern alkaline glaze combinations in its fired form. Research on this regional form of stoneware glaze is now underway. Sherds at the sites are the only evidence that we presently have, but some whole pots will undoubtedly be discovered soon.

BRISTOL GLAZES

The last form of glaze to become popularly used for stonewares was prepared from ceramic chemicals purchased from ceramic suppliers, a very modern manner in which to prepare stoneware glazes. It is termed the "Bristol" type of glaze. During the Victorian period in England, the utilitarian stoneware industry was influenced by both the taste and technology of the times. A smooth white glaze was developed from ceramic chemicals, supposedly by potters in Bristol, England, to cover the usual drab buff body of their stoneware. It quickly supplanted both the old British salt-glazed utilitarian pots, with their ferruginous dips that produced bands of brown, and the common all-brown-toned slip-glazed pots. The clean white look of the new Bristol glaze was immensely popular with a public now greatly concerned with sanitation. Potters from the then industrialized areas of Ohio were quick to see the advantages of this form of glaze and presented their own similar developments at the New Orleans Exposition of 1884. During the next two decades the use of this glaze by almost all industrialized potteries **spread across the entire North American continent.**

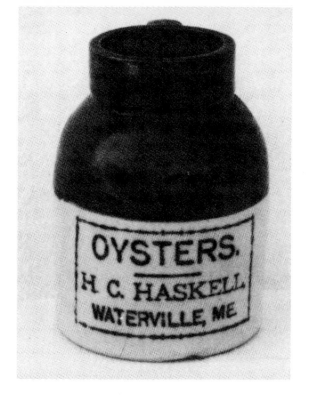

A very small pot or jug for oysters. It is only 4-7/8 inches tall and has a brown slip glazed interior and upper half (Albany type) while the lower exterior is probably a creamy Bristol glaze. "OYSTERS/H.C. HASKELL/ WATERVILLE, ME." stenciled on the front. Probably first quarter of the 20th century. *Courtesy of M. Lelyn Branin.* $100

A very large pitcher of about two-gallon capacity. It is an example of an early and poorly formulated white Bristol type of glaze. The pin hole type of defect appears in many areas both inside and out. Attributed to Bexar County, Texas probably 1905-1915. $125

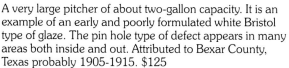

An example of the "Bristol Ware" advertised in 1885 by the Tilsonburg Pottery, Ontario. This jar is a direct copy of British wares of this period, even insofar as the tiny oval impressed mark. The shoulder and lip were dipped in a ferruginous slip, then the whole was covered inside and out with a white Bristol form of glaze. *Courtesy of David L. Newlands.* $195

Before 1920 the use of this glaze on the exterior of a pot in combination with Albany type slip glaze on shoulder, mouth, and interior became exceedingly popular. This was in direct imitation of the British stoneware vessels in which the upper portion, or sometimes upper and lower portions, of the pots were dipped into a ferrugionous solution before glazing with the Bristol type of glaze. The British use was for decorative purposes only, I am sure, since the dip was an old method of decorating salt-glazed wares as well. It performs no function save the addition of a more appealing color.

After about 1920 the Bristol glaze was almost always used alone, producing the coarse, white-glazed, mid-twentieth century American stoneware with which we are all familiar. In the quest for a more attractive product, potters at times added color, such as cobalt, directly to this glaze. Additional decoration in color was obtained by using decalcomania or stamped decoration. Decoration was also accomplished by sponging or spraying coloring oxides (mainly cobalt for blue, copper for green, and iron for brown over the glaze. The old method of hand painting decorative designs with slip clays containing coloring oxides, used by earlier salt glaze potters, no longer fit into the industrialized pattern prevalent in the production of twentieth-century utilitarian stonewares.

The main glaze used upon utilitarian stoneware in the United States in the twentieth-century period was some variation of the Bristol type of opaque, feldspathic glaze in white. At the time of this glaze's development, ceramic chemicals were readily available in the United States. Use of glazes prepared from purified chemicals rather than natural raw materials made possible a degree of glaze standardization that previously had not been available to utilitarian stoneware potters.

The Bristol type glaze employs materials, such as the feldspars, that are also used in porcelain glazes, but it has a high clay content so that it adheres to unfired pots. The combination of china clay with a rather large amount of zinc oxide gives the characteristic opaque white color. The zinc oxide also acts as a flux to lower the firing temperature so that most mixtures of the glaze mature at rather low stoneware temperatures between 1150 degrees C and 1200 degrees C. It has a very glossy, smooth, untextured surface.

A very typical formula given in Parmelee is the following mixture by weight:
Canadian Felspar 59.62 percent.
Whiting (ground marble or limestone) 8.03 percent.
Zinc Oxide 6.50 percent.
Florida Kaolin (china clay) 13.81 percent.
Flint (ground flint rock or sand) 12.04 percent.

The ingredients are fairly common compounds with which most of us are familiar. During the earlier period of their use, they were mixed and placed in a suspension in water and used as a dipping glaze. At the present time this same type of glaze is used to a great extent in industrial manufacture of glazed tile, various coloring stains being added. Most present-day glazing is done with high pressure air spray guns.

The basic color of this glaze is white. It will cover most rather dull buff and tan stoneware bodies and conceal a rather unpleasant body color beneath a coat of glistening opaque white. When used by utilitarian potters, this glaze was rarely colored, although it produces pleasing colors with the addition of cobalt, iron, and copper oxides. During the first quarter of this century, it was often used in combination with Albany type slip glazes to produce brown-and-white utilitarian wares. The color of this glaze may become pinkish or tan flecked if it is applied over a body rather high in iron content. Otherwise, it varies only from cream to dead white. At times it is not totally opaque, but more often it is a very opaque white. These variations are caused by altering the formula slightly. Potters are great experimenters and like to make their own glaze variations.

There are relatively few defects associated with this glaze. This is due in part to the fact that, by the end of the nineteenth century, kilns were better developed and firing with a large degree of control was possible. There are underfired examples of Bristol-glazed vessels, but the major defects of this glaze are due to its great viscosity. During the firing, gases from the body escape out through the glaze. If the glaze fails to seal over these tiny outlets, defects known as pinholes result. Blisters may also be seen and are common in early examples of the glaze. This glaze also has a tendency to "crawl" or agglutinate and pull together, leaving small patches of the body without glaze. Areas of blistering-off by direct flames are much less common in the later forms of kilns in which this glaze was generally used. A properly formulated Bristol type glaze will not craze or crackle, but this defect may be seen in older pots, particularly after they have been subjected to heat during use.

The survival of this glaze in the present industrialized ceramic industry is undoubtedly due to its dependability and durability. Its beauty is another matter, for it hardly approaches the realm of artistic consideration.

This very large garden pot is in a bowl form with a top diameter of about 20 inches. It has no bottom so that it could be used as a planter. Made at the Bluebird Pottery, Crooksville, Ohio by Edwin Worstall as a wedding present for his bride, Eva about 1890. This shows a white Bristol form of glaze being used in Ohio prior to 1900. It is decorated with banding and sponging in cobalt slip. *Courtesy of the Ohio Historical Society, Ohio Ceramic Center at Roseville.* $900

This 1-1/2 gallon decorated field jug is attributed to the Akron, Ohio, area about 1890. The white Bristol form of glaze was already being used at that time by Ohio potters. This jug has an incised, cobalt-outlined bird and "Joseph Patton, Copley, Ohio" inscribed in cobalt on the front. Floral designs of the same type appear on the reverse. *Courtesy of Nancy and Bob Treichler. Photographer: Doug Moore.* $1400-1600

CONCLUSIONS

All of the five major stoneware glaze types have variations produced by innumerable factors that come into play. These glazes were used with ingredients from different areas, over clays from different areas, by hundreds of different potters, and in a number of different forms of kilns. Within the kilns each firing varied slightly, if not greatly, as to the temperature ranges to which each pot was exposed as well as the varying atmospheric conditions within the kiln. I have therefore attempted to present some of the basic technology involved in the use of these glazes, major reasons for the texture and color variations which are evident after firing, and a discussion of their most important defects. Many defects in vessels may result during the firing process. These defects, of both body and glaze, will be presented during the discussion of the effects of firing.

Chapter 6
Passage Through Fire

In many ways the firing process is the most important process in the production of ceramics. Before firing, the dry clay pots are very fragile and can perform no function except that of pleasing the eye of the beholder with an artistic form. If glazes are present on raw wares they appear as a powdery coating of dull color, usually white, tan, or rusty red, which may be easily brushed off. The pots are water soluble and will return to their original state, a lump of wet clay, if dampened sufficiently.

Before firing, the clay almost always contains small amounts of water, even when appearing bone-dry on the surface. This water, if subjected to freezing temperatures, will form tiny bits of ice and will crumble the unfired pot as the expansion accompanying freezing takes place. Many early potters stopped making vessels during the coldest months of the year if they did not have a heated building to keep the pots from freezing.

The subjection of clay vessels to high temperature is necessary for the production of the final, useful articles. For earthenwares less formal kilns, even bonfires, are suitable. Stoneware temperatures can be reached only in a well-constructed kiln that has the ability to hold enough heat to attain temperatures up to nearly 1300 degrees C. Kilns, therefore, must be understood if one wishes to understand the beauties, as well as the scars, that result from firing.

Southern Groundhog Kiln

215

Updraft Kiln   Morganville NY

Downdraft Kiln
D'Hanis, TX

Crowntype Downdraft Kiln
Lee Co., TX

KILN TYPES

The structures within which almost any burning process takes place are called kilns. For the high temperature firing necessary for stoneware pottery, a kiln must be a well-constructed structure that has a firebox large enough to accomodate adequate fuel, a chamber called a "firing chamber" in which the pots are placed to receive the heat, and some form of venting for the heat to leave the kiln. Channels called flues are sometimes constructed both to carry the heat from the firebox to the pots and from the firing chamber out of the kiln. Chimneys, when present, serve as terminal flues.

Kilns may be round or rectangular. Round kilns are often described as "beehive" types, but there are a number of variations. The number of fireboxes may vary from one to five or six. These fireboxes are arranged so that they feed the heat as evenly as possible into the kiln. Since wood was the most common fuel used by earlier potters, the fireboxes of these kilns are rather large. After the heat leaves the firebox it rises. In the case of simple updraft kilns, the heat rises up through the pottery in the firing chamber. It then exits through an opening, or several openings, in the top of the kiln. The exit of heat may be slowed down by covering or partially closing these openings with a movable lid or damper. In the more modern form of round "beehive" kiln that began to be prevalent in this country about the beginning of the twentieth century, the heat from the firebox first rises to the top of the kiln. This top, or crown, is closed, and the heat therefore is forced downward through the firing chamber and is drawn out through flue channels in the floor or just above the floor, then up and out one or more chimneys. These more modern kilns are called downdraft kilns because the heat is pulled back down through the pots before it exits. The advantages of this form of firing are that it is much more economical as well as quite even in heat distribution. Early potters lost underfired pieces in almost every kiln load because of poor distributuion of heat. Simple round updraft kilns were one of the major types of

kilns used by American stoneware potters. Round downdraft kilns, which we most often see today, were not in common use in America until the early twentieth century.

Rectangular kilns are somewhat simpler in that they have only one firebox at the front, followed by a loading or firing chamber for the pots, and either a rear chimney or openings over the vault for the exit of the heat. Although these kilns are usually cross draft, that is, the heat passes transversely through the wares from front to back, rectangular kilns may also be mainly updraft or downdraft. The American groundhog form of kiln was essentially cross draft. Rhenish rectangular stoneware kilns were mainly updraft from a low front firebox. These kilns have openings over the vault to release the smoke and heat, and have no chimney. Many present-day rectangular kilns employed by artist potters have fireboxes or gas burners at the level of the firing chamber and flue channels under the floor that pull the heat down, then out through a tall chimney. They, therefore, fall into the downdraft classification.

The firing process was very damaging to the early kilns, particularly to the firebox areas. Repairs were often needed before the kiln could be readied for another firing.

Kilns are spoken of by potters as being "set," "stacked," or 'charged" when they are loaded. Each piece of pottery is "set" into its special place with hopes that it will remain in that position throughout the firing. If the setting is not done correctly, according to the peculiarities of the burning of each different kiln, it will not fire well. There is always the possibility that some of the supports used to prop the pottery will give way and the pots will fall out of position, leaving a mass of fused and distorted pots after firing. Different kilns are set in different ways.

KILN FURNITURE AND LOADING

The various clay forms used in loading kilns to assure the proper position of the pots are spoken of as kiln furniture. There are two different types of kiln furniture. Pieces formed ahead of time either on the potter's wheel or by rolling and cutting flat strips and squares of clay are the true furniture. Saggers, jug saggers, and large rings or discs used between wide-mouthed vessels were generally made on a wheel. These as well as flat strips or squares of clay for use between vessels and the small rings, rectangles, or triangles which were used as test pieces were all allowed to become bone-dry before the loading process. These major pieces may be used a number of times if not damaged in firing.

Since no shelves were used in most utilitarian stoneware pottery kilns, a second type of supporting furniture was needed, and it was made at the time of loading. Soft scrap clay, frequently with added coarse sand, was formed by hand into all sorts of coils, spools or separators, and patties. These soft pieces of clay could be easily adjusted to keep the stacks level and separated. They were also often dipped into sand so that they did not adhere to the pots. Such pieces were always discarded after firing.

Of the pre-formed kiln furniture, the most complicated pieces are called saggers. These are nothing more than small, usually round, lidded boxes made of a very coarse clay. They were not commonly used by American utilitarian stoneware potters, although they were used in England for utilitarian wares. They are used for all sorts of different finer wares, and were used for the fine salt-glazed tablewares made in England during the eighteenth century. Saggers serve as protective coverings over pots so that no damage is done to the glazes by open flames. When used for salt-glazed wares saggers were mainly employed for assistance in stacking, for holes were cut into the side walls to allow the entrance of the salt vapor. Most American potters stacked their wares much as German salt-glaze potters did, using, instead of saggers, squares and strips of clay cut and dried before firing.

One type of kiln furniture that is found only rarely in association with stoneware kilns is the cockspur, or stilt. This small device usually consists of either a ring of clay with the top notched by the finger or three small coils of clay joined at the center to form a small three-legged trivet. These pieces of kiln furniture are commonly used in earthenware glost firing, in which the glaze often appears on the bottom of the vessel. The little supports hold the vessels off of the shelf, and the small contact points make only small scars in the glaze and can be easily smoothed. I have seen one of these cockspurs at an excavated stoneware site in Texas. The potters in this case seem to have placed spurs on the interiors of their milkpans to keep them from sticking together in firing, since the resultant scars are visible in some of their pans.

A form of furniture rather commonly found at old stoneware pottery sites is called the jug sagger or stacker. It consists of a short, truncated cylinder in which one large section has been cut out of one side and usually one or two smaller holes or notches cut in the remaining sides. These saggers were used to assist in the stacking of jugs. The large cut is such that the handle of the jug may extend through it. The form is placed upside down over the jug neck, the handle protruding through its opening. Scars resulting from the placing of this form of sagger over the neck may usually be seen. If the exterior of the jug was salt-glazed, there will be a ring around the jug of unglazed clay at the point of contact of the sagger. The salt glaze is also frequently thin and without noticable texture in the area of the shoulder and neck that was covered by the sagger, even though holes were made for the admission of the salt.

During the last decade or so of the nineteenth century ingenious methods of forming certain types of pots so that they fit together to form a solid stack in the kiln were developed. The large milk bowls with wide heavy rims were formed so that one hung within the other very easily. The upper rim and the area just beneath the lower edge of the rim were kept free of glaze or cleaned. No furniture was necessary to hold these bowls in an upright stack, but small rolls of clay were sometimes used as separators between the rims.

A sagger from William Roger's Yorktown Pottery. It was used for salt-glazing mugs at this eighteenth century pottery. *Courtesy of The National Park Service.*

Kiln furniture prepared before loading. Two broken wheel-made rings and a portion of a disc used between large jars are at the top. A five-inch diameter jug sagger or stacker, viewed from the top, is at the center base. On the left side fragment of square tile and on the right bits of flat strips, both used in stacking, are seen. The strip with a large hole at the lower right is a draw-trial.

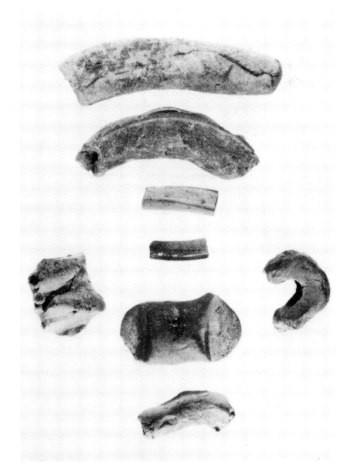

An assortment of fired, hand-formed pieces of clay used in the setting or stacking of kilns. The large flattened rolls at the top were placed between large jars and jug bases. The smaller rolls just below were used between bowl rims. On the left and right are wads used between vessels; the one on the right shows the impression of a jug mouth. Between these pieces a roll flattened at both ends, sometimes called a spacer or a spool, was placed between upright stacks.

A form of jug that has a heavy flat ledge just beneath the shoulder was also manufactured so that this ledge served as support for a jar of the same capacity (usually one gallon). The ledge was unglazed and the unglazed rim of an open jar was placed on this shelf-like area, upside down. (Glaze is not used on the rims or bottoms of most stoneware vessels.) The stack consisted of a jug and jar, another set of the same on top, and so forth. The handles of these stacking jugs were shorter than most jug handles so that they could be placed beneath the jar. Jugs of this form are referred to as stacker, or shouldered, jugs. Shouldered jugs were also fired in the usual manner of stacking used for other vessels — mouth to mouth and bottom to bottom. Stacking jugs were frequently made in two parts in jigger molds.

The process of setting or loading the kiln began when the pots and the previously made kiln furniture were all completely dry. Kilns are loaded according to their form. The small, very low groundhog kilns were frequently of the "single-shot" type. This means that the pots were arranged on the floor of the kiln singly and no upright stacking took place. The low vessels such as milk bowls fit next to the sides of the kiln, and the vessels were packed in order of ascending height with the tallest churns and storage jars in rows through the middle of the long firing chamber. The potter had to crouch on his hands and knees to load such a kiln. At "single shot" kiln sites investigations have revealed almost a complete absence of any sort of kiln furniture. There is also an absence of scars from stacking on vessels fired in these kilns. Rims are completely glazed, but bottoms are usually free of glaze. The floor of such a kiln was covered with fine sand or a layer of local quartz that had been heated and broken into small sharp pieces. These spicules of rock served much like small stilts beneath the pots so that they did not stick to the floor of the kiln. Pots salt glazed in kilns with such a floor often show glaze over most of the bottom surface, since the points of the quartz chips held them up enough that they contacted salt vapor.

As the kilns, be they rectangular or round, increased in height, the height of the stacks of pots increased. Stacks were usually not high in groundhog kilns, but two or three vessels might be placed one over the other. Accessory kiln furniture was necessary in taller kilns.

Since utilitarian potters made a certain number of vessels of each size and shape, vessels of the same size and form were more easily stacked together. The assemblage fired in one single load varied somewhat from that in another according to demand. At times this was a seasonal demand. Preserve jars of one- or two-gallon size were in demand during the early summer for preservation of fruits, and jugs were in great demand in the fall in areas in which **syrup was made from sorghum cane.** In winter months, large jars for the storage of lard and sausage were most popular.

As taller stacks of pots were formed in upright kilns, more hand-formed rolls and patties of clay were needed at the time of stacking. These pieces of furniture were made of soft clay during each specific loading in order to wedge the pots apart so that the stacks would remain upright. The pieces called "spools" or "spacers" by some potters were made to fit between the upright stacks. Scars from these attachments are common, particularly on salt glazed vessels. If cut and dried strips and squares or wheel-made rings and discs were not prepared previously, small patties, coils, and balls of clay were made at the time of loading and placed between the vessels in the stacks as they were built up. All of this type of hand-formed furniture was considered disposable after the firing and was tossed into the waster heap.

When separate firing openings were present in the kiln, sanded scrap clay was placed around and over the bricks that were used to close up the loading door. All round wood-fired kilns, and most ground-hog kilns, have special doors used only during loading and unloading. These must be sealed by this plastering of clay or mud before the firing begins. A small ground-hog kiln might have one single door for loading, firing, and unloading, but even in the groundhog type the single door was not common.

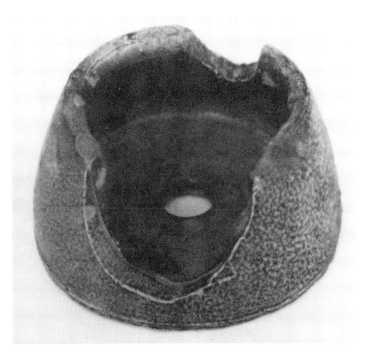

A close view of a jug-stacking device showing the large cut for the handle and other openings to admit salt vapor. These pieces are turned over the jug shoulder to handle. Heavy salt glaze can be seen on the exterior of the device, which is from a pottery in Hardeman County, Tenn. c. 1870. *Courtesy of the Tennessee Department of Conservation, Division of Archeology.*

The circular scar from a jug stacker is seen around the upper shoulder of this Albany type slip-glazed jug. In salt-glazed pieces the scar is represented by an unglazed area in this same position.

221

A one-gallon jug which was made in two jigger molds, then joined at the shoulder. The lower exterior is salt-glazed, while the upper exterior is unglazed, indicating that this was used as a "stacker" jug in the kiln. "Wm. RADAM's/MICROBE KILLER" appears in relief on the shoulder area while "RED WING POTTERY/RED WING, MINN." appears in relief on the bottom. $250

A one-gallon preserve jar with bail handle. This was used as a "stacking" piece in conjunction with a one-gallon open jar. The shoulder and interior which were covered during firing are glazed in a brown slip glaze very like Albany but known to be from the Alazan Creek in San Antonio. The shoulder ledge is unglazed and the lower section is white Bristol glazed. Stenciled "PRICE-BOOKER MFG. CO./SAN ANTONIO, TEXAS" for a local pickle company. Elmendorf, Texas c. 1900. $100

A one-gallon jug in a medium green alkaline glaze. The form of this jug was influenced by the late 19th century development of the "shouldered" form and imitates it shyly. Impressed "W.F. HAHN/TRENTON/S.C." Probably 1880-1900. $210

Jug stacker in
position.

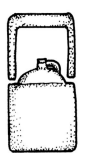

Stacker jug and
jar in position

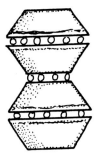

Mouth to Mouth
and Bottom to
Bottom stacking

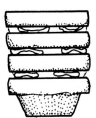

Hanging Stack-
ing of Wide
Rimmed milk
bowls

Stacking in an Upright Kiln

Stacking in a low Groundhog Kiln

223

FIRING THE KILN

In the firing of raw pottery (that which has never been subjected to firing before), the heat of the kiln must be increased very carefully during the early period. Almost all American utilitarian pottery was fired from a raw state to the high temperature of body and glaze maturation in one process, and almost all of the early potteries used wood as fuel. During the process of industrialization, pottery and brick kilns were converted to burn coal. At the present time gas, natural or bottled, is the common form of fuel used in large potteries unless electricity is relatively inexpensive in the area.

The early slow period of firing is necessary to drive off both any excess water that might be present in the vessels themselves and the water that is naturally combined with the clay. This combined water is released at about 600 degrees C. If the increase in the heat is too rapid before this water is freed, it forms steam under pressure and produces cracks in the ware which are quite distinctive. These are called water cracks. They frequently penetrate only the outer layer of the body clay. If the pot is not uniform in thickness, these cracks tend to occur in the thicker parts of the body, usually around the base. Small bubbles may also be formed by steam pressure between the layers of the clay body. Whole wall sections may be blown off of the pot by this steam pressure.

The length of time necessary for the completion of firing varies according to the size and construction of the kiln. A small groundhog of about twenty feet total length can be completely fired with wood in 12 or 18 hours. The early period of firing is not particularly interesting, for nothing may be seen within the kiln. As the temperatures increase, however, the firing process becomes more and more fascinating. The increasing heat within the kiln soon starts to show color. As a red heat is developed, a glow can be seen within the kiln and around every orifice leading into the chamber in which the wares are sitting, the firing chamber. Even the pieces of pottery begin to glow with a dull red color. Long tongues of flame begin to enter the firing chamber and flow around the pots. Wood-fired kilns are probably the most exciting to watch, since the wood flames are long and can be seen within the kiln.

The last few hours of firing—the very most exciting as well as the most exhausting—are frequently called the "blast-off" period. The name was in use long before space flights used the same term for their period of departure. In the blast-off period fuel is added as rapidly as it is consumed in an effort to keep the heat rising rapidly. A stoker must be with the kiln constantly during this period if wood or coal are used. In wood-burning kilns with low chimneys, flames come out of every orifice, and tall flames may rise eight to ten feet above the chimney. Smoke is plentiful, especially if fat pine wood is being used during this period. Within the kiln the vessels have become a glowing light yellow in color. Surface glazes glisten and appear wet as they melt. It is at this period that the potter begins to pull out some of his draw trails if a dipped glaze has been used. Draw trails are small rings or strips of clay of the same body as the pots. If slip or alkaline glazes are being used, they are dipped into the same glaze as the pots. When the firing begins to near completion, these pieces are withdrawn from the kiln with a long metal hook. The proper melt of the dipped glaze determines the conclusion of firing for all but salt glazed pieces. When salt is the glaze of choice, the first salting may take place at this high temperature.

In the first salting, approximately one-third of the required amount of salt is poured into the kiln through a series of holes in the top of the kiln called saltports. These have been closed until this time by brick or ceramic lids placed in or over them. If there are no saltports in the vault of the kiln, about one-third of the salt is thrown into the firebox with a small shovel. Almost immediately, intense white smoke, then black smoke, then the odor of chlorine gas issue from every orifice of the kiln. The fire is then stoked again with fuel so that within an hour or so the temperature has come back up, and the kiln is ready for the second dose of salt. If draw trial pieces have been placed within the kiln, some are withdrawn after this salting. After the potter examines the deposit on the draw trials, a third dose of salt is generally given to the wares as soon as the temperature is right again. Draw trials are inspected and if all appears well, the firing is concluded.

After the last salting, the fire stoking is stopped and all orifices within easy reach covered. When dipped glazes are being fired, this is done as soon as the tests appear mature. The firebox door is closed with brick or a piece of metal, all spy hole bricks are replaced, and the low chimney, if present, is covered by a sheet of metal.

Dampers may be closed in the more sophisticated kilns with tall chimneys. The glow within the kiln slowly fades, but usually at least two, if not three, days are allowed to pass before the kiln is opened.

A large jug which is 22 inches high and probably about 4 gallon capacity. It is covered with a light tan salt glaze and has a brown, probably local, slip glazed interior. A large eagle with outspread wings is incised on the mid-front area. The breast itself is in the shape of a shield with prominent stripes. A large Masonic emblem with compass and angle is in the center of the shield. The left claw holds a sheaf of arrows and the right claw an American flag. Inscribed on the shoulder "MADE BY A. STEADMAN." Absolon Steadman, New Haven, Conn., 1828-1831. *Courtesy of Barry Cohen. Photographer: Henry Cox.* $15,000-20,000

A small salt-glazed bank which stands 8-3/4 inches tall with its ornate finial. Decorated in cobalt with a small bird on a branch and dots around the vessel neck. Dated 1876 in cobalt on the reverse. Attributed to West Troy Pottery, Troy, N.Y. *Courtesy of Peter Schriber. Photographer: Mawson.* $3500

A small bottle form flattened into a flask. It is 7-3/4 inches high and covered with an almost honey colored salt glaze. On the front "C.H. Smith/Sept. 1860" is hand inscribed within a large heart with a bow or flower at the top of the heart. On the reverse "Cornwall/N.Y." is inscribed within the same heart form. The inscription was rubbed with cobalt and the heart outlines, bownots, and part of the lip also have been colored blue. *Courtesy of Jeremy L. Banta.* $1800

UNLOADING THE KILN

A waiting period is absolutely necessary, for no one can enter the kiln the first day after firing. By the second day the pots are frequently still much too hot to pick up with a bare hand. Rapid cooling will cause rapid contraction of the clay and the pots will crack badly. Even after forty-eight hours—the cooling period for a relatively small kiln—as the door is opened, high pitched snaps, pings, and tinkles may be heard as the pots contract.

As the door is taken down, a revealing peek or so may indicate some of the things that happened during the firing. This first look at least will indicate whether the firing was within the proper temperature range and will satisfy the potter or disappoint him. All of the beauties as well as the defects are now indelibly fixed in both the body and the glaze of the pot.

The emergence of the first few pots as they are handed out of the kiln into daylight sets the mood for the rest of the unloading—elation or disappointment. The traditional utilitarian potter depended upon this unloading or "drawing" of the kiln in a very practical manner. Saleable pots were his bread and butter. Potters generally fired one, possibly three or four, times a month. The loss of a kiln load of pots meant the loss of income from the entire period of throwing, glazing, drying, and firing.

THE IMPERFECT POT

There are always some pots that crack before firing and are discarded. Each fired load also has a few losses. Utilitarian potters seldom tried to rescue a few underfired pots by refiring them, but tossed them in the waste heap with other defective pots. These heaps now tell those who investigate them just what a specific potter was making and peculiarities of his forms and glazes that may distinguish his wares in the absence of marks. Few old pottery sites remain in industrialized or urban areas, but many remain in remote countryside areas all over the United States.

The defects caused by some movement within the firing kiln, overheating, underfiring, normal stacking, poor throwing, body clay abnormalities, and glaze abnormalities, are all evident after the firing. The colors of the body clay as well as the glaze of the finished pots show the effect of the atmosphere most prevalent within the kiln during the firing period—oxidizing or reducing.

The major problems experienced in early kilns were easily visible as soon as the kiln was opened. Extensive cracking from too rapid cooling was one. These cracks or "dunts" may be large or small. The next problem was caused by the slipping or falling of some of the stacks of ware during the firing. Tumbled stacks allowed the pots to come in contact with one another and the glazed surfaces adhered to other pots. A large amount of ware could be lost in this manner. The opening of a kiln exposing an entire load of underfired dry-looking ware was certainly a depressing situation and a major problem. At times the immaturity was spotty, being most prevalent in areas of the kiln receiving insufficient heat. This ware was not marketable if the body clay was still completely unvitrified and the glazes rough and dry. Such vessels would leak and, with no smooth surfaces for cleaning, also be rather unsanitary and undesirable.

Although an entire load was seldom lost from overfiring, occasional pieces might be slumped and others bloated from overheating. "Slumping" is the term used to describe deformation of the pot by excessive heating. The clay body begins to soften and the pot itself will slump or bend, especially in any area that supports weight. "Bloating" is the process in which large bubbles are formed within the clay body of the pot. The outer surfaces of the body have become vitrified, and the gases cannot escape to the outside as they can before this process is complete. Both slumping and bloating may be seen in overfired pots. Many early vessels with these faults were sold, however. Overheating also caused melting of overhead brick from time to time, and large drops of dark, foamy, glazelike material from these melted bricks were deposited upon vessels. Occasionally these deposits were too large for the vessel to be saleable, but many such areas are visible on surviving pots that were sold and used.

Some defects within the body clay were visible only after firing. Many potters abandoned a pottery after only a year or so of working because of continual problems with the only clays available in the area. Cracking of the ware either in drying or firing was one of the most serious problems of the body clay. Other problems were caused by the inclusion of rather large particles of other compounds such as lime and iron within the clay. Lime particles caused a problem in the clay that resulted in the popping off of pieces of the surface clay and glaze during the firing. These defects are called "popouts" and scar the surfaces of the pot with shallow pits, usually about the size of a thumbnail. Frequently a particle of lime one or two millimeters in diameter is seen at the base of such a pit. Ware of this type did not compete well with better-looking wares. Large particles of iron melt in reducing firings, and resultant depressions or holes in the pot walls, with a glossy black material issuing from them, mar the surface. Both of these defects may be remedied somewhat by the laborious process of making the body clay into a thin water suspension and screening it as the initial step in its preparation. Potters would often prefer to change their shop location than to bother with this process.

A one-gallon preserve jar with an underfired Albany type slip glaze. The glaze is wrinkled and unmelted all over the exterior, mature on the interior. It is dull black with yellow-green mottling. Attributed to Elmendorf, Texas c. 1890. $75

A five-gallon capacity, small-mouthed jar with bilateral, vertical strap handles. This jar is remarkable in that it was overheated in the kiln and the body clay is full of large bubbles. This is called "bloating." The pot has a brown alkaline glaze inside and out. From Rusk County, Texas, c. 1870. $575

A one-gallon, salt-glazed jug dug in New Orleans, Louisiana. Although it shows evidence of having lost its handle at a later period, this jug was deformed or slumped at the time of firing. Even in this state it was sold and barged down the Ohio and Mississippi Rivers, for its form, glaze, and characteristic clay indicate that it was produced along the Ohio River in Ohio, Indiana, or Kentucky. $100

A one-gallon, salt-glazed jug with an Albany type slip glazed interior. A large cobalt floral spray was brushed on the front just under the mark. This jug was overheated and slumped slightly in firing, but not discarded. Impressed "PFALTZENGRAF & CO./YORK, PA." Second half of the 19th century. $500

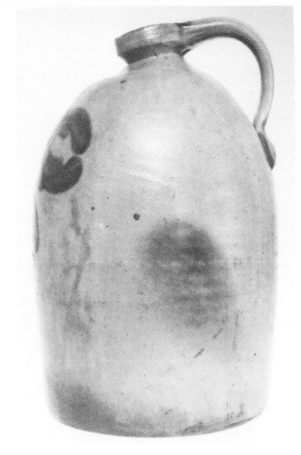

A pair of lids melted and adhering to the broken base of a jug or jar found at the Dunkin Pottery, Bastrop County, Texas, c. 1870. A set of ashtrays (4 inches in diameter) that fused together and cracked and bloated as the kiln overheated. Found at the Meyer Pottery Site, Bexar County, Texas, c. 1945-50.

Kiln Accidents: An artistically melted jar (found at the R. Cole Kiln Site) and a bloated jug with adhering fired fragments from another pot that exploded during firing (from the L. Sugg Kiln Site.) Both sites were salt-glazing potteries in central North Carolina. *Courtesy of The Potter's Museum. Photograph by Bill Jenko.* L-R: $200, $475

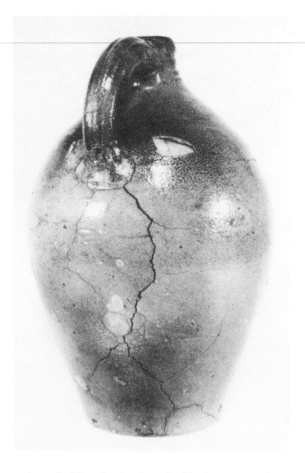

An early 1/2-gallon jug from the Manhattan area shows extensive water cracking on the back of the body. The large cracks caused by steam expansion during firing do not extend through the entire wall, and the jug will hold liquid. Salt glaze exterior, Manhattan, N.Y., New York area, c. 1800. $550

This three-gallon open jar is covered inside and out with an Albany type slip glaze. Numerous dark spots on the surface were caused by the burning out of iron during firing. The light spots are areas in which a large lime particle expanded during firing and fractured off the overlying body and glaze surface. These are called pop-outs. William Saenger, St. Hedwig, Texas, c. 1880. $150

A three-gallon churn with incised lines around the shoulder and wheel-thrown bilateral handles at the shoulder. It is covered with a transparent, medium olive green alkaline glaze inside and out. The clay used in this pot contained many small particles of iron which melted and spotted the surface during the firing. The one large spot, about three centimeters wide and ten centimeters long, is very striking. East Texas, c. 1875. $395

A two-gallon jug and a two-quart jar glazed with a dark brown slip glaze of the Albany type. The flames contacted the abnormal areas of the glaze early in firing and peeled much of the slip from the surface. The slip remaining in the areas did not develop a normal glaze, and what remains is a dry, yellowish color, easily scraped off. William Saenger Pottery, St. Hedwig, Texas, c. 1880. L-R: $220, $100

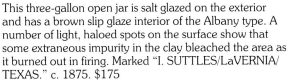

This three-gallon open jar is salt glazed on the exterior and has a brown slip glaze interior of the Albany type. A number of light, haloed spots on the surface show that some extraneous impurity in the clay bleached the area as it burned out in firing. Marked "I. SUTTLES/LaVERNIA/TEXAS." c. 1875. $175

A two-gallon jar with open loop horizontally attached handles. The exterior is covered with a glossy light gray salt glaze and the interior is only "toasted" by salt. Several bits of clay are stuck to the lower front of the pot resulting from a firing accident, probably explosion, of a nearby pot. A slender bird reaching out to eat a bunch of grapes is incised on the mid-front surface and filled with cobalt. This is impressed "BOSTON" in large letters. The work of Jonathan Fenton, Boston, Mass. 1793-1796. *Courtesy of Peter E. Schriber. Photographer: Mawson.* $900

The cleanliness of the clay to begin with was important, since inclusion of vegetable matter, such as roots, made the turning difficult and burned out in the firing, leaving a hole or defect in the fired clay.

One other factor involving the clay was sometimes caused by poor throwing. Certain clays are insufficiently plastic and make it difficult for the thrower to pull up walls of any height on the spinning wheel. The optimum situation in throwing is to have the final walls and bottom of the pot even in thickness. Poor throwers, even with good clays, have a tendency to leave thick bottoms and lower walls, rising to thin walls at the top of the vessel. This promotes cracking from poor drying of the thick section as well as poor heating of the same area during firing. As the clay particles shrink and begin to fuse together in either the drying or the vitrification period, the tension of this shrinkage pulls on the areas that are not either completely dry or vitrified and results in cracking. Too thin a bottom will also crack away from the thicker base of the walls.

Defects in decoration and glaze that were not evident before are also seen after the firing. In the case of decoration, most incised or impressed marking or decoration remains about the same. The main defects visible after firing involve the use of decorating slips containing coloring oxides. Too little oxide in the mixture will result in a thick decoration that may burn to black rather than remain the usual blue or brown desired. At times decoration may also run and streak the pot.

Defects in the glaze visible after firing are numerous. First of all, vessels with a salt glaze will reveal no true glaze or glossy surface if the body did not contain sufficient silica for the formation of a glaze. Dry, scummy looking patches of glaze, which may even be rubbed off of the surface, will be visible. If the pot did not receive sufficient salt during the salting process, the surface will also be dry and have no glaze development. This may be a general defect, or it may be one-sided if one side of the pot was in such a position during firing that it did not receive enough salt vapor. This is true of interiors on salt-glazed pots which were not glazed with a slip or covered by another pot during the firing. Too much salt causes heavy drips and runs as well as fusion of vessels to kiln furniture but usually did not prohibit the early potter's sale of the pot.

The defects seen after firing in all of the dipped forms of glaze used on common stonewares are much the same. Underfiring, with its resultant very dry and rough glaze surfaces, has been discussed. Small areas of underfiring may be seen on glazed pots, especially at the basal area in pots fired in a groundhog kiln. These kilns are known to distribute heat to the bottom of the kiln poorly. Small underfired areas were usually overlooked by purchasers.

Blistering and peeling are defects caused by the action of direct flames upon the glaze surface before it is hot enough to melt. Small or large areas of the pot surface may be completely without glaze, exposing the body clay. The flames have caused the glaze surface to dry and peel off, much as the surface of the skin is blistered and peeled by a burn. This defect is most common on exterior surfaces. Fly ash in the kiln during wood firings will often settle on the uppermost area of a pot. This is easily seen in slip glazed pots where this ash has a bleaching effect.

Melted debris from the overhead areas of the kiln—such as salt, melted kiln brick, and surplus glaze from a pot positioned higher in the kiln—may drip upon the surface of the glaze and mar the surface upon which they are deposited. Such melts and drip deposits in utilitarian wares were often the result of high firing temperatures rather then a defect in the glaze composition.

Other defects seen in dipped glazes after firing are the result of improper composition of the glaze itself. The presence of insufficient clay of the proper type in the glaze mixture placed upon a raw or unfired pot will allow the glaze compound to dry and shrink more rapidly than the pot itself shrinks, and the entire glaze layer will peel off even before the pot is fired. If a glaze clay has a very high or low shrinkage factor, even the pure clay is unsuitable.

This was one of the problems frequently encountered in the preparation of local slip glazes. They did not "fit" the pot because of the differing shrinkage factors. This same effect may also be seen during the firing. Some clays shrink much faster than others when exposed to heat, and a rapidly shrinking surface clay or glaze will shrink, split, and crack or "crackle" the glaze surface. A glaze or slip glaze that does not shrink as rapidly as the pot which it encases may literally be pushed off the pot in sharp slivers. This is called "shivering" and is the opposite of crackling. A high silica content in the body clay improves it for salt glazing, but tends to make dipped glazes shiver off.

A two-gallon salt-glazed jug which shows very large areas of material, probably a mixture of salt and melting brick, which dripped on it from above as it was being fired. The areas are a glossy black against a light gray salt glaze. "GOODWIN & WEBSTER/HARTFORD" impressed on front. Hartford, Conn., c. 1830-40. $1500

A one-gallon preserve jar with a tie-down rim and alkaline glaze inside and out. The area in which the glaze is peeling off probably was licked by flames before the glaze began to melt, causing the glaze to peel from the jar. John M. Wilson Pottery, Guagalupe County, Texas, c. 1860. $300

A one-gallon jug covered with a local brown slip glaze (Leon slip glaze). Areas over the shoulder and handle show speckling and bleaching from fly ash and possibly some salt vapor contacting this area during firing. Meyer Pottery, Atascosa, Texas, 1900-1920. $300

233

A large blue-green drop of salt, which dripped from deposits on the roof of the kiln, is seen on a one-pint salt-glazed jug of ovoid form. Attributed to W.C. Knox, Limestone County, Texas, c. 1870. $450

A jar, of about three-gallon capacity, which shows considerable crazing of the alkaline glaze with dark stain in the cracks covering all but the base area. This crazing probably was emphasized by exposure to heat as this jar was used as a container for rendered lard. Pottersville, Edgefield, S.C., 1830. $200

A large salt-glazed storage jar of approximately five-gallon capacity. A fish is inscribed on the upper front area and a tree in the same position was inscribed on the reverse. The base bears the following inscription "made by William North, April 14, 1835." The interior is lined with a thin brown slip glaze, probably local. This pot shows blisters in the salt glaze formed when the surface glaze was no longer fluid but gases were still escaping from the body within the hot kiln. Provenience: probably southern Ohio. $375

If a glaze or a glaze clay is too low in its melting point to withstand the temperatures necessary for the firing of stonewares, it will become fluid in the heat and run toward the lower portion of the pot, sometimes even running completely off and dripping down into other pots or the kiln floor.

"Crawling" is a peculiar defect in glazes. The glaze mixture tends to agglutinate in the firing process, leaving some spaces on the surface of the pot without glaze. The name refers to the fact that it crawls off of these areas, making a thick area or "bead" of glaze where it agglutinates. Although it somewhat mars the surface, minimal crawling does not make the pots unusable. This agglutinating property is especially prevalent in glazes prepared with wood ash and is frequently seen on alkaline-glazed pots. On these pots it is not considered a defect.

"Pinholing" is another major defect seen in stoneware glazes. It appears when the glaze mixture is very stiff. As gases produced by the heat and vitrification process continue to escape from the glaze itself or the vitrifying body of the pot, tiny holes are produced through the glaze by these escaping gases. When the glaze mixture is not sufficiently fluid to melt back over this hole, or has cooled to such a state, a tiny opening resembling that made by a pin in solid substances remains through the glaze surface of the fired pot. At times a small bump produced by a blister under the glaze surface remains around the pinhole. This defect is common in the Bristol glaze family, but may be seen on any glaze surface, even a salt-glazed one. In the latter instance, the defect occurs when the glaze produced by salting has cooled slightly and become viscous, making it difficult for the gases to free themselves from the body and glaze.

Finally, glaze defects can be caused by the method of stacking the pots in the kiln. These were anticipated and acceptable defects in the case of most small potteries. Any area of a pot that has contacted another area, be it pot, furniture, or kiln wall, during the firing must be free of glaze or the surfaces become fused together by the melted glaze. For this reason bases and mouth rims were generally unglazed in utilitarian stonewares. Any glaze remaining on these areas after dipping into the glaze solution was wiped away with a damp sponge. Small amounts of glaze may be seen as thin streaks across the bottoms of some pots for this reason. When separating rolls or spools of clay were placed between upright stacks in the kiln, an attempt was made to place these between unglazed areas. If placed between glazed surfaces, scars resulted from the adhesion of the kiln furniture.

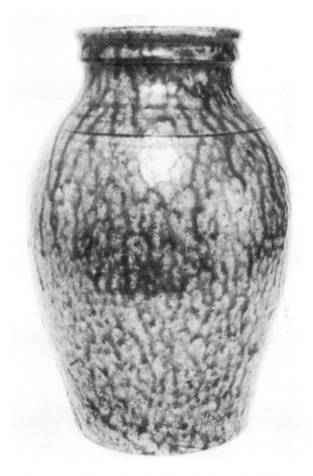

A tall, ovoid, alkaline glazed jar. Possibly the work of John Leopard of Rusk County, Texas between 1855 and 1879. This jar has a one-gallon capacity and may have been used for storage. It has a lid ledge within the mouth. The heavily agglutinated, crawled, or separated alkaline glaze on the exterior is a brownish to olive color. The interior glaze is smooth and more olive in color. $750

235

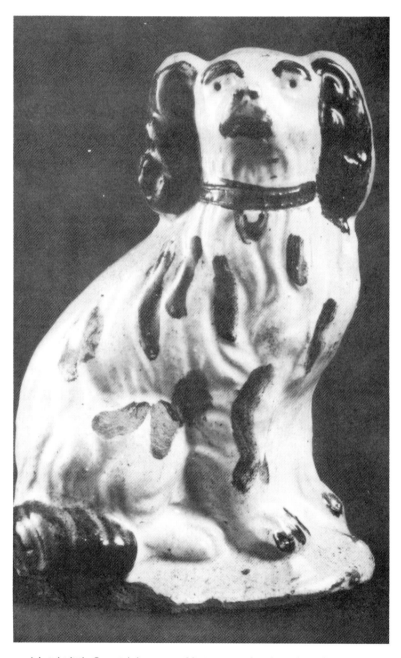

A tall jar with bilateral strap handles; probably used as a storage jar. The alkaline glaze here shows a marked agglutination or crawling on the exterior. The interior is smooth. If the interior had not fired properly, the piece would not have been useful. Rusk County, Texas, c. 1860. $675

A bright little Spaniel door stop. He is covered with a white slip under a transparent glaze and decorated with brown. He was properly named a "King Charles Spaniel" by his producers, the Owen Sound Pottery, Owen Sound, Ontario. 1895-1907. *Courtesy of the Royal Ontario Museum.* $6000

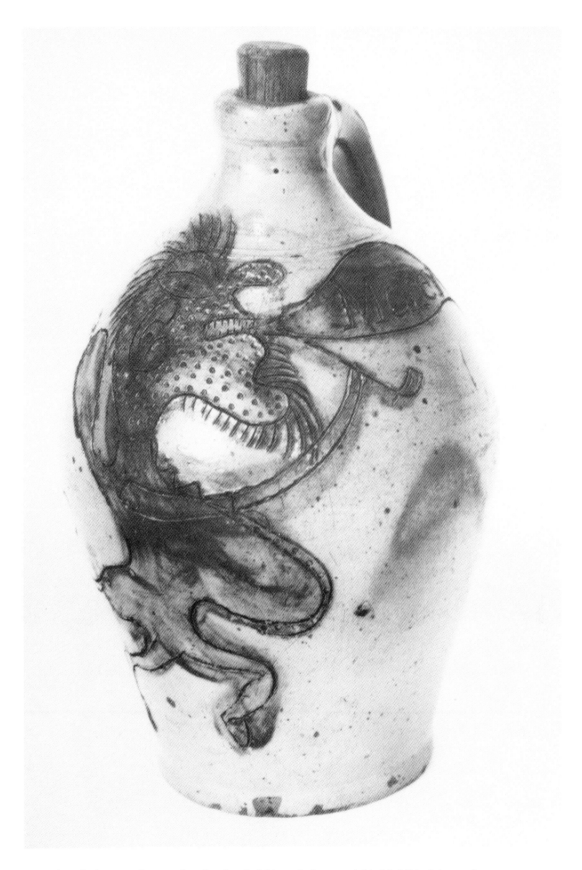

A wicked satanic figure colored with cobalt blue winds around this 11-1/2 inch jug under a gray salt glaze. He has a pockmarked face, rough whiskers, a humped back and a looped tail. Out of his mouth issues a cartoonlike loop bearing the word "MONEY" inscribed by hand. Probably New York state, early 19th century. *Courtesy of Jeremy L. Banta.* $12,500

In salt glazing many scars seen after firing are the result of kiln furniture protecting the contacted pot surfaces from any deposition of glaze. Striking patterns are sometimes produced by the toasting ability of a thin salt vapor stealing in between the bits of kiln furniture and clay wadding, leaving dark patterns around the protected spots. The scars usually remain lighter in color and have a dry, unglazed surface.

I am sure that absolutely perfect pots might become dull in the eye of the present-day collector. Fortunately many of these defects were not sufficient to prohibit the sale of the pot, and the resultant variations make the present-day student more, rather then less, interested in old utilitarian pots. The one firing defect that made the pot of no value at all was cracking through the entire wall. The pot would no longer hold liquid or dry solids and therefore was functionally useless. Some potters tested each piece of ware with a tap by a metal tool. The sharp, high ring of unmarred vitrified ware assured them that they would have no complaints from customers. **Those pots without a good ring**

went into the discard heap. At other times poorly vitrified pots were sold. These frequently exhibit the resultant defect caused by poor vitrification only after they have been used. This is called spalling and areas of body may crumble off, carrying any glaze with them. This leaves a pitted, eroded surface on the pot. Other potters are said to have dipped the pots in water as they came from the kiln. This sudden temperature change caused the enlargement of cracks that were not visible as the pots came from the kiln. Most potters simply unloaded, discarding only very obviously defective pots. The defects acceptable to nineteenth-century customers sometimes are not understandable to us today. Underfired as well as slumped and bloated pots were often sold. The demand for utilitarian stoneware, especially in areas remote from sources of manufactured items was such that defective pots were discarded only if they would not hold water. The discerning housewife of today, with the plentitude of manufactured items which we have available seldom ever buys "seconds" of ceramic wares.

This three-gallon, wide-mouthed jar was not well vitrified when it was fired. This is evidenced by the spalling of body clay and glaze from the lower section of the pot. It has a salt-glazed exterior, Albany type glazed interior. Crude cobalt drawing of a floral form and "B.J. KRUMEICK/MANUFACTURE/NEW-ARK" impressed. New Jersey, c. 1840. $575

A one-gallon, salt-glazed jug. The large area extending up the side as well as a small patch just below the shoulder show that salt was prevented from reaching these areas and forming a glaze by the manner of stacking within the kiln. These areas are a salmony brown color which stands out against the rather deep blue-gray color of the glazed areas. G.W. Suttles, La Vernia, Texas, c. 1880. $200

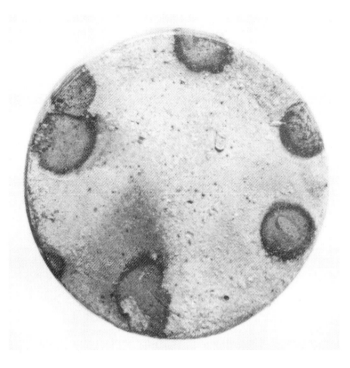

This one-gallon salt-glazed jug base shows scars from clay pads used as separators in the setting of the kiln. During firing salt vapor reacted with the rest of the base, forming a thin salt glaze. The covered areas have a toasted halo around bare body clay. Meyer Pottery, Atascosa, Texas, c. 1890.

The lid to a one-gallon jar. Such lids were frequently not glazed. This one shows a browning of the surface as it was reached by a small amount of salt vapor during firing. Only the outermost edge shows glaze development. The pale areas, which almost form a pattern on the outer ledge, are bare clay body areas that were covered by tiny clay wads during firing. William Saenger, Elmendorf, Texas, c. 1890.

The base of a salt-glazed, one-gallon preserve jar. Evidence suggests that this jar probably was sitting upon another jar of the same form in the kiln: salt-glaze was formed on the outer edges of the base, but the central area was covered and remains unglazed. Star Pottery, Elmendorf, Texas, c. 1895.

Three bottles which hold about eight ounces each were designed to hold beer, ginger beer, and ale. The bottle on the left is salt glazed while the others have a white Bristol type glaze over a top dip of ferruginous solution. British, mid to late 19th century. $125-200 ea.

Chapter 7
From Foreign Shores

A number of utilitarian stoneware vessels that appear in North America were manufactured in other countries and brought here as the result of foreign trade. The majority of these vessels were manufactured abroad as containers for products that were imported for use or consuption by Americans. Foreign tablewares or common earthenwares are not included in this consideration. The common foreign wares of the colonial periods have already been fully presented by Ivor Noel-Hume, and I see no reason to repeat his discussion of these wares. This discussion will therefore be limited to the utilitarian stoneware vessels from other parts of the world which were fairly common in North America during the nineteenth and first half of the twentieth centuries.

BRITISH IMPORTS

The foreign products most extensively used in this country during the early period were British, and I shall therefore begin with a discussion of the common vessels which we see from that nation. The vessel forms always appear to me to be a little strighter and neater than American and German vessel forms. They do have ovoid forms in some instances, such as jugs prior to 1860, but tend to be more commonly cylindrical than American forms of the same period. The straightening of the sides was complete in the industrialized Victorian potteries of the 1875 period and remained that way into the twentieth century. British vessels were wheel turned and were carefully smoothed on the exterior by the potters. Wide-mouthed vessels were usually smoothed on the interiors as well, and no throwing ridges are visible.

In British pots prior to 1860, salt glaze is the most prevalent form of glaze. The salt-glazed vessels were usually a medium gray to dark brown color. If a dark body was not used, these vessels were very often dipped into a thin ferruginous solution before firing to give them a final brown color. Traces of this dip may be seen on some of the vessel bases. A few dark brown slip glazes were also used during this period.

After 1860 the white feldspathic glaze that we call the Bristol form of glaze in America became common in Great Britain and was used for the glazing of the thousands of beer and ale bottles which we see so commonly here. This same glaze was also used for larger jars and jugs manufactured as containers for liquor, preserves, and even chemicals. Almost all of these Bristol-glazed pots had the upper half of the pot dipped into a ferruginous solution before the final glaze was applied. This gives the very typical British brown-and-white jar, jug, or bottle. In most instances the brown, being underglaze, produced a lighter brown than that seen in Ameriican pots in which the upper half had been glazed with an Albany type slip glaze and the lower section dipped into a Bristol form of glaze. The Bristol glaze as seen on imported British wares is always a very shiny, smooth, well-matured glaze with no sign of the many defects obvious during the early period of its use in North Ameriica.

Large and small ink bottles seem to have continued to be salt glazed throughout the nineteenth century. Many small containers such as those for various ointments and tooth wash, mustard, and even fish and meat pastes also were of British manufacture. Some of these are of white-glazed stoneware, while others have ironstone or porcellaneous bodies. Jars in the same form were also manufactured in the United States during the late nineteenth and early twentieth centuries. These two types may be differentiated positively only by the presence of printing of the pot lid or base which states where the product was manufactured.

One last word about the jugs and larger jars. Frequently these are seen still within wicker covering that was placed on them to make shipping and handling safer. I might add that in the past few years there has been a vast influx of antique and semiantique articles from Great Britain, and many of these brown-and-white Victorian jars and jugs have been imported recently.

A few pieces of stoneware with ovoid forms and very nice finishing details, such as extruded handles and rouletted bands, appear from time to time in North America, but they are not particularly common. These were produced in Great Britain during the second half of the nineteenth century and were imported for sale as utilitarian vessels rather than as containers that came along with imported products. They almost always have a ruddy brown, glistening, slip glaze. A few pieces of hard-burned earthenware, mainly in the form of large pan-shaped bowls, also appear. Most of these are not lined with a common clear or brown transparent lead glaze, as are the American earthenware vessels, but with an opaque white glaze.

A brown salt-glazed jar of about two-gallon capacity. This jar was recovered from the wreck of the Mary Bowers which sank in Charleston Harbor in 1864. The jar still contained camphor when raised from the wreck. *Courtesy of The Institute of Archeology and Anthropology, University of South Carolina.* $375

A slip-glazed jar with coggled decoration and a shiny brown slip glaze and a large jug of about three-gallon capacity with a tan and dark brown salt glaze, the top of the jug having been dipped in a ferruginous solution before firing. They are British mid to late 19th century. L-R: $200, $300

Two small jars of the type used to market polishes and blacking. The larger has a brown toned salt glaze while the short one has a dark brown slip glaze and "BLACK-ING" impressed on the front. British, mid 19th century. L-R: $175, $200

Salt-glazed ink containers and one covered in a brown slip glaze. The small containers were for individual use, while the large ones have tiny pouring spouts. All are British mid to late 19th century. The large bottle has a capacity of about one pint. L-R: $125, $100, $150, $95

Three examples of typical late Victorian British containers covered with a white Bristol glaze with neck and shoulders stained by an underglaze ferruginous dip. The beer or ale bottle is about one pint capacity, the flattened spirits jugs of one quart, and the large jug with its ceramic screw-in closure has a capacity of about three gallons. L-R: $95, $150, $90

GERMAN IMPORTS

By far the most common stoneware vessel produced in Germany as a product container and imported into the United States was the tall, cylindrical, Rhenish jug. These are almost always salt glazed on the exterior and were used as containers for mineral waters, wines, and distilled liquors and cordials. Since these vessels are perfectly vitrified, there is no need for any interior lining glaze.

Many of these jugs have the impressed marks of the Rhenish and Dutch companies who manufactured the beverages for which they were used. It was not until recently that I learned that little stoneware was manufactured in Holland, and that the Rhenish had manufactured stoneware containers for them for the past several centuries. Mustard pots of Rhenish salt-glazed stoneware are also rather common. Their colors vary from a gray-white to a medium brown, depending upon the iron content of the clay used for the vessels.

Quite a number of utilitarian vessels of salt-glazed Rhenish ware do appear in North America. Their importation was not limited to the nineteenth century, but we shall consider only that period in this discussion. Some of these German salt-glazed wares are very light in color. These almost white stoneware pots are usually products of the Westerwald area. They exhibit no interior glazes other than traces of salt. Their traditional forms have changed very little over the past two centuries, and rather wide-mouthed jars with a slightly ovoid form and bilateral open-loop handles are common. This handle form changed over a hundred years ago in North America but is being manufactured in Germany even today. Many have painted cobalt decoration or even incised decoration filled with cobalt slip. It is at times very difficult to be sure that these are not very early American vessels, but they can sometimes be distinguished by the fact that they are of a very white clay and usually much more carefully decorated, especially when incised. Dark-bodied, salt-glazed pots from areas other then the Westerwald area of Germany also appear, but are less common. These darker salt-glazed wares frequently show an interior glaze of the slip or loam type, deep brown in color. These may be confused at times with the pots made by Jacob Wingender and his sons after they emigrated from Germany to New Jersey about 1850. I think that any pieces being considered for classification as the product of the Wingenders should be carefully studied and compared with known pieces of their work. In the few pieces known to be their work that I have seen, the same decorative patterns are consistently used. A few pieces of brown slip or loam-glazed German utilitarian stoneware also show up from time to time in this country. Their main distinguishing characteristic is that they are of the same semi-ovoid form as the salt-glazed, wide-mouthed jars with the characteristic open loop handles on both sides near the upper rim. The glaze is a smooth, shiny brown that could be confused with American glazes of this same type.

A pair of salt-glazed German jugs. These were commonly used as shipping containers for wines, spirits, and mineral waters. Probably late 18th century or very early 19th century. $150

A pair of late 19th or early 20th century German salt-glazed jugs. The quart size bears an impressed mark of a mineral water. The larger, about two gallon capacity, has an impressed Dutch merchant's mark and a paper "Cognac" label. Although these containers frequently bear the names of Dutch merchants, they were manufactured in Germany. L-R: $95, $50

A salt-glazed German bottle which was flattened on all four sides after turning to resemble a "case" gin bottle. The impressed stamp indicates that it was made to hold mineral water. 19th century. *Courtesy of W.E. Grove.* $225

A pitcher, mustard jar, and small wide-mouthed jar of the vitreous light colored clay typical of the Westerwald area in Germany. There is no interior glaze on these salt-glazed pots. Cobalt banding and simple decoration are present on the pitcher and jar. The mustard has a Rotterdam merchant's name impressed. Late 19th or early 20th century. L-R: $125, $50, $65

A large pitcher of about one-gallon capacity and a storage jar of about one-half gallon capacity. Both are salt glazed with cobalt slip decoration. Interiors are glazed with a brown slip glaze. These pieces are probably late 19th century and are of German manufacture. L-R: $195, $175

FRENCH IMPORTS

French stonewares are uncommon in the United States. I have seen more of this type of ware unearthed in New Orleans than from any other early American city. Small French bottle forms have been found in Savannah, Georgia, and Charlestown, South Carolina. They undoubtedly occur in French areas of Canada. This form of stoneware characteristic of the areas producing stoneware in northern France was unglazed both inside and outside before about 1875. The many bottles that are seen in this form of stoneware have a characteristic, almost artistic, ovoid form with an elegant neck finished off with one or two accessory rings below the top lip. Many of these appear in New Orleans. They range in size from about half-pint to quart capacity, although one- and two-liter capacity sizes also occur in New Orleans with the same fancy neck finish and a full ovoid body form. These were used as containers, particularly for inks and oils.

The French unglazed stonewares have a rather typical dry and slightly rough surface. Sometimes faint toasting of ash from wood firing, as well as some color variation from flashing within the wood firing kiln, appears on the surface. The colors vary from a light gray with reddish flashing to a deep, ruddy gray color. The jugs seem more often to be dark, while the bottles are usually rather light in color. No true glaze deposit is visible on either interiors or exteriors of these pots.

After 1875 the Beauvais area began to use the salt glaze technique, and ink bottles of a form very like the British (a cylindrical body, small neck, and pouring spout in the lip), became common. Mustard jars are also common in this very thick, salt-glazed ware, usually a ruddy brown in color. The word "depose" impressed in the body of some of these bottles and jars means that they were manufactured for export.

Rarely are pieces of the very strange salt-glazed ware from the La Borne area of France seen. This ware is not covered by a thick deposit of salt; as a matter of fact, a typical salt glaze texture rarely appears upon these pots. The salting was accomplished by placing a tiny cup of salt on or between the pots as they were placed in the kiln. The resultant deposit is generally little more than enough to give an uneven toasted appearance to the body that is very little different from the unglazed stonewares. I do not believe that these wares were ever imported to North America in any quantity as utilitarian vessels. My own examples are twentieth-century pieces brought home by an American soldier. These late examples show a semi-opaque, white interior glaze.

A one-quart size ink bottle, individual ink, and mustard jar. The large bottle and the mustard jar bear French marks. They are of the heavy, dark, salt-glazed ware manufactured around Beauvais, France, during the last quarter of the 19th century and into the 20th century. L-R: $125, $95, $150

247

A storage jar with a simple overhanging lid of about one gallon size and a small porridger from the area of LaBourne, France. These pieces are very thinly salt glazed. The salt is placed in small cups within the kiln as it is loaded and the resultant glaze is thin and uneven. Both pieces have a semi-transparent, colorless interior glaze. These are late 19th to early 20th century. L-R: $100, $45

A pair of unglazed stoneware bottles. They are gray to brown in color with a dull surface and no glaze inside or out. These are small, having a capacity of one-half and one pint. Produced near Beauvais, France. Late 18th and early and mid 19th century. *Courtesy of W.E. Grove.* $100

One pint bottle and one quart jug of brownish unglazed stoneware. Both are ornately turned, but were probably shipping containers. French, early and mid 19th century. *Courtesy of W.E. Grove.* L-R: $40, $95

An ornately turned, flattened, one-quart jug of hard-burned unglazed stoneware. This piece is a ruddy brown in color. It is from the Beauvais area of France. Early and mid-nineteenth century. $90

248

ORIENTAL IMPORTS

One other part of the world in which stoneware was manufactured as a utilitarian ware has contributed to our ceramic melange as well. Oriental vessels turn up from the eighteenth century onward along the eastern coast of North America. Earlier oriental vessels may be seen from time to time in Mexico and California as a result of the Manila Galleon trade. A large amount of tableware was imported from China, particularly during the eighteenth and early nineteenth centuries. The utilitarian vessels came along as well, almost always as containers for the exotic foods for which Americans began to develop a taste. The major form of food import before the influx of Chinese immigrants into this country was preserved ginger. Jars which must have contained ginger preserved in heavy syrup appear in many early and mid-nineteenth port cities. These are usually of stoneware, most often with a transparent or white feldspathic glaze and blue decoration under the glaze. I have seen them in all of our early southern port cities and have purchased two in inland cities as well.

Most of the other Oriental containers were imported after Oriental immigrants became rather common in North America. These immigrants opened Chinese restaurants and also kept their own food preferances relatively unchanged from those of their homeland. This necessitated the importation of other forms of oriental foods and seasonings. The soy sauce container is one of the most common oriental stoneware containers found here. It is usually in a low fat form and has a central opening in the top as well as a small spout on one side of the shoulder. These containers, most often of about one-quart capacity, are found in most areas in which transplanted Chinese were living. The containers are seen in larger sizes, the equivalent of one-gallon capacity, appearing especially in the Pacific states. A very unique ovoid jar form, usually with a dark brown to black glaze and a mouth opening of about two inches or a little more in diameter and having capacities of from one pint to one quart, is fairly common. These were containers for various oriental pickles and preserves. The oriental distilled alcoholic beverage container was also commonly of stoneware. These bottles have no handles and a fully belly, tapering up toward a narrow neck with a flaring mouth ring. All of the above forms of utilitarian containers made in China, have most commonly a dark slip or loam glaze or a dark brownish glaze of the alkaline form made by the combination of wood ash with local clays. Very large globular jars, usually with the dark brown wood-ash glaze, are seen occasionally and were undoubtedly food containers as well. They vary from about four to eight-gallon capacities.

White porcelain bottles with a clear and colorless glaze and a rather typical cylindrical bottle form occasionally appear. These were frequently used to bottle Japanese saki, a form of rice wine.

None of these oriental stonewares have handles of the types seen on European and American vessels. If any handles at all are present, they are small loops near the top of the vessel used for the insertion of a cord with which to secure the lid and also with which to handle the vessel.

A Chinese stoneware preserved ginger jar which has underglaze blue decoration and a semi-opaque white glaze. This probably dates from the mid 19th century. The porcellanous bottle is Japanese and 20th century in period. This white clay bottle covered with a transparent glaze was used as a container for saki, Japanese rice wine.

Almost all other oriental ceramics imported for the daily use of the immigrants or for use in Chinese restaurants are made of porcelain. These are really tablewares and will not be discussed here. Ginger containers also appear in true porcelain with underglaze blue decoration. These are probably very late nineteenth century or twentieth century, as are most of the tablewares.

It is necessary for a person interested in American stonewares to have a little information about some of the common foreign vessels appearing in the same medium. Oriental vessels are generally quite different in form and may be easily distinguished, but European vessels are sometimes confusing, since they frequently employ glazes that are essentially the same glazes used by the American branch of the craft. Form and manner of marking and decoration are the two major differences in these obviously related pieces.

The groups discussed above are the main forms of foreign utilitarian stoneware that surface from time to time in this country. For the most part, they are easily distinguished from American wares, although in the past they have been confused at times. Detailed studies of American stonewares that have been made in the past few years have made the differences somewhat clearer.

A Chinese soy sauce container about one quart capacity. These jars are also seen in larger sizes. The glaze is a dark, brown, shiny, clay and wood ash type. Late 19th and 20th century period. $150

A jar of about two quart capacity and a bottle of one quart size. Both are covered by a thick, dark, brownish-black glaze, probably a natural clay glaze. The jar was used as a container for pickles and preserves while the bottle is the typical container for Chinese distilled liquor. Chinese, late 19th and 20th century. $275 ea.

Chapter 8
Destination and Destiny

SELLING THE POTTER'S WARES

THE LOCAL TRADE

The manner of distribution of North American pottery wares to their final destinations was essentially related to the size and production of the pottery. Most pots from small local shops were destined to be used within about a one hundred mile radius of the pottery. Intensive study has shown that this surely was true of the small shops operating during the second and third quarters of the nineteenth century in Texas. The pots were sold for household use in the surrounding local areas and the price was usually fixed by the gallon capacity, commonly ranging between five and ten cents a gallon retail. Special pots such as jugs marked with merchant's names cost about double the price of a plain jug.

Pots were always for sale at the pottery, but since some of these potteries were in rather remote areas, most of the ware was transported in small lots to be sold individually to the householders along a regular route or in larger lots to merchants in nearby towns. It was customary for some potteries to distribute the wares themselves. A wagon would be loaded with pottery stacked in straw after a kiln was unloaded. Often the potters themselves would drive the wagon. At times employees or family members would drive. Sometimes shops had one employee who helped with common work around the shop when there was nothing to transport, but who routinely drove the wagon and team both to pick up supplies and clay and to transport the wares to market. One month the haulers might go along a route southward from the pottery with the ware, the next

month westward, and so on. If any merchants had placed orders, these were delivered as soon as the orders were ready. Frequently there were drummers or haulers with their own wagons who purchased loads wholesale at the pottery and then distributed them to customers. If the potters did not provide their own transportation, this was the most common early method of distribution.

Although wagon and mule team were the most common method of transportation, a few potters did use a wagon and team of oxen. One story told to me in East Texas was that John Leopard had a team of oxen and a wagon that he took from Henderson, Texas, to Shreveport, Louisiana with loads of pottery during the 1860-1870 period. It took him seven days to go and return home from Shreveport, a distance of fewer than one hundred miles that now takes less than two hours to drive one way in a car.

Potters also sometimes traded pottery for farm products, then took the produce back to a small town and sold it to a local merchant. Eggs, watermelons, and corn were a few of the farm products traded for stonewares in East Texas in the early days of the twentieth century. This bartering was a common method of trade when transportation was limited or cash was difficult to obtain.

WATER TRANSPORT

The longest distances that utilitarian stonewares traveled during the early and mid-nineteenth century were undoubtedly when trade items were transported primarily by water. Ocean vessel transportation was common for foreign stonewares, but was also utilized within North

America. For example, stonewares were brought to southern Atlantic and Gulf of Mexico ports from the larger and more important centers in New York and New Jersey. Many fragments of northern stonewares, often with marks, have been found by excavators in the larger port cities of the South, such as Charleston, South Carolina, and Savannah, Georgia. An inkwell in perfect condition with the C. CROLIUS/MANUFACTURER/MANHATTAN WELLS, NEW YORK mark turned up in an excavation in New Orleans.

Barge transportation down the Ohio and Mississippi Rivers was a boon to the potters of western Pennsylvania, Ohio, and Kentucky. Today even very large pieces, up to twenty gallons in capacity, made by the Eagle Pottery or Hamilton and Jones of Greensboro, Pennsylvania, and marked for merchants in Kentucky are not uncommon. Not to be outdone, Kentucky, Ohio, Illinois, and Indiana potters along the rivers made pots marked for merchants from Vicksburg, Mississippi, to New Orleans. Many pieces of pottery with Kentucky potters' marks, such as I. THOMAS of Maysville, are found along the southernmost sections of the Mississippi River. Many other pieces found in this area (either marked for Louisiana merchants or without any marks at all) are of the same

dense, very vitreous, dark gray clay so characteristic of all of the Ohio River potteries. The rivers proved a boon as well to the early industrialized shops producing earthenwares such as yellow-ware and Rockingham ware in East Liverpool, Ohio. Their products were routinely barged to New Orleans.

Trade in the Gulf of Mexico is also not to be forgotten. New Orleans was a center of mercantile development. Imported tablewares as well as utilitarian stonewares reached that port either by ocean transportation or down the Mississippi River and were then loaded on smaller ocean-going vessels and taken to ports in the Gulf of Mexico such as Mobile, Alabama, and Galveston, Texas, during most of the nineteenth century. Undoubtedly other canals and navigable streams were used for transportation by barges and sloops throughout the populated areas of the United States before the railway system was well developed.

An alert little stag figurine which is 14 inches long and 12 inches tall. He is decorated in cobalt blue under a salt glaze. The teeth are indicated by tiny spots of white slip. Hand modeled. Unmarked, possibly Shenandoah Valley. Probably mid-nineteenth century. *Courtesy of Edwa Osborn. Photography- Herb and Dorothy McLaughlin.*

RES. & POTTERY OF F.J. KNAPP
AKRON, OHIO.

EXCELSIOR STONE WARE WORKS OF W.ᴹ SHENKEL & CO
AKRON, OHIO.

An engraving showing the F.J. Knapp Pottery in Summit County, Ohio about 1874. The wagon contains a load of Pottery. From "Combination Atlas Map of Summit County, Ohio" by Tackberry, Mead, and Moffett, Philadelphia, Pa. 1874. *Courtesy of The Western Reserve Historical Society.*

The Excelsior Stoneware Works of Wm. Shenkel & Co. at Akron, Ohio. From "Combination Atlas Map of Summit County, Ohio", 1874. *Courtesy of The Western Reserve Historical Society.*

A view of the Marshall Pottery, Marshall, Texas about 1903. Workers seated in front of the small crown type downdraft kiln at the center. The shop is on the left and stacks of ware stand behind the wagon at the right. *Courtesy of Wesley Ellis.*

A flat boat on the Monogahela River in Western Pennsylvania. Stoneware pots are stacked on their sides within the deck area and a few have been set on the rear of the boat. *Courtesy of the Department of Anthropology, California State College.*

RAILWAY TRANSPORT

The railway system was an important system of distribution for all manner of goods across the United States and was advantageous to many potteries, particularly the large industrialized shops of the middlewestern states. Stoneware was frequently shipped in boxcar loads during the last two decades of the nineteenth century and much of the twentieth century. The method of stacking a boxcar with three loads of ware for three different destinations was described to me by one old potter. Each end was filled with pottery packed in straw, wooden separations were put up, and the central portion of the car was then packed with the wares for the nearest destination. While most smaller shops probably only shipped within the state in which they were situated, the middlewestern potteries took over the westward trade and shipped vast amounts to the Great Plains and western states. By the 1890s the industrialized middlewestern potteries also began to intrude on areas that had, prior to that time, been supplied by many small shops, sending wares into Missouri, Arkansas, and Texas. Stoneware vessels of the last decades of the nineteenth century and the twentieth century marked by such large potteries as the Macomb Pottery of Macomb, Illinois, the Uhl Pottery of Evansville, Indiana, and the North Star and Redwing Potteries of Redwing, Minnesota, are commonly seen in all of the western states as well as in Missouri, Arkansas, and Texas.

HIGHWAY TRANSPORT

During the second quarter of the twentieth century, trucks began to replace the mule and wagon, and larger loads could be transported around local regions. This was the common method of local distribution after 1930, and remains the method of general distribution presently used by many small art potteries. The one large pottery that now manufactures a limited amount of utilitarian stoneware and tons of flower pots, the Marshall Pottery of Marshall, Texas, also distributes its wares by truck.

THE COLLECTOR'S ROUTE

Although few pieces of old stoneware wandered far from their place of origin unless shipped by water during the nineteenth century, some of the remaining pieces of old stoneware which turn up for sale in their former local area are now transported from "Maine to California" and destinations in between by antique dealers. One may never guess where an old piece will turn up now because of this mixing and long distance transportation. Such was not the primary destination of the vessels, but it has become their secondary destination as they have become collectable antiques.

A salt-glazed preserve jar of about one-gallon capacity and 10-1/2 inches tall. It is incised with the cartoon figure of a man holding a bottle in his left hand as though to put it to his mouth. The entire figure is incised and his early nineteenth century clothing is painted in with cobalt blue. On the opposite side and inscribed legend reads: "There is a man in our land,/Upon his feet he cannot stand/The reason why you all know/He drinks too much afore he'll go." Probably New York, first half of the nineteenth century. *Courtesy of Edwa Osborn. Photography: Herb & Dorothy McLaughlin.* $10,000

A gray salt-glazed pitcher with an interior Albany type slip glaze. A bold floral design was trailed on the mid-front in cobalt slip. The stamp also appears to have been dipped in cobalt slip to color its impression: "N. CLARK & CO./ ROCHESTER, N.Y." Height: 11 inches. *Courtesy of Mr. and Mrs. Ralph Strong. Photographer: William G. Frank, Rochester Museum and Science Center.* $1200-1400

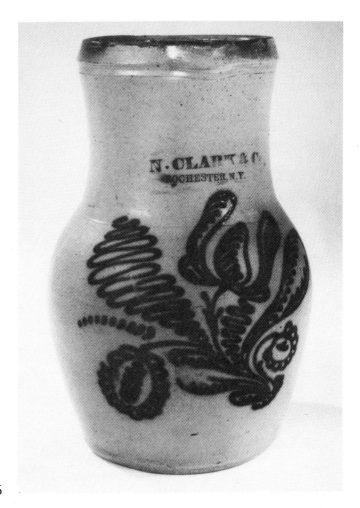

A wonderfully ornate presentation jug covered with applied hand-modeled floral designs, press-molded clasped hands, and six impressed stars and other stamped designs. It reads "TO JOSIAH DEFENBAUGH/E. HALL/U.S.A.-1858." Cobalt was trailed to inscribe the "to" and "1858" while the rest of the words are formed by impressed letters. Cobalt was also used to enhance the applied decoration. It even has its own decorated stoneware stopper. Made by E. Hall, Ohio. Ht. with stopper 12-1/8 inches. *Courtesy of Zanesville Art Center.* $9500-10,500

This large pitcher stands 10-1/2 inches tall and has a capacity of about one gallon. Around the belly of the pot it has underglaze brown slip painted in the form of stems and leaves enhanced by outlining and veining trailed in white slip. A small half-circle of brown scalloped with white is also painted under the spout. Pale yellowish alkaline glaze inside and out. Attributed to Collin Rhodes, Edgefield, S.C. about 1850. *Courtesy of the Ferrel Collection. Photographer: David Rasberry.* $1500

A large storage jar of about eight gallon capacity. It is covered inside and out with a yellowish olive green alkaline glaze. A band of white slip decoration extends around the shoulder and under each handle. Impressed: "CHANDLER/MAKER." Thomas Chandler, Edgefield, S.C. c. 1850. $4200

A four-gallon wide-mouthed jar with a dark brown Albany type slip glaze inside and over the upper exterior. The lower exterior is glazed in a light buff, possibly a Bristol type of glaze. The stamped mark is most interesting with its use of a British arms type mark over the rectangle enclosing the potter's mark. "E. SWASEY & CO./ PORTLAND, ME./U.S.A." *Courtesy of M. Lelyn Branin.*

257

A small whistle in the form of a jug (3 inches tall) and a
hand-formed "gourd" whistle and marbles. All unglazed.
Meyer Pottery, Bexar County, Texas c. 1930-1940.
Courtesy of Joann G. Wells. L-R: $375, $675

A miniature churn, three inches tall, glazed in a brown
Albany type slip. A very tiny jug 7/16 inch tall and also
glazed in brown slip. The little sewer pipe dog of a ruddy
color with a salt glaze, probably from Ohio. All pieces are
late 19th century or early 20th century. L-R: $175, $225,
$1200

DECLINE OF THE POTTER'S CRAFT

THE LOSS OF TRADE

The utilitarian potter's craft was destined, as were all of the handcrafts of the nineteenth century, to fade into a slow demise in the twentieth century. The cultural changes that have taken place during the twentieth century in North America have made the need for household articles common to the material culture of the nineteenth century obsolete. Modern America has become a highly industrialized society. Various inexpensive, industrially produced vessels of metal, glass, and plastic have taken the place of stoneware vessels for ordinary kitchen use. Methods of preservation of food have changed and, although some foods are still canned in modern glass jars, most foods which were once difficult to preserve (such as meats, butter, and vegetables) are now frozen in home freezers. These conserve them well for much longer periods. Families are generally smaller and there is not the need for large containers of preserved foods.

The household that keeps a cow for its own use or kills its own hogs each winter is now rare rather than common. Thus the need for one- and two-gallon preserve jars, five-gallon lard jars, five- to ten-gallon kraut and pickle jars, and even churns, milk bowls, and butter pots has vanished with the primary agrarian culture of the nineteenth and early twentieth centuries in North America.

There are still potters surviving in this country, but most are a new breed spawned from the renaissance of interest in handcrafts that has taken place in the United States during the last few decades. These are the artist or studio potters who create hand-formed pottery in earthenware, stoneware, and porcelain. Their products, although they may be wheel thrown, are basically decorative wares even though some, such as pitchers, bowls, or casseroles, may have some utilitarian purpose. They are, however, not usually produced in great numbers in identical form and are generally small in size. Most have added decorative touches such as unusual forms, painted, incised, and applied decoration, and decorative glazes.

A number of potters who originally were trained in a more or less utilitarian production, some being of old pottery making families, have had to modify their products in the last twenty years or so to fit into the studio pottery tradition in order to be able to continue their means of livelihood.

The last quarter of the nineteenth century was the period of the flowering of the utilitarian stoneware pottery craft in America. With the advent of the twentieth century industrially produced vessels, ceramic as well as glass and metal, were making inroads on the business of the small pottery shops. There was also a lack of interest of the younger men in training for traditional crafts as their life work. After World War I these young men had seen the world and were much more interested in becoming qualified to fit into the newer types of work available. At that time the remuneration which a craftsman might expect to receive from the sale of his product was hardly enough to buy food for a family. The wave of the great depression drowned most of the small shops that had managed to survive up until that period.

A few potteries survived the depression as well as the change toward industrialization by modifying their products. One pottery, the Meyer Pottery of Atascosa, Texas, made just about any form that anyone asked for. They made jiggered flower pots and produced glazed vases and jars for florist's use, tried tablewares such as plates, low modern-looking salad bowls, mugs with club or organization names upon them, and all manner of souvenier ware. The souvenir product was not glazed but painted with oil paint. Although much of their ware was still wheel thrown, press molds became common for certain forms. Some of the souvenir ware was only dipped into multi-colored swirled paint to give a marbled appearance, while other pieces were painted with intricate desert and bluebonnet scenes. This struggle for survival took place in many, many small pottery shops at that period and most succumbed. They could not compete with the mechanically pressed and slip cast products which the industrialized potteries were producing in America at low prices or with the inexpensive ceramic articles being imported, particularly from Mexico and the Orient.

A floral jardiniere (no drain hole) with a hand-ruffled or fluted edge. Deep olive green alkaline glaze inside and out. Lanier Meaders, Cleveland, Ga. c. 1970. $175

A set of rimless mixing bowls with a yellowish-green Leon slip glaze. Made at the Meyer Pottery, Bexar County, Texas probably between 1930 and 1940 in an attempt to imitate modern forms. Three-quart, two-quart, and one-quart capacities. Prices given are from Large to Small. $450, $425, $275

A tall vaselike form which was probably made expressly as a decorative piece. It is salt-glazed on the exterior only and decorated with incised double curved lines and cobalt bands and spots. Height: 18-1/2 inches. Impressed: "J.B. OWEN" in a circle. c. 1930. $1200

Showing a move toward studio pottery types, a Mexican Sombrero of yellowish glaze stoneware. Impressed: "SAN ANTONIO POTTERY, SAN ANTONIO." c. 1930. $475

Although pieces were decorated with a creamy white slip over Albany slip glaze around Des Moines, Iowa and Ripley, Illinois, this piece came from central Pennsylvania. The flowery manner of decoration here does not resemble that of the western pots and so this piece remains an enigma. It appears mid to late 19th century, but may have been a plain jug decorated and refired recently. $500

MODERN SURVIVALS

During the 1950s the few surviving pottery shops stopped the production of almost all of their basically utilitarian products because there was no longer a market for such wares. Many amplified their essentially decorative forms and became studio potteries. This change indicated the nearly complete extinction of the craft of utilitarian stoneware production in this country.

At the present time the Marshall Pottery continues to produce a hand-thrown line of two forms of pitchers in three sizes and five-gallon churns, some of which are modified into water coolers. A few other small items are wheel made, such as mugs and small jars that are decorated with hand-painted cobalt designs. These vessels are turned by eight professional potters, but the preparation, glazing, and firing of these pots is done in an industrial setting along with the pressed stoneware and earthenware vessels produced in large amounts at this plant. The hand thrown wares have become extremely popular during the past ten or fifteen years, more as decorative items than necessary household vessels.

During recent years two or three other potteries have been established for the production of imitations of old utilitarian stonewares with blue decoration. These are sold at relatively high prices, and the collector should beware of these as well as fakes produced by redecoration and refiring of old pots. This "faked" decoration will always be over the glaze, never under or within, and it can usually be detected by a sharp eye.

The craft of the utilitarian potter is hanging to life by a mere thread, which will soon break. Most of the old pots have also met their destiny, having been used, broken, and discarded.

Those old pots that do remain in fair condition have now a second destiny-to be treasured, admired, and preserved. Attics, cellars, barns, and even trash heaps have been scrounged for surviving pieces of early ware. The most valuable are the oldest pieces and those with the most striking decoration, but there are collectors for

The remains of John Hunt's groundhog kiln in Rusk County, Texas. Photograph about 1976.

every type. Some collect by region of manufacture, others by the form of the decoration, a few according to vessel form, and many for the decorative appeal of these vessels placed about in their homes. The interest in old pots has increased steadily over the past fifteen to twenty years.

This renewed interest inspires the present owners to look at the pots much more thoroughly and to ask questions about the reasons for various forms, marks, defects, and colors. It is to enhance the understanding of the processes involved in the manufacture of these vessels that this book has been written.

As a rank amateur in the craft of pottery, I have learned to understand the tremendous adversities which were overcome daily and to admire the skill which was necessary for the production of this ware by the almost forgotten utilitarian stoneware potters of North America. This study of the history and technology of their vanishing craft will, hopefully, give deeper insight to others who are admirers and students of American utilitarian stonewares.

A scattering of sherds at the site of the Wilson-Durham Pottery in Guadalupe County, Texas. The pottery ceased operation about 1903. Photograph c. 1970.

Some General Keys
for Stoneware Identification

Although these notes will cover the identification of many pieces of American stoneware, there are exceptions to each. The use of three different characteristics of each piece will help to fit them into most general groups. These are body, form, and glaze.

The Body Clay

1. This is usually rather coarse in texture with small particles of iron, mica, and other impurities visible within the clay. These particles, especially those of iron, produce speckling in the fired body, especially when it has been fired in reduction.

2. The color of the body clay may be from almost white to a dark gray or brown. Many bodies in the brown range will have a terra-cotta color which confuses this red-bodied stoneware with red-bodied earthenware at times.

3. The upper rims and bottoms of most utilitarian stoneware are left unglazed or wiped free of glaze and the body clay may be seen in these areas.

4. American stoneware is theoretically vitrified. Most pieces of old stoneware, unless badly cracked, will give off a relatively high tone when tapped with a piece of metal. There are many pieces which are only partially vitrified, but they have a higher tone than most earthenware.

The Form

Most of the main vessel forms such as jugs, jars, churns, and bowls show some temporal change during the nineteenth century. The odd pieces and pitchers and chamber pots show little change.

1. The very full-bellied ovoid form is generally representative of the period from the beginning of the American manufacture of stoneware in the late eighteenth century to about 1860. This form persists later in the Southern Highlands.

2. The very sloping shouldered form in jugs which gives them a bell shape is sometimes seen in early jugs of sizes under three gallons, especially in the deep South.

3. A straight-sided cylindrical form in jars and jugs is usually indicative of a date after 1860, more often after 1870.

4. The "shouldered form" of jug or jar with a tooled flat ledge at the shoulder is indicative of a late date, after 1890.

5. The very straight-sided, cylindrical form of the open or wide-mouthed jar is common, but almost always dates after 1860, usually after 1870.

The Glaze

1. Salt-glazed vessels generally date from the period prior to the twentieth century. The absence of a slip-glazed interior usually indicates manufacture prior to 1860 or in a remote area. The major exceptions to this statement are the wares produced in the central North Carolina area around Seagrove where salt-glazing was commonly done until about 1925 or 1930.

2. Alkaline glazed vessels almost always have the same glaze inside and outside of

the vessels. They are always from the deep southern states. They date before 1900 in most instances, but the use of this glaze continued well into the twentieth century in small, remote potteries in Alabama, Georgia, and North Carolina.

3. Vessels glazed inside and out with slip or natural clay glazes are most commonly after 1875 in date, and this form of glaze was popular in many small potteries, especially in the deep South, until about 1940.

4. A heavy salt deposit on top of a slip glaze will bleach its color and mimic an alkaline form of glaze. A normal interior or section of the exterior will indicate what happened. No normal salt texture develops when the salt and slip glazes melt together.

5. The white form of the Bristol glaze became popular in the industrialized potteries of the North and Middlewest by about 1890. After 1900 it became popular in most industrialized potteries all over the country. The persistence of the use of other forms of glaze was mainly in small potteries in rather remote areas.

6. Combinations of a white Bristol form of glaze and an Albany type slip glaze are common until about 1915. After that most vessels had a Bristol glaze both inside and out.

A Test for Lead in a Glaze:

This simple test may be helpful to some persons who have difficulty separating the dark brown to black forms of lead glaze used upon some utilitarian earthenware vessels from those vessels fired to stoneware temperatures and using a form of dark brown to black Albany type slip glaze. This slip glaze does not contain lead.

Solutions needed:
a. Household vinegar or 5% acetic acid
b. A saturated solution of potassium iodide---potassium iodide crystals may be dissolved in distilled water--20 gm. in 20 cc. H_2O. (either available at a pharmacy).
c. A dilute solution of hydrofluoric acid (available as "Whisk-Away" rust remover for clothing at most groceries).

Method: Mix equal parts of acetic acid and potassium iodide solution (1 c.c. each). Apply one large drop of this mixture to the glaze to be tested. On top of this place one drop of the hydrofluoric acid. Within five minutes, often within only one, a yellow-orange precipitate will appear within the drop if lead is present in the glaze. This test has been modified from that presented in "Eighteenth Century English Porcelain" by George Savage, London, 1964 (pp. 54 and 55). It may also be used to test for soft or lead-containing porcelain glazes. This type of glaze was characteristic of early soft-paste forms of porcelain and is sometimes even now used over a vitrified porcelain body.

Glossary
of Ceramic Terms

AGGLUTINATION: To unite by adhesion. Some glazes, especially wood ash glazes, tend to agglutinate as they melt.

ALBANY CLAY: A natural alluvial clay found along the Hudson River in New York State. It forms a glaze at stoneware temperatures and was widely used in the United States. The other commercially mined slip clays, especially those from Ripley, Michigan, and Elkhart, Indiana, are so nearly like this after firing that most dark brown and black slip-clay glazes are called "Albany type" unless known to be a specific clay.

BARTMANN: Rhenish salt-glazed jugs with an applied relief of a bearded face on the front of the neck; generally sixteenth and seventeenth century pieces.

BELLARMINE: The British name applied to sixteenth and seventeenth century Rhenish "Bartmann" jugs.

BLISTERING: The development of blisters in a glaze caused by unvented gasses trapped within the glaze as it melts. If the blisters burst and melt down, small pinholes are left in the glaze.

BLOATING: The undesirable blistering within the body caused by trapped gases. In stoneware this usually happens if the pot is heated above the vitrification point.

BODY CLAY: The clay from which the body of a pot is formed.

BOLT: A colloquial term for the long, flattened, piece of clay, usually twenty or more pounds in weight, which is formed of damp clay as it comes from the pug mill. Clay is stored for wheel throwing in this form.

BRICK CLAY: Clay suitable for making ordinary bricks, usually firing pink to red at earthenware temperatures.

BRISTOL GLAZE: A stoneware glaze developed in England during the nineteenth century and used most extensively in North America during the twentieth century. It was the first glaze made from ceramic chemicals used for utilitarian stoneware.

CHINA CLAY: The purest white clay, Kaolin. Vitrifying at high temperatures, it is used in porcelain body pastes.

COCKSPUR or SPURS: Small pointed pieces of kiln furniture used to hold glazed wares off of a shelf; usually used for earthenware. Some spurs are single points while others, known also as stilts, have three raised ends.

COGGLE: A small wheel of wood or metal turned on an axle and used to make decorative impressions in soft clay. It is essentially the same as a roulette wheel, but coggled designs are usually thought of as those made only by a small-toothed or cogged wheel.

CRACKLE: Purposeful cracking of a glaze for decorative or artistic appeal.

CRAWLING: A glaze defect characterized by agglutination and beading up of the glaze, leaving a bare patch of body.

This is so common in ash glazes that it is not considered serious in that glaze.

CRAZE: Cracking of a glaze after use; not purposeful, as in crackle.

DRAWTRIAL: A small piece composed of the same ceramic body and glaze currently being fired in a kiln. These pieces are placed so that they may be drawn out of the kiln through a spy hole to test the maturation of both glaze and body.

DUNTS: Cracks formed in pottery during firing and cooling; usually caused by stress in the formation of the pot or expansion and contraction of the pot or glaze.

EARTHENWARE: Pottery made of a porous body and usually fired below 1100 C; covered at times with a soft glaze.

FELDSPAR: A group of natural minerals which are used as a flux in the body and a major ingredient in the glaze of high temperature ceramics, both stoneware and porcelain. They have a high content of alkaline earths.

FERRUGINOUS: Containing red iron oxide.

FIRECLAY: A type of clay that needs high temperatures to mature. Firebrick, drainage pipes, sanitary wares, and stone-wares are made from such clays.

FLASHING: The interesting or annoying color variations produced when volatile substances in the kiln settle on areas during firing.

FLUX: An oxide which promotes ceramic fusion. Stoneware fluxes are usually alkaline earths such as calcium, barium, sodium, potassium, and magnesium oxides.

FLY-ASH: Fine ash that circulates in the kiln and settles on pots to give glaze variations. It occurs mainly in wood firing.

FROG-SKIN GLAZE: A greenish yellow stoneware glaze used by potters in North Carolina. It may be produced by throwing a small amount of salt into a hot kiln of Albany-type slip-glazed ware.

GREEN WARE: This term is used to describe unfired vessels; the pots have been formed, and are dry enough to fire.

GLAZE: A layer of glass fused into place on a pottery body.

JIGGER or JIGGER MACHINE: A machine in which soft clay is formed in a spinning mold. A template forms the second contour as the machine turns. The jigger forms shallow vessels such as plates over a mold, while the template cuts the base or exterior. This term is also used for "jollying" by most American utilitiarian potters.

JOLLY: This is the opposite of the jigger. The mold is deep and forms the exterior of jars and large bowls, while a template is used on the interior contour.

JUG SAGGER: A piece of kiln furniture made to fit over the mouth, handle, and shoulder of a jug in the kiln. It is really a stacking piece.

KAOLIN: The Chinese name for china clay, the finest white, high temperature clay.

KILN: A structure built to conserve heat. A pottery kiln is used to fire pottery objects.

KILN FURNITURE: Movable furnishings used in stacking pottery in a kiln; includes shelves, supports, stacking pieces, and all forms of separators.

LEATHER HARD: The state of drying of formed, unburned pots in which they are of the firmness of leather. An excellent stage for the application of certain types of decoration and glazing.

MOLD: A form consisting of one, two, or several parts. It is generally made of plaster of paris for pottery, and plastic clay or slip are placed inside the mold. The plaster absorbs water from the clay and a soft pot or portion of a pot able to hold its own shape may be removed from the mold as soon as the pot is stiff.

PIN HOLES: Tiny holes remaining in a very viscous glaze even after the gasses have escaped and the blisters smoothed out. A common defect of Bristol glazes.

PEELING: Also called "shelling" or "flaking." The glaze peels off of the clay of the body as it dries or fires because of unequal shrinkage and poor bonding. Glaze may also be peeled off by the action of direct flames early in firing, before the glaze has begun to melt.

PIPE CLAY: A fine white clay vitrifying at a fairly low temperature; used for forming white clay tobacco pipes.

PLASTIC CLAY: Clay in a state of moisture in which it can be formed by moderate pressure and retain that form without collapse.

POP-OUT: The condition produced when small pieces of the body pop out and off during the firing process. One of the most frequent causes of this problem is granules of limestone within the clay which expand during heating.

PORCELAIN: A special type of stoneware that is pure white, completely vitrified, and sometimes translucent.

POTTER'S CLAY: Clay for making pottery; especially a pure clay, containing little iron, that may be used to make stonewares.

PRESS MOLDING: Forming pots or decorative objects by pressing plastic clay into or over absorbent plaster molds.

PUG MILL: A machine for mixing and compressing plastic clay. A central shaft with blades in a spiral pattern is rotated within a cylinder. The clay must have been mixed with water to be of proper consistency before it is placed in the mill. The shaft may be turned by horse, water, or electric power.

RAW: The name for the state of clay which has not been burned.

REFRACTORY: Resistant to high temperatures.

ROULETTE WHEEL: A small rolling wheel, usually of wood, fixed on an axle with a handle. The wheel itself is carved with a design pattern which is impressed into the clay as it is rolled along.

SAGGER: A refractory clay box inside of which pots may be protected during firing. Salt glaze saggers have holes cut in them to allow the vapor to react with the pot and form a glaze.

SALT GLAZE: A stoneware glaze derived from common table salt. The firing temperature must be high enough for the silica in the clay to combine with volatile sodium to form the glaze.

SGRAFFITO or SCRAFFITO: Scratched or incised decoration on a pot. This is most effective when the incising is done through a colored slip. In stoneware, Albany slip is frequently incised to reveal the light body of the pot.

SHIVER: The process in which glaze is compressed and splits off of a stoneware pot in long slivers. This is caused by unequal shrinkage of pot and glaze -- the pot contracts more than the glaze and forces it to split and fall off.

SLIP: A homogenous mixture of clay and water.

SLIP CASTING: The formation of a pottery object by using a watery suspension of clay poured into an absorbent mold, usually made of plaster of paris.

267

SLIP CUP or SLIP TRAILER: A small cup made of clay with an opening at the top and a very small opening at one side of the base. The small opening was fitted with a goose quill and the cup used to trail colored slips over pots for decoration.

SLIP GLAZE: A mixture of natural clay and water that is used as a glaze. These clays will melt into a glaze at high temperatures without any added ingredients.

SLUMP: To sag or become distorted in form; a defect found in vessels fired at too high temperature.

SPALL: To chip or crumble. This happens after use in stoneware pots that have not vitrified well in firing.

SPONGE DECORATION: A type of decoration produced by the application of a sponge dipped in colored slip or glaze, usually in an irregular pattern over the body of a pot.

STONEWARE: A hard, strong, vitrified pottery ware usually fired above $1200^{\circ}C$. This type of ware may be covered with a hard glaze when desired.

SPRIGGING: The process of adding more clay to the surface of a pot. This may be hand-formed or molded clay and of the same or different clay from that of the pot.

STACKER: A colloquial term for a jug separator and also for a jug with a tooled shoulder upon which a jar rim could rest in kiln stacking.

THROWER: A person who forms pots upon a quickly rotating wheel using his hands, simple tools, and water as a lubricant.

"TIGER" GLAZE: An agglutinated, dark brown glaze, the clumps being separated by light margins of transparent, colorless salt glaze. It was produced by salt glazing over a refractory, iron-containing slip. Produced by Rhenish potters in the sixteenth and seventeenth centuries.

TOPPING: A colloquial expression for the formation of large jars, jugs, and churns by throwing a base section and a top section separately, then adding the top section to the base to form a large pot.

TURNER: A person who trims a pot either upon a potter's wheel or lathe. This term is very often used somewhat colloquially for "thrower."

VITRIFICATION: A process occuring in pottery at high temperatures which causes the silica and other ingredients in clay to melt into a glassy mixture without deformation of form.

WHEEL: A rotating disc on which pots are formed from a ball of soft clay; the wheel may be powered by hand, foot, or mechanical means.

WHITING: Chalk or calcium carbonate prepared as a fine powder.

An Annotated Bibliography
for American Stonewares

This bibliography has been prepared in place of a checklist of potters, since I feel that a complete checklist of American stoneware and earthenware potteries cannot yet be prepared. A vast amount of research has been done in some areas, while nothing at all has been investigated in others. The pattern has been such over the past few years that we may look forward to more and more publications on potteries of a single state or even a section of one state. The research done for these publications will give us a much more correct and in-depth list of the potters working in these areas. After a number of these are in print, a combination of their checklists might furnish an adequate amount of information to enable compilation of a proper checklist of American potters and potteries.

Almost all of the publications listed below are full length books or catalogs. Many short articles on potteries have appeared in various antique magazine or newspaperlike publications over the past few years, and they may be found by the interested reader using the indices of these publications. Most of these articles are more specific studies of one pottery that can be found listed in any major publications on the area. There have also been a few publications in archeological journals or reports of excavation. Such articles are difficult for an average person to locate and have, therefore, not been included.

The list is arranged by region to facilitate its use.

UNITED STATES
GENERAL

Barber, Edwin Atlee. *The Pottery and Porcelain of the United States and Marks of American Potters.* 3rd edition, revised and enlarged. New York, New York: J and J Publishing, 1976.
This book, originally written in 1893, has information not included in some of the other general books. The checklist is most helpful for tablewares, not stonewares.

Counts, Charles. *Common Clay.* Atlanta, Georgia: Droke House/Hallux, 1971.
A study of several present day traditional potters in the deep South.

Guilland, Harold F. *Early American Folk Pottery.* Philadelphia, Pa.: Chilton Book Co., 1971.
A nice introduction, but the reproductions from the American Index of Design are arranged so that they are very difficult to use for reference.

Ketchum, William C., Jr. *The Pottery and Porcelain Collector's Handbook.* New York, New York: Funk and Wagnall, 1971.
Although this book has an overview of American stonewares, earthenwares, and tablewares, it is only an overview with little in-depth information. The checklist is useful, but not dependable and much too brief.

Northeast Historical Archeology, Vol. 6, Nos. 1 and 2, Spring, 1977. Papers from the Rochester Conference on Ceramics in America.

Myers, Susan. *A Survey of Traditional Pottery Manufacture in the Mid-Atlantic and Northeastern United States.*

Mitchell, James R. *Industrial Pottery of the United States.* Barka, Norman and Sheridan, Chris. *The Yorktown Pottery Industry, Yorktown, Va.*

Michael, Ronald L. *Stoneware from Fayette, Greene, and Washington Counties. Pennsylvania.*

Greer, Georgeanna H. *Groundhog Kilns.*

Springsted, Brenda Lockhart. *Ringoes: An Eighteenth-Century Pottery Site [N.J.].*

Quimby, Ian M.G. (editor). *Ceramics in America.* Winterthur Conference Report, 1972. Charlottesville, Va.: University Press of Virginia, 1973.

Contains information on the early potteries at Yorktown, Virginia; Salem, North Carolina; and Cheesequake, New Jersey. Stonewares and earthenwares from these sites are discussed.

Ramsey, John. *American Potters and Pottery.* Clinton, Mass.: Hale, Cushman, and Flint, 1939.
Still the standard book for information on American potteries. The marks section is excellent, but not extensive. The checklist is useful, but not always correct, especially for the southern states.

Schwartz, Marvin D. *Collector's Guide to Antique American Ceramics.* Garden City, N.Y.: Doubleday & Co., 1969.

Smith, Elmer L. and Bradford L. Rauschenberg, *Pottery, A Utilitarian Folk Craft.* Lebanon, Pa.: Applied Arts Publishers, 1972.
A short book, but it does show many pieces of stoneware and earthenware not appearing in other publications. Stress is on northeastern wares.

Smith, Joseph J. *Regional Aspects of American Folk Pottery.* The Historical Society of York County, catalogue of a show May to October 1979. York, Pennsylvania: 1979.
A small catalogue presenting various pots, mainly from the eastern United States, both earthenware and stoneware are included.

Smithsonian Institution, the National Museum of History and Technology.

The John Paul Remensnyder Collection of American Stoneware, catalogue of a show November 1978-November 1979. Washington, D.C.: Smithsonian Institution, 1979.
Superb stoneware pieces from the northeastern United States are discussed and some are presented in photographs in this short show catalogue.

Spargo, John. *Early American Pottery and China.* Rutland, Vt: Charles E. Tuttle, 1974.
General discussion of American china manufacture as well as earthenware and stoneware. Limited in scope, stressing manufacture in the northeastern and Atlantic states. Originally written in 1926. Very little was changed for the 1974 edition.

Stradling, Diana, and J. Garrison, (editors). *The Art of the Potter.* Redware and Stoneware. Articles from The Magazine Antiques. New York, N.Y.: Main Street, Universe Books, 1977.
Articles selected from *The Magazine Antiques* between 1922 and 1974 which discuss American utilitarian earthenwares and stonewares.

Webster, Donald Blake. *Decorated Stoneware Pottery of North America.*
Rutland, Vt.: Chas. E. Tuttle, 1971.
A discussion of American stonewares with emphasis on the various forms of decoration.

LOCAL

GEORGIA

Burrison, John A. *Georgia Jug Makers: A History of Southern Folk Pottery.* PhD Dissertation. Univ. of Pennsylvania, 1973.
A very intensive history and study of the potters of Georgia. In-depth checklist included.

Burrison, John A. *The Meaders Family of Mossy Creek.* Catalogue of a show. Atlanta, Ga.: Georgia State University, 1976.
A show catalogue presenting an intensive study of the Meaders family potters.

ILLINOIS

Denker, Ellen Paul. *Forever Getting Up Something New: The Kirkpatrick's Pottery at Anna, Illinois.* Dissertation for M.A. degree. Univ. of Deleware, 1978.
A thorough study of the Kirkpatrick brothers who finally settled in Anna, Illinois. They were ingenious potters.

Madden, Betty I. *Arts, Crafts, and Architecture in Early Illinois.* Urbana, Ill.: University of Illinois Press, 1974. Chapter 15 "Jug Towns," pp. 181-194.
The chapter on "Jug Towns" of Illinois contains the best general information on early earthenware and stoneware potteries in that state. A brief checklist is also included.

Meuginoi, Elinor. *Old Sleepy Eye.* Delos L. Hill and Ozella I. Hill. Tulsa, Oklahoma: The Printing Press, 1973.
The advertising used by "Sleepy Eye" Milling Company for their flour, including ceramic items made by the Western Stoneware Company, Monmouth, Ill.

INDIANA

Loar, Peggy A. *Indiana Stoneware.* Indianapolis Museum of Art. Catalogue of an exhibit April - May, 1974. Speedway Press, Inc., Indianapolis, Indiana, 1974.
A catalog of a show presented in 1974 with some history of the potteries and a short checklist. All that is now available on Indiana stonewares and earthenwares.

MICHIGAN

Dewhurst, C. Kurt and Marsha Mac Dowell. *Cast in Clay: The Folk Pottery of Grand Ledge, Michigan.* Lansing, Michigan: The Museum, Michigan State University Folk Culture Series, Vol. I, No. 2, Michigan State University.
A show catalog presenting a history of the Grand Ledge Sewer Pipe industry and a large number of whimseys made by the workmen.

MINNESOTA

Viel, Lyndon C. *The Clay Giants, The Stoneware of Redwing, Goodhue County, Minnesota.* Des Moines, Iowa: Wallace-Homestead Book Co., 1977.
An excellent study of the large potteries of Redwing, Minnesota. They supplied stonewares to a large area of the country during the very late nineteenth and early twentieth centuries.

MISSISSIPPI

Mississippi State Historical Museum. *Made by Hand.* Catalogue of a show January-May 1980. Mississippi Dept. of Archives and History, Jackson, Miss. 1980.

Greer, Georgeanna H., "The Folk Pottery of Mississippi," pp. 45-54.
The only information so far published Mississippi potteries. All of the information was derived from library sources and no field work has been done.

MISSOURI

Van Ravensway, Charles. *The Arts and Architecture of German Settlements in Missouri.* Columbia, Mo.: University of Missouri, 1977. Chapter 21 - "Pottery," pp. 459-482.
The chapter on pottery wares of the area shows that considerable research has been done and is an excellent reference. Unfortunately it does not consider the potteries in other areas of Missouri.

NEW ENGLAND

Barret, Richard Carter. *Bennington Pottery and Porcelain.* New York, New York: Bonaza Books, 1958.
A study of the products of both the stoneware and decorative ware potteries of Bennington. Many photographs are included.

Branin, M. Lelyn. *The Early Potters and Potteries of Maine.* Middletwon, Ct.: Wesleyan University Press, 1978.
An in-depth history of the stoneware and earthenware potteries of Maine. Excellent checklist and other information in appendices.

Osgood, Cornelius. *The Jug and Related Stoneware of Bennington.* Rutland, Vt.: Charles E. Tuttle, 1971.
An exceedingly complete study of the stonewares produced at the Norton family potteries in Bennington, Vt.

Pappas, Joan and Harold Kendell. *Hampshire Pottery.* Manchester, Vt.: Foreward's Color Productions, Inc., 1971.
A brief color plate presentation of the wares of this pottery. Although some early stonewares are pictured, the emphasis is on products of the art pottery era.

Spargo, John. *The Potters and Potteries of Bennington.* Southampton L.I., N.Y.: Cracker Barrel Press, reprint of 1926 edition.
An intense study of the Bennington potteries. Much of the book is devoted to the fancy wares of the Fenton pottery. All of the Norton stoneware marks are listed with dates.

Watkins, Lura Woodside. *Early New England Potters and Their Wares.* Archon Books, 1968. Reprint of 1st edition, 1950.
It is the recognized source for such information and has an excellent checklist. Earthenware and stoneware are discussed.

Watkins, Lura Woodside. *Early New England Pottery.* Sturbridge, Mass.: Old Sturbridge Village, 2nd printing, 1966.
A short summary of the work of the early potters in New England.

NEW JERSEY

New Jersey State Museum. *New Jersey Pottery to 1840.* Catalogue of a show at the Museum, Trenton, March to May, 1972.
Although this is a show catalogue, a great deal of the informatiion presented here is not to be found in any other reference.

Monmouth County Historical Association. *New Jersey Stoneware.* Catalogue of an exhibit May - June, 1955. Freehold, N.J.: Transcript Printing House, 1955.
An early show catalogue with consider-
able information on some of the early potteries.

NEW YORK

Ketchum, William C., Jr. *Early Potters Potteries of New York State.* New York, N.Y.: Funk and Wagnall, 1970.
An historical study of New York potteries with a long and in-depth checklist. Very good documentation on many potteries.

Munson-Williams-Proctor Institute Museum of Art. *White's Utica Pottery.* Catalogue of a show November 1969 to February 1970. Utica, N.Y.: The Widtman Press, Inc., 1969.
A show catalogue presenting a number of pieces made at this pottery as well as historical information on the pottery.

Rochester Museum and Science Center. *Clay in the Hands of the Potter,* an exhibition of pottery manufactured in the Rochester and Genessee Valley Region c. 1793-1900. March - August, 1974. Rochester, N.Y.: Rochester Museum and Science Center, 1974.
A show catalogue which contains considerable information about the excavation of pottery sites in the area. Both earthenware and stoneware are discussed.

Taylor, David and Patricia. *The Hart Pottery, Canada West.* Picton, Ontario: Picton Gazette Publishing Co. Ltd, 1966.
Information on the Hart family in both New York and Canada West.

NORTH CAROLINA

Bivins, John Jr. *The Moravian Potters in North Carolina.* Chapel Hill, N.C.: Univ. of N.C. Press, 1972.
A very complete history of the Moravian potteries at the settlements of Salem and Bethabara. It includes the history of the late as well as the better known early period potteries.

Bridges, Daisy Wade (editor). *Potters of the Catawba Valley,* Volume IV, Journal of Studies, Ceramic Circle of Charlotte. Charlotte, N.C.: Mint Museum, 1980.

An excellent catalogue containing the family histories where several generations were potters.

Conway, Bob and Gibreath (Editor). *Traditional Pottery in North Carolina.* Waynesville, N.C.: Mountaineer, 1974.
Mainly a pictorial presentation of work being done by the presently operating studios in North Carolina. This is not traditional utilitarian ware, but a modification toward art pottery.

Schwartz, Stuart C. *North Carolina Pottery: A Bibliography.* Charlotte, N.C.: Mint Museum of History, 1978.
A bibliography of all of the material that has been written on the stoneware, common earthenware, and art pottery of the area. It also includes some general bibliography on potteries of the South.

Zug, Charles T. III. *The Traditional Pottery of North Carolina.* Chapel Hill, N.C.: Univ. of N.C. Printing Dept., 1981.
A new catalogue of an extensive exhibit at the Akland Art Museum. The traditional earthenwares as well as salt- and alkaline-glazed stonewares are presented with some historical information. Unfortunately most of the pieces were not photographed, but some of the outstanding ones are included in the catalogue.

OHIO

Adamson, Jack E. *Illustrated Handbook of Ohio Sewer Pipe Folk Art.* Barberton, Ohio, 1973.
Presents a vast assortment of whimseys made by workers at sewer pipe factories in Ohio.

Blair, C. Dean. *The Potteries of Summit County, 1828-1915.* Akron, Ohio: Summit County Historical Society, 1965.
A history of the stoneware and earthenware potteries of the county. An excellent checklist as well as a reprinted 1903 catalogue of the Robinson Clay Products Company.

PENNSYLVANIA

James, Arthur. *The Potters and Potteries of Chester County.* Exton, Pa.: Schiffer Pub. Co., reprint 1980.
An intensive history of a large number of potteries functioning in Chester County, Pennsylvania. An in-depth checklist is included. Both earthenwares and stonewares are discussed.

Guappone, Dr. Carmen A. *New Geneva and Greensboro Pottery.* McClelland-town, Pa.: Guappone's Publishers, 1975.
A short history of the stoneware potteries of the area with photographs of many pots.

Lasansky, Jeannette. *Made of Mud: Stoneware Potteries in Central Pennsylvania 1834-1929.* Lewisburg, Pa.: Union County Bicentennial Commission, 1977.
An excellent history of the stoneware potteries working in central Pennsylvania. Many photographs and an in-depth checklist.

Myers, Susan H. *Handcraft to Industry.* Washington, D.C.: Smithsonian Institution Press, 1980.
A serious study of the development of pottery industry in Philadelphia, Pennsylvania. It contains the best information on these potteries available.

Powell, Elizabeth A. *Pennsylvania Pottery, Tools, and Processes.* Doylestown, Pa.: Bucks County Historical Society, 1972.
This short book presents a number of pieces of Pennsylvania earthenware and stoneware. The emphasis on the manner of forming, decorating, and even firing gives an excellent view of the technical side of the craft.

Schaltenbrand, Phil. *Old Pots: Salt-Glazed Stoneware of the Greensboro-New Geneva Region.* Hanover, Pa.: Everybody's Press, 1977.
An excellent discussion of the stonewares from the Greensboro- New Geneva region of Pennsylvania. There is much information about the techniques used in these semi-industrialized potteries.

SOUTH CAROLINA

Ferrell, Stephen T., and T.M.Ferrell. *Early Decorated Stoneware of the Edgefield District, South Carolina.* Catalogue of a show March - May, 1976.

Greenville, S.C.: Greenville County Museum of Art, 1976.
This show catalogue contains excellent photographs of some of these unusual pieces -- decorated alkaline-glazed wares --and has some historical information on the potteries.

TENNESSEE

Smith, Samuel D. and Stephen T. Rogers. *A Survey of Historic Pottery Making in Tennessee.* Nashville, Tenn.: Division of Archeology, Tennessee Department of Conservation, 1979.
A very complete study of pottery making in Tennessee with a checklist and much information on the location, types of ware made, and even types of kiln remains.

TEXAS

Greer, Georgeanna H. and Harding Black. *The Meyer Family, Master Potters in Texas.* San Antonio, Texas: Trinity University Press, 1971.
History of a pottery that functioned for over fifty years in Bexar County, Texas.

Humphreys, Sherry B. and Johnell L. Schmidt. *Texas Pottery, Caddo Indian to Contemporary.* Catalogue of a show at the Star of the Republic Museum, Washington, Texas, 1976.

This show catalogue has a little information on some utilitarian stoneware potteries in the state.

Malone, James M.; Georgeanna H. Greer; and Helen Simons. *Kirbee Kiln: A mid-Nineteenth Century Texas Stoneware Pottery.* Austin, Texas: Texas Historical Commission Office of the State Archeologist, 1979.
An archeological study of both kiln and artifacts at an early alkaline-glazing site in Texas.

Steinfeldt, Cecelia and Donald Stover. *Early Texas Furniture and Decorative Arts.* San Antonio, Texas: Trinity University Press, 1973.
Contains a section on the stonewares of the area around San Antonio, Texas, with information supplied by Georgeanna H. Greer.

VIRGINIA

Barka, Norman F. *The Archeology of Kiln 2 Yorktown Pottery Factory, Yorktown, Virginia.* The College of William and Mary Yorktown Research Series No. 4. Williamsburg, Va., 1979.
An archeological study of the second kiln found at William Rogers' Yorktown pottery. Kiln structures and artifacts are discussed.

Rice, A.H. and John Baer Stondt. *The Shenandoah Pottery.* Berryville, Va.: The Virginia Book Co., reprint, 1974.
This is an exact reprint of the book written in 1929. The information is still very good and the checklist acceptable.

Wiltshire, William G., III. *Folk Pottery of the Shenandoah Valley.* New York, N.Y.: E.P. Dutton & Co., Inc., 1975.
A large book of color plates of outstanding pieces of earthenware and stoneware from the Shenandoah Valley area. It also has a checklist of potters working in the area.

WEST VIRGINIA

Hough, Walter. *An Early West Virginia Pottery.* Washington, D.C.: Smithsonian Institution, 1898.
A very old and scarce publication. The presentation of the Morgantown Pottery in Morgantown, West Virginia, is very complete. Photographs of tools and wares.

CANADA

Collard, Elizabeth. *Nineteenth Century Pottery and Porcelain in Canada.* Montreal, Canada: McGill Univ. Press, 1967.
A general discussion of imported wares as well as wares produced in Canada. Considers coarse earthenwares, tablewares, and stonewares.

Newlands, David L. *Early Ontario Potters: Their Craft and Trade.* Ryerson, Canada: McGraw Hill, 1979.
An intensive study of the early stoneware and earthenware potteries of Ontario. Has a photographic list of marks which is excellent.

Taylor, David and Patricia. *The Hart Pottery, Canada West*. Picton, Ontario: Picton Gazette Pub. C., Ltd., 1966.
This contains some history of the Hart family potteries in New York State as well as in Canada.

Webster, Donald. *Early Canadian Pottery*. Greenwich, Conn.: New York Graphic Society, 1971.
A general history of Canadian common earthenware, stoneware, and tableware production.

PIPES

Sudbury, Byron. "Historic Clay Tobacco Pipe Makers in the United States of America." The manufacture of American short-stemmed tobacco pipes with many references and photographs.
Section II reprinted from *The Archeology of The Clay Tobacco Pipe* edited by Peter Davey. Oxford, England: B A R International Series 60, 1979.

Bibliography

Adamson, Jack E. *Illustrated Handbook of Ohio Sewer Pipe Folk Art.* Barberton, Ohio, 1973.

Barber, Edwin Atlee. *The Pottery and Porcelain of the United States, and Marks of American Potters.* 3rd edition, revised and enlarged. New York, New York: J. and J. Publishing, 1976.

Barka, Norman F. *The Archeology of Kiln 2 Yorktown Pottery Factory, Yorktown, Virginia.* Williamsburg, Virginia: The College of William and Mary, Yorktown research series No. 4, 1979.

Barret, Richard Carter. *Bennington Pottery and Porcelain.* New York, New York: Bonanza Books, 1958.

Bivins, John, Jr. *The Moravian Potters in North Carolina.* Chapel Hill, North Carolina: The University of North Carolina Press, 1972.

Blair, C. Dean. *The Potteries of Summit County, 1918-1915.* Akron, Ohio: Summit County Historical Society, 1965.

Branin, M. Lelyn. *The Early Potters and Potteries of Maine.* Middletown, Connecticut: Wesleyan University Press, 1978.

Brears, Peter, C.D. *The English Country Pottery.* Rutland, Vermont: Charles E. Tuttle, 1971.

Bridges, Daisy Wade (Editor). *Potters of the Catawba Valley, North Carolina.* Volume IV, Journal of Studies, Ceramic Circle of Charlotte. Charlotte, North Carolina: Mint Museum, 1980.

Burrison, John A. *Georgia Jug Makers, A History of Southern Folk Pottery.* Ph. D. Dissertation, University of Pennsylvania, 1973.

Burrison, John A. *Alkaline-Glazed Stoneware: A Deep South Pottery Tradition:* Southern Folklore. V. 39, No. 4, pp. 377-402. December, 1975.

Burrison, John A. *The Meaders Family of Mossy Creek.* Catalogue of a show. Atlanta, Georgia: Georgia State University, 1976.

Cardew, Michael. *Pioneer Pottery.* New York: St. Martin's Press, 1969.

Chaton, Robert and Talbot, Henri. *La Borne et ses Potiers.* Delayance, France, 1977.

Collard, Elizabeth. *Nineteenth Century Pottery and Porcelain in Canada.* Montreal, Canada: McGill University, 1967.

Conway, Bob and Gilbrieath (Editors). *Traditional Pottery in North Carolina.* Waynesville, North Carolina: Mountaineer, 1974.

Counts, Charles. *Common Clay.* Atlanta, Georgia: Droke House Hallux, 1971.

Denker, Ellen Paul. *"Forever Getting Up Something New" The Kirkpatrick's Pottery at Anna, Illinois.* Dissertation for M.A. degree, University of Delaware, 1978.

Dewhurst, C. Kurt and MacDowell, Marsha. *Cast in Clay, The Folk Pottery of Grand Ledge, Michigan.* Lansing, Michigan: The Museum, Michigan State University, folk culture series, Vol. I, No. 2, Michigan State University, 1980.

Eaton, Allen H. *Handicrafts of the Southern Highlands.* Chapter XIV, Pottery and the users of Clay, pp. 209-219. Reprint. New York: Dover Press, 1973.

Ferrell, Stephen T. and Ferrell, T. M. *Early Decorated Stoneware of the Edgefield District, South Carolina.* Catalogue of a show March - May, 1976. Greenville, South Carolina: County Museum of Art, 1976.

Evison, Vera I.; Hughes, H.; and Hurst, J. G. *Medieval Pottery from Excavations.* London: John Baker, 1974.

Freeman, John Crosby. *Blue Decorated Stoneware of New York State.* Catalogue and Study Guide - 1. Watkins Glen, New York: American Life Foundation, 1966.

Glassie, Henry. *Pattern in the Material Folk Culture of the Eastern United States.* 4th printing, paperback. University of Pennsylvania, 1976.

Gobels, Karl. *Rheinisches Topferhandwerk,* Frechen, West Germany: Stadtfrechen, 1971.

Gobels, Karl. *Keramik-Scherben aus Frechen.* Reinland Verlag BMBH, Koln, West Germany, 1980.

Greer, Georgeanna H. and Black, Harding. *The Meyer Family, Master Potters in Texas.* San Antonio, Texas: Trinity Press, 1971.

Guappone, Dr. Carmen A. *New Geneva and Greensboro Pottery.* McClellandtown, Pennsylvania, 1976.

Guilland, Harold F. *Early American Folk Pottery.* Philadelphia, Pennsylvania: Chilton Book Co., 1971.

Homer, Frank. *The Potter's Dictionary of Materials and Techniques.* New York, New York: Watson-Gupthill, 1975.

Hillebrandt, Heinrich; Mayer, Otto Eugene; and Hugot, Leo. *Steinzeug Aus Dem Raerener und Aachener Raum.* Aachen, West Germany: J. A. Mayer, 1977.

Hodgman, Charles D. *Handbook of Chemistry and Physics.* Cleveland, Ohio: Chemical Rubber Pub., 1936.

Hough, Walter. *An Early West Virginia Pottery.* Washington, D. C.: Smithsonian Institution, 1898.

Humphreys, Sherry B. and Schmidt, Johnell L. *Texas Pottery, Caddo Indian to Contemporary.* Catalogue of a show at the Star of the Republic Museum, Washington, Texas, 1976.

Loar, Peggy A. *Indiana Stoneware.* Catalogue of an exhibit at the Indianapolis Museum of Art April - May, 1974. Indianapolis, Indiana: Speedway Press, Inc., 1974.

James, Arthur. *The Potters and Potteries of Chester County.* Reprint. Exton, Pennsylvania: Schiffer Pub. Co., 1978.

Ketchum, William C., Jr. *Early Potters and Potteries of New York State.* New York, New York: Funk and Wagnall, 1970.

Ketchum, William C., Jr. *The Pottery and Porcelain Collector's Handbook.* New York, New York: Funk and Wagnall, 1971.

Lasansky, Jeannette. *Made of Mud—Stoneware Potteries in Central Pennsylvania, 1834-1929.* Lewisburg, Pennsylvania: Union County Bicentennial Commission, 1977.

Madden, Betty I. *Art, Crafts, and Architecture in Early Illinois.* Chapter 15, "Jug Towns", pp. 181-194. Urbana, Illinois: University of Illinois Press, 1974.

Malone, James M.; Greer, Georgeanna H.; and Simons, Helen. *Kirbee Kiln, A Mid-Nineteenth Century Texas Stoneware Pottery.* Austin, Texas: Texas Historical Commission, Office of the State Archeologist, 1979.

Menginoi, Elinor. *Old Sleepy Eye.* Delos L. Hill and Ozella I. Hill. Tulsa, Oklahoma: The Printing Press, 1973.
    The advertising used by "Sleepy Eye" Milling Company for their flour, including ceramic items made by the American Stoneware Company, Monmouth, Illinois.

Mississippi State Historical Museum. *Made By Hand.* Catalogue of a show January - May, 1980. Mississippi Department of Archives and History, Jackson, Mississippi, 1980. Greer, Georgeanna H. *The Folk Pottery of Mississippi.* pp. 45-54.

Monmonth County Historical Association. *New Jersey Stoneware.* Catalogue of an exhibit May - June, 1955. Freehold, New Jersey: Transcript Printing House, 1955.

Munson-Williams-Proctor Institute Museum of Art. *White's Utica Pottery.* Catalogue of a show November 1969 to February 1970. Utica, New York: The Widtman Press, Inc., 1969.

Myers, Susan H. *Handcraft to Industry.* Washington, D.C.: Smithsonian Institution Press, 1980.

Newlands, David L. *The New Hamburg Pottery, New Hamburg, Ontario. 1854-1916.* Waterloo, Canada: Wilfred Laurier University Press, 1978.

Newlands, David L. *Early Ontario Potters, Their Craft and Trade.* Ryerson, Canada: McGraw Hill, 1979.

Northeast Historical Archeology. Vol. 6, Nos. 1 and 2, Spring 1977, Papers from the Rochester Conference on Ceramics in America.

New Jersey State Museum. *New Jersey Pottery to 1840*. Catalogue of a show at the museum. Trenton, New Jersey: March to May, 1972.

Noel Hume, Ivor. *A Guide to Artifacts of Colonial America*. Knopf, New York: 1972.

Osgood, Cornelias. *The Jug and Related Stoneware of Bennington*. Rutland, Vermont: Charles E. Tuttle Co., 1971.

Parmelee, Cullen W. *Ceramic Glazes*. Boston, Massachusetts: Cahner Publishing Co., 1973 - 3rd edition.

Pappas, Joan and Kendell, Harold. *Hampshire Pottery*. Manchester, Vermont: Foreward's Color Productions, Inc., 1971.

Powell, Elizabeth A. *Pennsylvania Pottery, Tools, and Processes*. Doylestown, Pennsylvania: Bucks County Historical Society, 1972.

Quimby, Ian M. G. (Editor). *Ceramics in America*. Winterthur Conference Report, 1972. Charlottesville, Virgina: University Press of Virginia, 1973.

Ramsey, John. *American Potters and Pottery*. Clinton, Massachusetts: Hale, Cushman, and Flint, 1939.

Rhodes, Daniel. *Kilns*. Philadelphia, Pennsylvania: Chilton, 1968.

Rhodes, Daniel. *Stoneware and Porcelain*. Philadelphia, Pennsylvania: Chilton, 1959.

Rhodes, Daniel. *Glay and Glazes for the Potter*. Philadelphia, Pennsylvania: Chilton, 1973 revised edition.

Rice, A. H. and Stoudt, John Baer. *The Shenandoah Pottery*. Berryville, Virginia: The Virginia Book Co., Reprint, 1974.

Rochester Museum and Science Center. *Clay in the Hands of the Potter*. (an exhibition of pottery manufactured in the Rochester and Genesse Valley Region, c. 1793-1900. March-August, 1974.) Rochester, New York: Rochester Museum and Science Center, 1974.

Rosenthal, Ernst. *Pottery and Ceramics*. Baltimore, Maryland: Penguin, 1954.

Schaltenbrand, Phil. *Old Pots, Salt Glazed Stoneware of the Greensboro-New Geneva Region*. Hanover, Pennsylvania: Everybody's Press, 1977.

Smith, Elmer L. and Ranchenberg, Bradford, L. *Pottery, A Utilitarian Folk Craft*. Lebanon, Pennsylvania: Applied Arts Publishers, 1972.

Smithsonian Institution, The National Museum of History and Technology. *The John Paul Remensnyder Collection of American Stoneware*. Cagalogue of a show November 1978-November 1979. Smithsonian Institution, Washington, D. C., 1979.

Stienfeldt, Cecelia and Stover, Donald. *Early Texas Furniture and Decorative Arts*. San Antonio, Texas: Trinity University Press, 1973.

Savage, George and Newman, Harold. *An Illustrated Dictionary of Ceramics*. New York, New York: VanNostrand, Rheinhold, 1974.

Schwartz, Marvin D. *Collector's Guide to Antique American Ceramics*. Garden City, New York: Doubleday & Co., 1969.

Schwartz, Stuart C. *North Carolina Pottery, A Bibliography*. Charlotte, North Carolina: Mint Museum of History, 1978.

Smith, Joseph J. *Regional Aspects of American Folk Pottery*. The Historical Society of York County, catalogue of a show May to October, 1979. York, Pennsylvania, 1979.

Smith, Samuel D. and Rogers, Stephen T. *A Survey of Historic Pottery Making in Tennessee*. Nashville, Tennessee: Division of Archeology, Tennessee Department of Conservation, 1979.

Spargo, John. *The Potters and Potteries of Bennington*. Southampton, Long Island, New York: Cracker Barrel Press. Reprint of 1926 edition.

Spargo, John. *Early American Pottery and China*. Rutland, Vermont: Charles E. Tuttle Co., 1974.

Stradling, Diana and J.Garrison (Editors). *The Art of the Potter*, Redware and Stoneware. Articles from Antiques Magazine. New York, New York: Main Street Universe Books, 1977.

Sudbury, Byron. *"Historic Clay Tobacco Pipe Makers in the United States of America"*. Vol. II of *the Archeology of the Clay Tobacco Pipe*. pp. 151-341 B.A.R. International Series Reprint, Oxford, England, 1974.

Taylor, David and Patricia. *The Hart Pottery, Canada West*. Picton, Ontario: Picton Gazette Publishing Col, Ltd., 1966.

Troy, Jack. *Salt Glazed Ceramics.* Watson Gupthill, New York: Watson, 1977.

Van Ravensway, Charles. *The Arts and Architecture of German Settlements in Missouri.*
    Chapter 21 - Pottery, pp. 459-482. Columbia, Missouri: University of Missouri Press,
    1977.

Viel, Lyndon C. *The Clay Giants, The Stoneware of Redwing, Goodhue County, Minnesota.*
    Des Moines, Iowa: Wallace-Homestead Book Co., 1977.

VonBock, Gisela Reineking. *Steinzeug.* Koln, West Germany, 1976.

Watkins, Lura Woodside. *Early New England Pottery.* Sturbridge, Massachusetts: Old
    Sturbridge Village. 2nd printing, 1966.

Watkins, Lura Woodside. *Early New England Potters and Their Wares.* Archon Books, 1968.
    Reprint of 1st edition, 1960.

Webster, Donald Blake. *Decorated Stoneware Pottery of North America.* Rutland, Vermont:
    Charles E.Tuttle Co., 1971.

Webster, Donald B. *Early Canadian Pottery.* Greenwich, Connecticut: New York Graphic
    Society, 1971.

Wiltshire, William, III. *Folk Pottery of the Shenandoah Valley.* New York, New York:
    E.P. Dutton & Co., Inc., 1975.

Zug, Charles G. III. *The Traditional Pottery of North Carolina.* Catalogue of a show at the
    Akland Art Museum, Chapel Hill, North Carolina, University of North Carolina, 1981.

Personal Interviews:

E.J. Brown, Connally Springs, N.C. - July 22, 1973

Arthur Cole, Sanford, N.C. - June, 1973

Herman Cole, Seagrove, N.C. - July 1973

Sarah Dunkin, San Antonio, Texas - 1969

John Ellis, Marshall, TX - March, 1976

William Gordy, Cartersville, GA - 1972

Lobel Hunt, Henderson, TX - 1974

E.J. Humphreys, Marshall, TX - November 1978

Mapp, Bacon, Level, Ala. - 1974

Lanier Meaders, Cleveland, GA - 1972-73

Frank Meyer, Atascosa, TX - 1970

James Wilson, Jr., Seguin, TX - 1973

Index

More Titles from Schiffer Publishing

Fireworks: New England Art Pottery of the Arts and Crafts Movement Paul Royka. American art pottery is one of the most dynamic collecting fields, with prices soaring up to $200,000 for one piece. Paul A. Royka examines New England art pottery made from 1872 to 1928. Sold through auctions and galleries and found in attics and homes throughout the United States, the pieces illustrated here have a combined value of over one million dollars. The most comprehensive work of its kind, Fireworks examines the origins of the Arts and Crafts Movement and the influences manufacturing companies had on it. It provides help in identifying marks, evaluating, and pricing the works of Chelsea Keramic Art Works, Dedham, Low, Grueby, Hampshire, Crook, Merrimac, Walley, Marblehead, Saturday Evening Girls, and Dorchester Pottery. A beautiful book with more than 450 color photographs, it is a must for the pottery collector and a wonderful gift for any art lover.

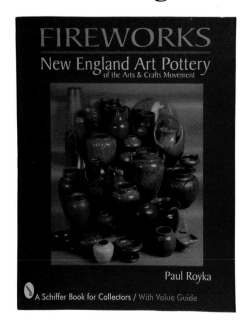

Size: 8 1/2" x 11"	450 color photos	192 pp.
Price Guide		
ISBN: 0-88740-988-1	hard cover	$69.95

Watt Pottery: A Collector's Reference with Price Guide Dennis Thompson & W. Bryce Watt. For over 40 years a family firm in central Ohio produced pottery that graced kitchens and dining rooms of Americans coast to coast. Wares once given as advertising premiums or sold inexpensively in department stores are now valuable collectibles. Watt Pottery tells the history of this pottery and traces its product and pattern development. Original research and 800 precise photos help identify pieces, including the very popular hand-decorated ones, and distinguish Watt ware from other pottery pieces. Full sections on marks, patterns, and all know mold shapes and numbers make this book a collector's dream.

Size: 8 1/2" x 11"	800 photos	240 pp.
Price Guide		
ISBN: 0-88740-614-9	hard cover	$39.95

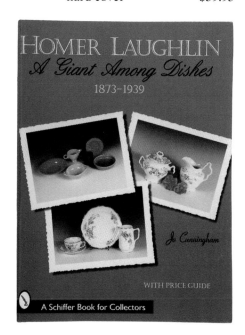

Homer Laughlin China: "A Giant Among Dishes" 1873-1937 Jo Cunningham. The proud history of one of America's most prolific and best known dinnerware manufacturers is presented with over 500 color photographs and new research from the company archives. Today the popularity of Fiesta® and many other Homer Laughlin dishes from the 1870s to the 1930s is well known to ceramics collectors. This book gives the factual history of all the shapes, decorations, and variations that have been found. Current market value ranges are given in the captions.

Size: 8 1/2" x 11"	520 color photographs	192 pp.
Price Guide		Index
ISBN: 0-7643-0417-8	hard cover	$29.95

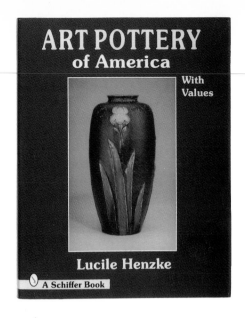

Art Pottery of America, *Revised* Lucile Henzke. This is a completely new study of American art pottery by the author of the leading, pioneer book published twelve years ago. Arranged alphabetically by the potteries, the text includes important historical data, photographs of each pottery's representative forms, and a complete series of the identifying marks. Here the novice as well as advanced collector will gain knowledge to help identify and interpret the art pottery produced in America from the late nineteenth and early twentieth centuries.

Size: 8 1/2" x 11"   549 color & b/w photos   368 pp.
Price Guide   Index
ISBN: 0-7643-0159-4   hard cover $45.00

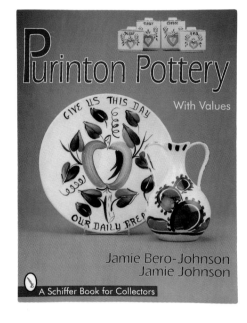

Purinton Pottery Jamie Bero-Johnson & Jamie Johnson. More than 1100 color photographs chronicle this pottery from its early, primitive Peasant Ware stages after the company was founded in Wellsville, Ohio in 1936, to the ever-popular Apple and Pennsylvania Dutch patterns of the 1940s and '50s, with all known patterns and molds illustrated in chronological order. This book also identifies the various shapes made by Purinton and displays their children's wares, figurals, Christmas pieces, and experimental items. The authors go further, identifying pieces signed by the company's two most prestigious decorators, Bill Blair and Dorothy

Size: 8 1/2" x 11"   1100 Photos   224 pp.
Price Guide   Index
ISBN: 0-7643-0290-6   soft cover $29.95

Rookwood Pottery: The Glaze Lines Anita J. Ellis. The Rookwood pottery, founded in Cincinnati, Ohio, produced experimental decorated and commercial pottery from 1880 until 1967. This new book stands ahead of all other references by offering the most complete understanding of Rookwood products, and it places Rookwood's glaze lines in the context of the pottery's history. Author Anita Ellis conclusively explains the Decorated Wares, especially those made after 1915 which have always been problematic, and categorizes and defines the Commercial Ware for the first time. The book is unique in offering the most complete set of Rookwood pottery, potter and decorator marks; a thorough glossary of terms; and all the glaze lines. Over 200 beautiful color photographs of the elegant Rookwood pottery shapes illustrate the glaze lines.

Size: 8 1/2" x 11"   288 photographs   240 pp.
Price Guide
ISBN: 0-88740-838-9   hard cover $69.95

Schiffer books may be ordered from your local bookstore,
or they may be ordered directly from the publisher by writing to:
Schiffer Publishing, Ltd.
4880 Lower Valley Rd Atglen PA 19310
(610) 593-1777; Fax (610) 593-2002
E-mail: schifferbk@aol.com

Please include $3.95 for shipping and handling for the first two books and
50¢ for each additional book. Free shipping for orders $100 or more. Please
visit our web site catalog at **www.schifferbooks.com**
or write for a free catalog.

Printed in China

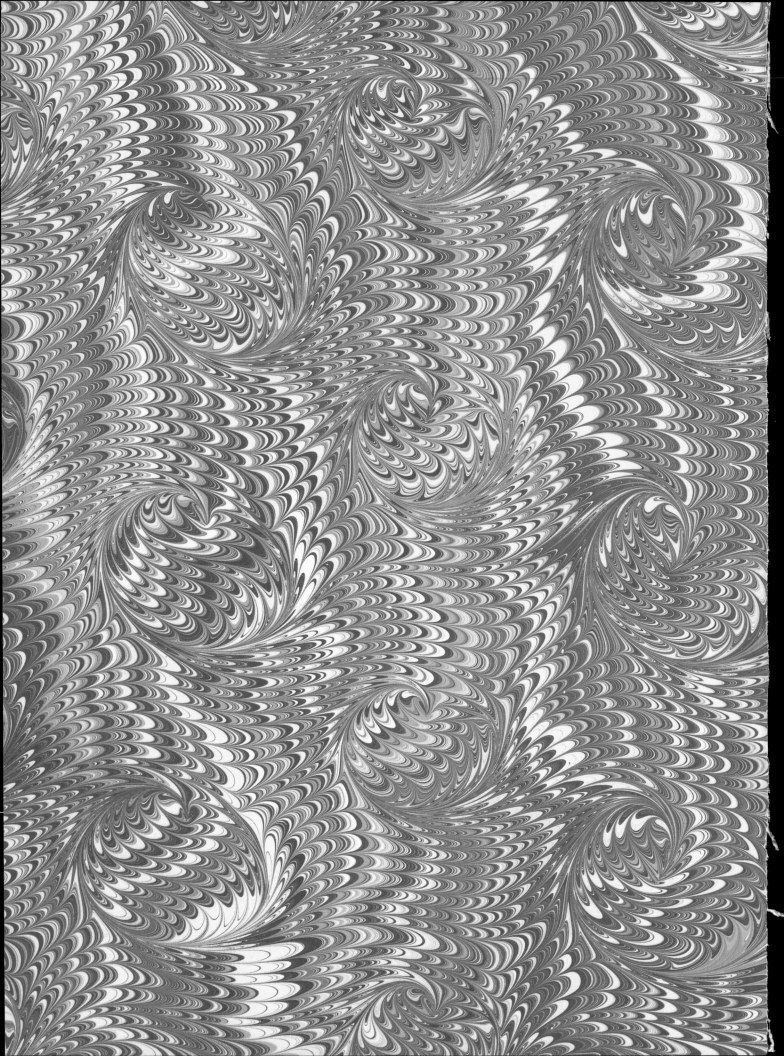